Financial Crime Issues

Petter Gottschalk

Financial Crime Issues

Fraud Investigations and Social Control

 Springer

Petter Gottschalk
Department of Leadership & Organizational Behavior
BI Norwegian Business School
Oslo, Norway

ISBN 978-3-031-11215-7   ISBN 978-3-031-11213-3   (eBook)
https://doi.org/10.1007/978-3-031-11213-3

This Springer imprint is published by the registered company Springer Nature Switzerland AG
The registered company address is: Gewerbestrasse 11, 6330 Cham, Switzerland

Preface

For far too long, corporate compliance has been an issue of the legal license to operate, where private and public enterprises might continue their operations even when politicians, shareholders, employees, citizens, activist groups, customers, and many other stakeholder groups react negatively to enterprise activities. Recently, a supplement perspective concerned with the social license to operate has emerged that in a growing number of cases has made it more important for corporations and other enterprises to achieve acceptance and potential support from various stakeholders in the community. This book presents the new perspective based on the emerging theory of social license. The new perspective of social license to operate might trivialize legal issues in corporate compliance work, where future compliance officers are trained in social issues rather than the law.

Oslo, Norway   Petter Gottschalk

Contents

Chapter 1
Introduction

Haines et al. (2022: 184) examined "how social control in the form of community pressure might be used to control corporate harm and shape business conduct in a more socially responsible direction." They suggested a social license to civilize, control, or repel corporate activity. They defined a social license as acceptance of a business or business activity within a particular community. The social license adds to the legal license to operate business activities. The social license forms part of a bottom-up and outside-in strategy where wrongdoing becomes social property independent of the criminal justice system.

The social license is predominantly centered on social permission for business activity where the media, social movements, and citizen watchdogs exert pressure, demand change, and bring enterprises to account. The social license if present is a visible manifestation of a commitment to corporate social responsibility regarding agreement between company and community in business operations.

Sale (2021) defined social license as the acceptance of business or organization by the relevant communities and stakeholders, and Cui et al. (2016: 775) referred to the social license to operate as "a community's acceptance or approval of a specific company project or of the entire company's ongoing operations in the community." Melé and Armengou (2016) referred to social license as the acceptance of the expansion of profit-seeking business that can affect community life. Further scholarly definitions of the expression are presented in the first chapter.

Haines et al. (2022) studied community pressure against unconventional gas exploration by a large resources company in New South Wales (NSW) in Australia. While the bottom-up and outside-in approaches by various stakeholders were successful in reducing corporate harm, a number of issues emerged related to authority, meaning, and value. For example, an issue was to identify who were entitled to represent the community. Those chosen and accepted to represent the community might be those considered mature enough for the role, while critical and eccentric voices can be deemed unsuitable.

© The Author(s), under exclusive license to Springer Nature Switzerland AG 2022   1
P. Gottschalk, *Financial Crime Issues*,
https://doi.org/10.1007/978-3-031-11213-3_1

In their case study, the social license went far beyond the legal license (Haines et al., 2022: 191):

> Company representatives felt that an a priori assertion of their legal right to access land would be met by anger and defiance. Relying on their legal rights would be seen as arrogant and likely to lead to lengthy court disputes, one argued 'we never tested it' (their legal rights). Unlike coal mines where land to be mined is acquired by coal companies, gas companies did not need to acquire land (as subsurface resources in NSW are owned by the state), but they did need access to land in order to access those resources.

Sale (2021: 785) studied Wells Fargo and Uber as cases of "how the failure to account for the public nature of corporate actions, regardless of whether a 'legal' license exists, can result in the loss of 'social' license. This loss occurs through publicness, which is the interplay between inside corporate governance players and outside actors who report on, recapitulate, reframe and, in some cases, control the company's information and public perception."

Most of Wells Fargo's profits and growth were coming from the Community Bank. Executives as well as other employees in the community banking division at Wells Fargo had their motives for financial wrongdoing. Both pressures and possibilities were their motives. Sanger et al. (2017: 2) found that there was an explicit and strong "pressure on employees to sell unwanted or unneeded products to customers." The banking division was a sales-driven organization. Hired people got instructions in these sales practices and would lose their jobs otherwise. While risking their social license, the threat of job loss seemed more serious. The threat of job loss became a reality after disclosure of the account fraud scandal (Sanger et al., 2017: 2):

> Approximately 5300 employees had been terminated for sales practices violations through the September 2016 settlements with the Los Angeles City Attorney.

Before the termination of all those employees "poor performance in many instances led to shaming or worse" (Sanger et al., 2017: 30). Investigators found that employees below the branch manager level – lower-level in-branch managers and non-managers – frequently cited branch managers as actively directing misconduct or offering inappropriate guidance to subordinates on what constituted acceptable conduct (Sanger et al., 2017: 37):

> Everyone was aware of what was implied when the manager would state "it's late in the day and we need a certain number of accounts by the end of the day."

An important possibility was compensation, as ambitious sales goals linked directly to incentive compensation (Sanger et al., 2017: 20):

> Employees were measured on how they performed relative to these goals. They were ranked against one another on their performance relative to these goals, and their incentive compensation and promotional opportunities were determined relative to those goals. The system created intense pressure to perform, and, in certain areas, local and regional managers imposed excessive pressure on their subordinates.

Because of such deviant practices, the Community Bank at Wells Fargo lost its social license as the process of publicness exposed additional frauds (Sale, 2021: 833):

> Take for example, the car loan repossession scandal. Between 20,000 and 570,000 customers of the bank were enrolled in and charged for car insurance without their knowledge, and when some of them failed to make payments on the unknown insurance, they had their cars repossessed. Even though Wells Fargo said it was "extremely sorry" and promised to refund customers and work with credit bureaus, its response lacked credibility.

The idea here is that the legal license was not necessarily violated, while the social license was certainly violated. Therefore, board members and executives could probably not be prosecuted in court, while the business suffered from social disapproval (Sale, 2021: 837):

> Although it is unclear what information the Wells Fargo board received, ex post investigations reveal that the company's decentralized nature and, perhaps, management evasion resulted in fragmented reporting, which in turn contributed to the sustained nature of the fraud. Yet, if the board had pressed with questions about management strategy and its downside risks, the board would have ensured dialogue about the types of underlying facts necessary to develop legitimacy, credibility, and trust and thus helped to protect the company's social license.

The typical outcome of social license violations seems to be the dismissal of executives at various levels in an attempt to regain trust, for example:

- CEO Carrie Tolstedt at Community Bank in the United States had to leave her position despite her attempts to blame individual employees (Sanger et al., 2017: 103): "Tolstedt emphasized that a large organization could not be perfect, and that the sales practice problem was a result of improper action on the part of individual employees."
- CEO Birgitte Bonnesen at Swedbank in Sweden had to leave her position after the money laundering scandal investigated by Clifford Chance (2020). The new Swedbank board decided to withdraw her final compensation (Johannessen & Christensen, 2020).
- CEO Thomas Borgen at Danske Bank in Denmark had to leave his position after a similar money laundering scandal investigated by Bruun Hjejle (2018).
- CEO Martin Winterkorn at Volkswagen in Germany had to resign because of the emission manipulation scandal (Jung & Sharon, 2019).
- CEO Thorsteinn Mar Baldvinsson had to step aside until the pending internal investigation into the Icelandic company's subsidiaries' alleged wrongdoing in Namibia was to be completed (Samherji, 2019a, b, 2020a, b, 2021).

In the Swedbank case, there was later determined that a violation of the legal license had also occurred. The former chief executive at Swedbank resigned from the position, while Clifford Chance was still conducting the internal investigation. Another executive resigned from the position of chief compliance officer when the bank publicized the report of investigation. Two years later, in 2022, the former chief executive at Swedbank, Birgitte Bonnesen, was charged with fraud and market manipulation by the Swedish prosecutor (Ismail, 2022: 7):

The revelations at that time led to a number of people in senior positions having to leave. The bank also received a record fine of four billion Swedish kroner, according to Swedish public broadcasting. One of those who were fired was Swedbank's top executive Birgitte Bonnesen. In January this year, the Swedish economic crime authority brought charges against Bonnesen for gross fraud and market manipulation.

In addition, the entire former management of Swedbank in Estonia was suspected of money laundering. The Estonian public prosecutor suspected that the management of Swedbank's Estonian bank contributed to laundering of 100 million Euros in the years 2014–2016. Some of the suspected money laundering was linked to Mikhail Abyzov, a former minister in the Russian government (Ismail, 2022).

Many more examples of dismissed chief executives come to mind. However, more interesting to mention are situations where blame is attributed downward in a corporate hierarchy to regain the social license to operate. An example is General Motors after the cobalt ignition switch failure. Rather than blaming CEO Mary Barra, several others had to leave. Bill Kemp, a senior lawyer in the automobile company, was one out of several who received blame for the lack of reaction to the ignition switch failure (Shepardson & Burden, 2014).

The social license to operate seems dependent on how the company is able to negotiate and achieve acceptance of the various impacts its operations might have on the local community. When the term was coined, it was especially concerned with environmental harm from mining companies and other physical business activities (Buhmann, 2016). Later, the use of the term has expanded to human rights and conditions for workers within the companies.

The term of social license to operate is related to several other constructs such as corporate social responsibility, stakeholder engagement, governance structure, and democratic processes (Cui et al., 2016).

From the perspective of social license, bottom-up as well as outside-in concerns should occupy board members' and top executives' attention. Negative statements by politicians, activists, employees, journalists, and others can indeed cause damage to the business as well as harm the career of people in trusted elite positions. While some companies initially attempt to respond by secrecy, the eventual publicness of wrongdoing, although not illegal, will cause damage. Therefore, as argued by Sale (2021) and Haines et al. (2022), the bottom-up approach of securing corporate social license contributes to corporate control of white-collar crime. The bottom-up approach to executive compliance focuses on organizational measures to make white-collar crime less convenient for potential offenders. Bottom-up control refers to the manner in which organizational members can use different types of control mechanisms – such as whistleblowing, transparency, resource constraints, and organizational culture – to monitor, measure, and evaluate executives' avoidance of deviant behaviors and influence them toward achieving the organizations' goals in efficient, effective, and socially acceptable ways (Zhong & Robinson, 2021).

Traditionally, white-collar and corporate crime research has focused on the role of the criminal justice system in policing, prosecuting, and punishing offenders and offenses. The frequent lack of police involvement, prosecution, and punishment has been explained by various theoretical perspectives that reflect the legal license to operate. However, the emerging perspective of the social license to operate illustrates punishment at violations that can cause termination of executives, market loss, and other serious harm to individuals and firms.

This book presents several case studies where fraud examiners reviewed the legal license, while the social license was ignored. There is an interesting avenue here for future white-collar and corporate crime research in distinguishing between punishment from violations of the legal license and punishment from violations of the social license to operate.

Surprisingly often, fraud examiners conclude with misconduct but no crime in their internal investigations of suspected white-collar and corporate offenses (Gottschalk, 2016, 2020, 2021). Fraud examiners are in the business of reconstructing past events and sequences of events when there are allegations and suspicions of financial crime such as corruption and embezzlement (King, 2012, 2020, 2021; Meerts, 2020, 2021). Investigation conclusions of misconduct but no crime implies that the client organizations did not violate the legal license to operate, where the legal license refers to laws that describe wrongdoing and punishment (Haines et al., 2022; Sale, 2021).

However, fraud examiners often identify misconduct and wrongdoing that represents violations of the social license to operate. Rather than punishment by the criminal justice systems, violations of the social license from wrongdoing lead to punishment by the local community and relevant stakeholders, where such punishment seems to grow in importance for accused enterprises in recent years (Baba et al., 2021; Haines et al., 2022; Hurst et al., 2020; Sale, 2021). Therefore – even when fraud examiners find that the legal license was obviously not violated – accused enterprises tend to change their business practices as a response to organized criticism to avoid harm to the business and individuals.

This book reviews fraud investigation reports and their consequences to provide insights into violations of the social license to operate. The current research is important, as the emerging stream of social license literature can illustrate that although white-collar and corporate crime suspicions tend to avoid the attention of the criminal justice system (Gottschalk & Gunnesdal, 2018; Gottschalk & Tcherni-Buzzeo, 2017), there are nevertheless consequences for offenders from external reactions that can harm and potentially threaten enterprise existence. As argued by Nason et al. (2018: 261), "social performance has become an increasingly important and expected performance criterion of contemporary firms." In fact, the threat of sanctions from powerful communities and stakeholders might in the future become more frightening than the threat of traditional criminal prosecution. Therefore, future fraud investigations might concentrate more on violations of the social license to operate and less on violations of the legal license to operate.

References

Baba, S., Hemissi, O., Berrahou, Z., & Traiki, C. (2021). The spatiotemporal dimension of the social license to operate: The case of a landfill facility in Algeria. *Management International – MI, 25*(4), 247–266.

Bruun Hjejle. (2018). *Report on the non-resident portfolio at Danske Bank's Estonian branch* (p. 87). Law Firm Bruun Hjejle.

Buhmann, K. (2016). Public regulators and CSR: The 'social license to operate' in recent United Nations instruments on business and human rights and the juridification of CSR. *Journal of Business Ethics, 136*, 699–714.

Clifford Chance. (2020). *Report of investigation on Swedbank* (p. 218). Law Firm Clifford Chance.

Cui, J., Jo, H., & Velasquez, M. G. (2016). Community religion, employees, and the social license to operate. *Journal of Business Ethics, 136*, 775–807.

Gottschalk, P. (2016). Private policing of financial crime: Key issues in the investigation business in Norway. *European Journal of Policing Studies, 3*(3), 292–314.

Gottschalk, P. (2020). Private policing of white-collar crime: Case studies of internal investigations by fraud examiners. *Police Practice and Research, 21*(6), 717–738.

Gottschalk, P. (2021). *Private policing of economic crime – Case studies of internal investigations by fraud examiners*. Routledge.

Gottschalk, P., & Gunnesdal, L. (2018). *White-collar crime in the shadow economy: Lack of detection, investigation, and conviction compared to social security fraud*. Palgrave Pivot, Palgrave Macmillan, Springer Publishing, UK.

Gottschalk, P., & Tcherni-Buzzeo, M. (2017). Reasons for gaps in crime reporting: The case of white-collar criminals investigated by private fraud examiners in Norway. *Deviant Behavior, 38*(3), 267–281.

Haines, F., Bice, S., Einfeld, C., & Sullivan, H. (2022). Countering corporate power through social control: What does a social licence offer? *The British Journal of Criminology, 62*, 184–199.

Hurst, B., Johnston, K. A., & Lane, A. B. (2020). Engaging for a social license to operate. *Public Relations Review, 40*. Published online https://doi.org/10.1016/j.pubrev.2020.101931

Ismail, K. (2022). Swedbanks tidligere ledelse i Estland mistenkt for hvitvasking (Swedbank's former management in Estland suspected of money laundering), daily Norwegian business newspaper *Dagens Næringsliv*, Monday, March 28, p. 7.

Johannessen, S. Ø., & Christensen, J. (2020). Swedbank vil ikke betale sluttpakke til toppsjef som matte gå av etter hvitvaskingsskandale (Swedbank will not pay final package to top executive who had to leave after money laundering scandal), daily Norwegian business newspaper *Dagens Næringsliv*, www.dn.no, published March 23.

Jung, J. C., & Sharon, E. (2019). The Volkswagen emissions scandal and its aftermath. *Global Business & Organizational Excellence, 38*(4), 6–15.

King, M. (2012). The contemporary role of private investigators in Australia. *Criminal Justice Matters, 89*(1), 12–14.

King, M. (2020). Financial fraud investigative interviewing – Corporate investigators' beliefs and practices: A qualitative inquiry. *Journal of Financial Crime*. Published online https://doi.org/10.1108/JFC-08-2020-0158

King, M. (2021). Profiting from a tainted trade: Private investigators' views on the popular culture glamorization of their trade. *Journal of Criminological Research Policy and Practice*. Published online https://doi.org/10.1108/JCRPP-07-2020-0050

Meerts, C. (2020). Corporate investigations: Beyond notions of public-private relations. *Journal of Contemporary Criminal Justice, 36*(1), 86–100.

Meerts, C. (2021). Struggles in cooperation: Public-private relations in the investigation of internal financial crime in the Netherlands. In N. Lord, E. Inzelt, W. Huisman, & R. Faria (Eds.), *European white-collar crime: Exploring the nature of European realities*. Bristol University Press.

Melé, D., & Armengou, J. (2016). Moral legitimacy in controversial projects and its relationships with social license to operate: A case study. *Journal of Business Ethics, 136*, 729–742.

Nason, R. S., Bacq, S., & Gras, D. (2018). A behavioral theory of social performance: Social identity and stakeholder expectations. *Academy of Management Review, 43*(2), 259–283.

Sale, H. A. (2021). The corporate purpose of social license. *Sothern California Law Review, 94*(4), 785–842.

Samherji. (2019a). *Statement from Samherji: Press release*, www.samherji.is, published November 11 by margret@samherji.is

Samherji. (2019b). *Samherji CEO steps aside while investigations are ongoing*, www.samherji.is, published November 14 by margret@samherji.is

Samherji. (2020a). *Samherji's Namibia investigation finalized*, Samherji ice fresh seafood, website https://www.samherji.is/en/moya/news/samherjis-namibia-investigation-finalized, Akureyri, Iceland, published by margret@samherji.is

Samherji. (2020b). *Fees for quotas were in line with market prices in Namibia*, Samherji seafood, www.samherji.is, published September 25 by Margrét Ólafsdóttir, margret@samherji.is

Samherji. (2021). Statement and apology from Samherji, Samherji seafood, www.samherji.is, published June 22.

Sanger, S. W., Duke, E. A., James, D. M., & Hernandez, E. (2017, April 10). *Independent directors of the Board of Wells Fargo & company: Sales practices investigation report* (pp. 113). https://www08.wellsfargomedia.com/assets/pdf/about/investor-relations/presentations/2017/board-report.pdf. Downloaded 2018, September 7.

Shepardson, D., & Burden, M. (2014, February 13). GM recalls 778K cars to replace ignition switches after fatal crashes, *Detroit News*. https://infoweb.newsbank.com/apps/news/document-view?p=AWNB&t=&sort=YMD_date%3AA&maxresults=20&f=advanced&val-base-0=ignition%20switch%20failure&fld-base-0=alltext&bln-base-1=and&val-base-1=GM&fld-base-1=alltext&bln-base-2=and&val-base-2=cobalt&fld-base-2=alltext&bln-base-3=and&val-base-3=2014&fld-base-3=YMD_date&bln-base-4=and&val-base-4=learned&fld-base-4=alltext&docref=news/14BF79CC1A B3B180

Zhong, R., & Robinson, S. L. (2021). What happens to bad actors in organizations? A review of actor-centric outcomes of negative behavior. *Journal of Management, 47*(6), 1430–1467.

Chapter 2
Theory of Social License

The theory of social license suggests that legal and social obligations and expectations provide separate but interacting issues for assessing the extent to which business conduct is aligned with norms in the community. While each business enterprise serves a number of purposes in the community such as employment and goods and services, the business conduct has to meet both legal and social requirements to operate. The community does not exist to serve the business enterprise. Rather, each corporate entity exists to serve the community with benefits without violating the legal and social license. The social license can be part of a bottom-up as well as an outside-in effort to enhance the social control of business activity (Haines et al., 2022). Business enterprises attempt to respond to indicate that their activities are not only legally legitimate but also socially legitimate (Saenz, 2019: 296):

> The expression is often used when a company's activities may face disapproval – especially when such disapproval could result in resistance that could harm their business interests. Failure to engage all segments of the community, to inform them, and to solicit their opinions is often seen as evidence of illegitimacy by those who are excluded. It is typically preferable for companies to communicate directly with the masses and not rely solely on those occupying leadership positions.

As mentioned in the introduction, Haines et al. (2022) studied community pressure against unconventional gas exploration by a large resources company in New South Wales (NSW) in Australia. While approaches by various stakeholders were successful in reducing corporate harm, a number of issues emerged related to authority, meaning, and value. For example, an issue was to identify who were entitled to represent the community. Those chosen and accepted to represent the community might be those considered mature enough for the role, while critical and eccentric voices can be deemed unsuitable.

P. Gottschalk, *Financial Crime Issues*,
https://doi.org/10.1007/978-3-031-11213-3_2

Sources of License Authority

Sources of license authority are a combination of people and knowledge. The main people sources of license authority are bottom-up activists and outside-in activists. The bottom-up approach to executive compliance focuses on organizational measures by employees to make wrongdoing less convenient for potential offenders (Haines et al., 2022). Compliance refers to obeying the formal and informal rules, regulations, and norms in force at a given time and place (Durand et al., 2019).

The main knowledge sources of license authority are insights, reflections, and assessments of benefits and harm (Rooney et al., 2014: 210):

> Other critical components include the reputation of the organization, previous relationships with communities, the level of transparency the organization operates with, and whether the organization is trusted to do the things they say they will. Social license relies critically on social aspects of knowledge diffusion, and contested "truth" claims often based on radically different ontologies, epistemologies, and axiologies.

Control by stakeholders is concerned with a negative discrepancy between the desired and current state of affairs. Control mechanisms attempt to reduce the discrepancy through adaptive action in the form of behavioral reactions (Direnzo & Greenhaus, 2011). Control mechanisms attempt to influence and manage the process, content, and outcome of work (Kownatzki et al., 2013). Control involves processes of negotiation in which various strategies are developed to produce particular outcomes. Control is therefore a dynamic process that regulates behavior through a set of modes, rules, or strategies (Gill, 2019).

There are various types of control mechanisms with various targets (Chown, 2021: 752):

> For example, prominent frameworks delineate controls based on whether they are formal or informal, coercive, normative, peer-based, or concertive. Controls are also divided based on whether they target employees' behaviors by implementing processes or rules that ensure individuals perform tasks in a particular manner, target their outputs by assessing employees based on measurable items such as profits or production, or target the inputs to the production process by controlling the human capital and material inputs utilized by the organization.

At its core, top-down control refers to the manner in which "an organization's managers can use different types of control mechanisms – such as financial incentives, performance management, or culture – to monitor, measure, and evaluate workers' behaviors and influence them toward achieving the organization's goals in efficient and effective ways" (Chown, 2021: 713). Similarly at its core, bottom-up control refers to the manner in which organizational members can use different types of control mechanisms – such as whistleblowing, transparency, resource access, or culture – to monitor, measure, and evaluate executives' avoidance of deviant behaviors and influence them toward achieving the organization's goals in efficient and effective ways. While the hierarchical structure remains with executives at the top of the organization in charge of the business, bottom-up control is a matter of stakeholder involvement in compliance. While top-down control is often a formal and rigid system, bottom-up control can be an informal and flexible system based on social influence (Haines et al., 2022: 185):

Criminalization, foundational analytical territory for criminology, forms part of a 'bottom up' strategy where it becomes 'social property', untethered from law and formal criminal justice. Criminalization as social property comprises a central element of 'social control influence' over corporate harm. This is justice in the vernacular with media, social movements and citizen watchdogs exerting pressure, demanding change and bringing business to account.

When noticing wrongdoing at the top of the organization, improvisation might be a key capability for organizational members and citizen watchdogs. Capability refers to the ability to perform (Paruchuri et al., 2021), while improvisation refers to the spontaneous process by which planning and execution happen at the same time (Mannucci et al., 2021). Rather than following formal reporting lines to people who are not trustworthy, improvisation is a matter of spontaneous action in response to unanticipated occurrences, in which individuals find a way to manage the unexpected problem.

Bottom-up approaches have been discussed so far in this section. It is matter of people in the organization who prevent potential offenders from wrongdoing and who detect offenses and offenders having committed misconduct and crime. A different approach in the same line of reasoning is the outside-in approach where outsiders rather than insiders prevent and detect wrongdoing in the organization. The outside-in approach involves various stakeholders in the community such as citizens, media, unions, politicians, and action groups.

The term stakeholder refers to someone with an interest or concern in something, especially in business (Gomulya & Mishina, 2017). A stakeholder is someone who can affect or be affected by the business, and a stakeholder is someone who associates with the business and does or does not derive utility from the association (Lange et al., 2022: 9):

Utility here describes the satisfaction, gratification, or need fulfillment that a stakeholder receives by virtue of interacting with or being associated with the business.

A stakeholder typically injects some kind of resource into the business with the expectation of receiving some form of return. Nason et al. (2018) argued that a stakeholder is someone who derives own identity to some extent from attributes of the business. Lange et al. (2022) argued that a stakeholder should not necessarily be viewed as someone having a single-minded focus on own utility but rather as someone having an outcome in mind that often will be of utility for groups of people based on a kind of solidarity. Nason et al. (2018: 259) suggested that a stakeholder provides "intense feedback when there are major discrepancies between their expectations and the firm's actual social performance."

The rise of social media, non-government organizations, as well as the knowledge level among citizens has led to the strengthening of stakeholder demands (Panda & Sangle, 2019: 1085):

As a result, firms often find themselves in conflicts. The cost of these conflicts for the firm is the opportunity cost of future projects due to loss of reputation, and for the stakeholders, it is the loss of opportunities, both social and economical, that could have been brought by the projects. The tension between firms and stakeholders creates a dynamic environment where following compliance is not enough, and social acceptance is equally important as government licenses. Such an acceptance is termed as 'social license to operate' (SLO).

SLO exists when a project is seen as having the broad, ongoing approval and acceptance of society to conduct its activities.

Panda and Sangle (2019: 1086) further argued that there is a growing awareness among stakeholders of their power to make their voices heard:

The rise of social media has resulted in organized movements against corporations as well as in the demand for greater transparency from firms. The number and type of stakeholders for a firm are no longer confined in their immediate surroundings. Most multinational corporations have 'global stakeholders' who may not directly have a stake in the firm but are interested in its social, economic, and environmental impacts. Firms practicing opaqueness are at a greater risk than those open to stakeholder inspection.

Panda and Sangle (2019) found that SLO is deeply rooted in the stakeholder theory. It is a theory of business ethics to promote managerial matters during different environmental situations. According to Waheed and Zhang (2022), the theory supports social issues by assisting the strategic decisions of organizations. It takes into account the evolving role of stakeholders, from being bystanders in a company to being a part in the decision-making processes (Panda & Sangle, 2019).

However, the monitored enterprise might find it easier to challenge the authority of outsiders compared to insiders who belong to the enterprise. Outsiders can be challenged whether they count in authorizing or denying the company their social license. Outsiders can be challenged whether they are entitled to speak based on their claimed membership and representation of the community.

One potential source of license authority is activist groups and non-government organizations that take cases to the courts. While a case is pending, the accused company tends to become passive by awaiting the outcome of the trial. However, bringing a case in front of a judge is only a matter of legal license to operate. The judge is to apply the law to the issues and cannot apply other criteria that citizens are concerned about.

Another potential source of license authority is name-and-shame lists where academics consider firms that are ethical and compliant versus firms that are not ethical and compliant. When Russia invaded Ukraine in February and March 2022 (Grønningsæter, 2022), the Yale School of Management in the United States updated on a daily basis a list of companies that had terminated their business in Russia as well as those that remained. The two lists were for a while updated every hour by Professor Jeffrey Sonnenfeld and his research team at the Yale Chief Executive Leadership Institute to reflect new announcements from companies in real time (Sonnenfeld, 2022a, b).

Substance of Social License

Sources of license authority are an issue of who has the right to speak and to be listened to, while the substance of social license is concerned with what they can and cannot say in terms of the content of their messages to grant or stop social permission for business activity. Furthermore, the substance of messages might be conflict or cooperation, where both are understood to be important aspects of influence. Haines (2022: 189) referred to cooperation:

> When a social license is understood as the development of trust, reciprocity and problem-solving between the community and the company, the aim of the social license is one of cooperation moving towards a shared goal.

Both by conflicting and cooperative messages from license providers by authority, the messages are a vehicle of social control. The vehicle provides criminological insights into criminalization, where two requirements are usefully emphasized. The first requirement for criminalization is that people think it is wrong what the company intends to do, is already doing, or has already done. The second requirement is that potential or actual wrongdoing deserves a consequence in terms of a warning, a sanction, or a punishment. Crime refers to acts that are considered bad and that should be punished.

As the term social license suggests, it is predominantly centered on permission for business activity that is not regulated by the law. The legal license refers to laws that describe wrongdoing and punishment. In the absence of laws for many instances and incidents of wrongdoing, the social license fills the gap by substance in messages from sources of license authority. The social license refers to "the acceptance or approval by the local – if not indigenous – communities and stakeholders of a business enterprise's operations or projects in a certain area" (Saenz, 2019: 297). The social license is "the set of demands and expectations held by local stakeholders and broader society about how a business should operate," and "a license is then said to be granted if the business is deemed to have met these demands and expectations – and thus is viewed as being socially acceptable" (Hurst et al., 2020: 1). The social license is "a social construction to which various stakeholders contributes" (Baba et al., 2021: 248). The social license is an expression "often used in the context of a possible disapproval of their activities, when such disapproval may result in resistance that could harm business interests," and the expression "refers to mainly tacit consent on the part of society toward the activities of the business" (Demuijnck & Fasterling, 2016: 675). Further scholarly definitions of the expression were presented in the introduction.

A distinction can be made between the static and the dynamic vision of social license to operate. The static vision suggests that obtaining the license mainly results from acceptable practice, while the dynamic vision suggests a continuous exchange to influence practice (Baba et al., 2021). The dynamic vision is a matter of maintaining relationships with stakeholders (Hurst et al., 2020: 2):

> While operational impacts will play a pivotal role in determining whether an entity is perceived as trustworthy, research also suggests that procedural fairness, quality of contact, promise keeping, and the development of a shared agenda are important in supporting organization-stakeholder relationships.

Procedural fairness in the quote refers to the extent a business listens to and respects opinions of relevant others. Quality of contact refers to the stability and content of relational exchanges between the business and relevant others. Promise keeping refers to authenticity in voice and action. Shared agenda refers to development of joint perspectives and values where the business can develop mutually supportive initiatives with the community and other stakeholders that are in line with expectations, aspirations, and perceptions (Hurst et al., 2020).

According to Rooney et al. (2014: 209), a social license refers to "an informal agreement that is granted by communities and relevant stakeholders to an organization or industry working in the local area":

> Organizations holding a social license may not even recognize they have one. However, when a social license is removed it becomes obvious to all, incurring both human and economic costs that sometimes can be irreparable.

There are various reasons why certain kinds of wrongdoing are not regulated by laws. One reason is that law making is often lagging behind citizens' perceptions of what is so wrong that it should be punished. Another reason is that law makers do not consider some forms of wrongdoing serious enough to regulate the matter by law. Furthermore, inefficient law enforcement and missing links in the criminal justice system can cause an absence of a clear institutional authority even when there are relevant laws.

The content of a social license is permission for business activity when requirements in messages from stakeholders have been met (Haines et al., 2022: 186):

> This social permission and the currency of the term provide a potentially important enabler for communities to control the activities of the business in their midst and reduce associated harms. At the same time, the absence of a clear institutional authority underpinning the social license means that its legitimacy as a business requirement can be challenged. The centrally social character of the social license also means that tensions around what is and what is not socially desirable business conduct often emerge simultaneously and can settle on the same activity. Legal and regulatory regimes are ordered around specific harms. A relatively straightforward orientation to hold a business to account for specific harm under the law (safety, environmental damage, fraud) from a social license orientation becomes a multi-faceted struggle over what is desirable, what is undesirable and who has the right to decide whether the business activity should or should not proceed.

Therefore, the social license is not as straightforward as the legal license. Rather, the acceptance of a company or industry's business practices and operating procedures depends on opinions in the community that might diverge between corporate employees, corporate executives, shareholders, investigative journalists, public activists, politicians from various political parties, and the general public. The messages from these kinds of sources might be questions in terms of their legitimate authority, their content, as well as their form as confrontational or cooperative. Nevertheless, the overall ambition of a social license is to bring about agreement between company and community and assert the license value as essential to industry operations.

Given the latter criteria of being essential to industry operations, both authority of actors and substance of their opinions become a matter of power and influence. Bottom-up initiatives as well as outside-in initiatives only become determinants for granting social license if the actors are able to be recognized as essential to business and industry operations. From the perspective of the potentially accused business, it is important to listen to the community in assisting the business obtain the permission of the community they work in and interact with through improving company relations and behavior toward representatives of the community. Since social license is not within a company's control, corporate "entities 'earn' social license through organizational actions that are both justified in the 'eyes of society' and not achieved through manipulation" (Sale, 2021: 821).

However, some businesses may choose a path of ignoring, manipulating, or challenging the substance of social license (Haines et al., 2022: 187):

> Critics of corporate use of the term argue that it represents a shallow form of reassurance where companies merely pay lip service to community concerns. It is used to legitimate company operations without serious attempts to reduce and manage the problems those operations engender. Similarly, it may be used by politicians with a business-oriented agenda to demonstrate that social issues have been considered, despite decisions being made against community desires. Other work shows how the processes ostensibly oriented around obtaining a social license and mutually beneficially agreement can be strategies for maintaining control used by companies to 'discipline' communities by marginalizing critical voices in association with professions from corporate engagement personnel to anthropologists. A central element of these company management strategies is influencing decisions regarding who represents the community.

While associating with those community members who support the business, the company may distance themselves from community members who disapprove of the business. This is in line with Sutherland's (1939, 1983) differential association perspective, where wrongdoers associate with those who agree with them and distance themselves from those who disagree with them. Yet another ignorance strategy toward stakeholders is window dressing that refers to the act or the instance of making something appear better than it actually is (Desai, 2016; Eberl et al., 2015).

Sale (2021) defined three stages of social license substance, legitimacy, credibility, and trust, that correspond to acceptance, approval, and identity. Legitimacy refers to a belief that a business has the basic right to operate. Legitimacy is an assessment of the appropriateness of an entity's actions (Bundy & Pfarrer, 2015; Fitzgibbon & Lea, 2018). Legitimacy implies that the company and its activities are reasonable and acceptable. According to Demuijnck and Fasterling (2016: 678), legitimacy "refers to the congruence between social values associated with or implied by activities and the norms and acceptable behavior in the larger social system." Legitimacy implies that the activities are neutral or desirable, proper and uncontroversial, and appropriate within a socially constructed space of norms, values, and beliefs.

In criminology, a typical characteristic of white-collar crime is the superficial appearance of legitimacy (Benson & Simpson, 2018). Legitimacy comes from the Latin legitimus meaning lawful (Melé & Armengou, 2016: 729):

> Today, the meaning of legitimacy is also related with the acceptance or justification of the existence of an institution beyond 'legality' (pertaining to the law).

Legitimacy is then a matter of acceptance of business exercise of power in a justified manner. Sometimes three forms of legitimacy are discussed. First, pragmatic legitimacy is based on the self-interested calculations of a company's most immediate stakeholders (Saenz, 2019: 297):

Pragmatic legitimacy is based on the self-interests of the public and is most often exchange or influential in nature. Under exchange legitimacy, society supports a company's policy based on the expected material benefits to the society, such as technological improvements or employment opportunities. Influential legitimacy is attained by being responsive to stakeholders and incorporating society's wider interests into the company's decision-making process.

Next, moral legitimacy is based on a positive normative evaluation of the company and its business activities (Saenz, 2019: 297):

Moral legitimacy hinges on whether a particular action is viewed as acceptable by a company's powerful stakeholders. Moral legitimacy is comprised of four aspects: consequential, procedural, personal, and structural legitimacy. Consequential legitimacy is result-oriented and is based on visible achievements such as increased employment, reduced emissions, and fewer numbers of workplace injuries. With procedural legitimacy, the focal point is not merely results of an action; rather, emphasis is placed on the morality surrounding the means to achieve a particular outcome (…) Structural legitimacy is based on the company's identity and whether or not it forms a part of a 'morally favored taxonomic category', whereas personal legitimacy is dependent on the character of the company's leaders.

Finally, cognitive legitimacy is based on a perception of the company as a natural phenomenon in the community compliant with established cultural norms (Saenz, 2019: 298):

Cognitive legitimacy can be split into two elements: comprehensibility and being taken for granted. The former attempts to make society understand the company through providing logical and easily understandable explanations for its actions and plans whereas the latter relies on the very existence of the company being taken for granted as an integral part of the social fabric.

Melé and Armengou (2016) emphasized the importance of moral legitimacy that might be achieved if the intended end of business operations contributes to the common good, if the means of business operations are acceptable, if stakeholder concerns are respected, and if possible risk of damage is minimized.

The next level of social license substance suggested by Sale (2021) is credibility that refers to the quality of being trusted and believed in (Gomulya & Mishina, 2017). It is a matter of approval by local communities, society, and stakeholders of a business enterprise's activities (Demuijnck & Fasterling, 2016). Credibility builds on approval by stakeholders (Sale, 2021: 825):

Credibility requires the prior existence of legitimacy. Here, however, the focus is on the company working with stakeholders to achieve more than just tacit approval. Instead, the company builds a relationship that involves initial trust and stakeholder voice in operations. Credibility, like legitimacy, requires action and interaction above the legally required line. For credibility to exist, the entity and the project must be 'believable', and the entity's promises must be both realistic and achievable. Put differently, before an entity can earn credibility, the stakeholders must perceive it to be honest. In addition to honest and open communication, credibility requires deliverables. The company must have certain characteristics, and the community must believe it has them.

The final level of social license suggested by Sale (2021) is trust, which is a stronger, more fundamental form of relationship. Trust is the acceptance of vulnerability to another's actions (Baer et al., 2021). Trust implies that vulnerability is accepted based upon positive expectations of the motives and actions of the entity. Kim et al. (2009: 401) defined trust as "a psychological state comprising the intention to accept vulnerability based on positive expectations of the intentions or behavior of another." The positive expectations can relate to what another does, how it is done, and when it is done. The positive expectations can relate to the reaction of another, where it is expected that the reaction will be understandable, acceptable, and favorable. Vulnerability means that trust can easily be violated without detection or correction of deviant behavior, causing potential harm to the trustor. Trust is thus associated with dependence and risk (Chan et al., 2020: 3):

> The trustor depends on something or someone (the trustee or object of trust), and there is a possibility that expectations or hopes will not be satisfied, and that things will go wrong. Trust is not absolute, but conditional and contextual.

Sale (2021) referred to the stage of trust as a transition from acceptance and approval to a state where the stakeholders identify with the entity. Stakeholders have confidence that entity actions will be either favorable or at least neutral to the community's interests. At the stage of trust, interests of the company and the community seem aligned.

Value of Social License

The value of a social license lies in both the defensive and the offensive dimensions. The defensive dimension is concerned with avoiding criticism and obstacles in business activities from skeptical representatives of the community. Executives do not like bad press and activist campaigns, and they want to avoid consumer reactions. Companies do not want critical attention from various supervisory authorities, and they would like to avoid becoming negative topics in municipal committees and government agencies. Companies want a social license that can "prevent demonstrations, boycotts, shutdowns, negative publicity, and the increases in regulation that are a hallmark of publicness" (Sale, 2021: 820).

The defensive dimension is a matter and concern of violation of the license or even loss of the license. Such circumstances "can lead to serious delays and costs for organizations, reduced market access, boycotts or protests, community anger, increased regulations, loss of reputation, and, in extreme instances, the failure of a project, organization and/or industry" (Hurst et al., 2020: 1). For example, in the Netherlands, the loss of the social license to operate caused Groningen gas to stop its operations making substantial volumes of gas being left in the ground (Beukel & Geuns, 2019).

Corporate enterprises certainly would like to avoid scandals, where a scandal refers to "an unexpected, publicly known, and harmful event that has high levels of initial uncertainty, interferes with the normal operation of an organization, and generates widespread, intuitive, and negative perceptions" externally (Bundy & Pfarrer,

2015: 350). A corporate scandal forces executives to make accounts, where an account refers to a statement made by the scandalized entity to explain negative behavior that has become subject to inquiry by stakeholders and outsiders (Gottschalk & Benson, 2020). A scandal can develop into a crisis, where a crisis refers to a fundamental threat to the organization, which is often characterized by ambiguity of cause, effect, and means of resolution (König et al., 2020). Scandals and following crises can cause the community explicitly to refuse to negotiate or cooperate with suffering enterprises. Generally, to avoid scandals and crises, enterprises would like to refrain from business activities that might stir up controversies (Demuijnck & Fasterling, 2016).

The offensive dimension of social license value is concerned with benefits and advantages in business activities from supportive and enthusiastic representatives of the community. Executives do like favorable press, and they enjoy consumers' expression of satisfaction. Companies want positive attention – or no attention – from various supervisory authorities, and they prefer to avoid becoming topics in municipal committees and government agencies, unless they are called upon as resources to solve state problems. As a resource, an enterprise can be an enabler of solutions preferred by politicians that they cannot accomplish without the help of the enterprise. Ideally as a resource, the enterprise has unique expertise in the field that can be applied to solve problems perceived challenging in the community.

The value of social license in the offensive dimension includes "the generation of legitimacy, trust, and credibility among stakeholders; improved corporate reputation; long-term business success; ongoing access to resources; improved market competitiveness; strengthened stakeholder relationships; and positive effects on employees" (Hurst et al., 2020: 1).

Companies would like to strengthen their reputation and brands by positive public attention where the social license is a visible and clear manifestation of benefits exceeding costs and advantages exceeding disadvantages. Therefore, as argued by Haines et al. (2022: 187), "the high value placed on a social license" can be seen in the damaging effects of communities expressing their distrust and rejection of company activities as well as in the enabling effects when the company is defended by the community against outside criticism:

> A social license is a visible manifestation of a commitment to corporate social responsibility. The literature centers on promoting the importance of a fair process in business dealings with communities with reciprocity, listening and promise-keeping central to ensuring that companies not only are tolerated by communities but when problems arise, can be defended by those communities against outside criticism. The emphasis is on elucidating how companies can develop trust and acceptance both by local communities and more broadly within society.

The positive dimension of being defended by communities might include an enabler where the "social license can 'make' a business by contributing to its survival and success" (Sale, 2021: 821). The value of a social license thus refers both to avoidance of negative effects of rejecting corporate activities and to achievements of positive effects of accepting corporate activities.

The value of a social license to operate is emphasized in situations where the enterprise is dependent on the local community as a source of labor and services and where the enterprise will influence living conditions for both employees and others in the community. The value is also emphasized when the license will enable the enterprise to establish operations quickly, while a lack of license will cause delays of sometimes several years and potentially make the business activity much more expensive (Melé & Armengou, 2016).

An example of delay caused by lack of social license to operate can be found in Norway where an actionist group was fighting a railroad project, first in the media and then in courts. The construction project had already been put on halt for 1 year when the case was on trial in Norwegian courts. The actionist group lost in a district court and later in a court of appeals. But they did not give up, so they appealed the verdict to the Norwegian Supreme Court. The issue was where the new railroad line should be located through a minor city in Norway (Bentzrød, 2022a, b).

Another recent example in Norway is wind turbine parks. Community members living close to one of the wind turbine parks complained that they could not sleep because of the noise from the turbines. One local resident said that she could not only sleep but she got headache that developed into a migraine because of the noisy sound from the windmills. Then she was hospitalized for 2 days to recover (Jørgensen & Mannsåker, 2022):

> Several neighbors to Tysvær wind farm report serious health issues as a result of loud noise from the wind turbines. For Lillian Soma Øvregård in Hervik, it went so far that last week she was hospitalized for two days.

As a consequence of the massive community protests against the noise, the company operating the windmills stopped them daily from 7 pm to 7 am. Their financial loss from this decision was substantial. In the meantime, the company tried to identify technology that would reduce the volume of the sound and the harmful kind of the sound so that it might be possible in the future to run the windmills also during nighttime (Jørgensen & Mannsåker, 2022).

The value of a social license can be understood within institutional theory where the main goal of organizations is to survive. This requires not only economic success but also social acceptance (Saenz, 2019). Institutional theory suggests that opportunities are shaped by individuals, groups, other organizations, as well as society at large. The theory argues that business enterprises are much more than simple tools and instruments to achieve financial goals and ambitions. The theory says that organizations are adaptable systems that recognize and learn from the environment by mirroring values in society (Kostova et al., 2008; Pillay & Kluvers, 2014; Shadnam & Lawrence, 2011).

Australian Case Study

The research by Haines et al. (2022) was extensively referenced in this chapter. Their research was concerned with a case in Australia. Their data collection centered on the activities of one particular company prominent in coal seam gas operations in New South Wales. They found that the company framed the social license to appeal to different audiences such as investors in annual reports, local residents in local newspapers, and broader constituencies in national broadsheet.

The sources of license authority included landowners who had to grant access to the coal seam operations to make business possible for the company (Haines et al., 2022: 191):

> In tangible terms, what the gas company offered landholders was annual payments for exploration wells sited on their land providing much-needed secure income to farmers particularly during periods of drought or low prices for their produce. The location of sealed roads built to enable company vehicle access could be negotiated so that they also assisted farmers. Negotiation could also proceed by way of comparison – namely that gas was less destructive than coal. Since exploration zones for coal often overlapped those for coal seam gas, allowing a gas exploration company access meant that it could be protected against encroachment by coal mines.

The substance of the social license rested on reciprocity and humanity, as well as on proper relationships, where the coal seam gas exploration business was being welcomed into and becoming part of the community (Haines et al., 2022: 191):

> The emphasis was on a fair process that would lead to a trusted relationship. Yet, the level of commitment required of the company to demonstrate their dedication to obtaining and maintaining social license ranged from a discrete transactional relationship bound in scope and time to an enduring relationship that encompassed a broad range of social and environmental concerns. The requirements to enable an enduring relationship were onerous. Community relations officers within companies could struggle to convince their superiors of the importance and depth of obligation that this level of commitment involved.

The value of the social license was an enhancement of as well as a replacement for law. The laws were not sufficient to regulate business activity. The social license represented and regulated more than what was legally permitted (Haines et al., 2022: 191):

> Those negotiating access for the company also understood that legality did not negate social expectations around company access to land. Company representatives felt that an a priori assertion of their legal right to access land would be met by anger and defiance. Relying on their legal rights would be seen as arrogant and likely to lead to lengthy court disputes; one argued 'we never tested it (their legal rights)'. Unlike coal mines where land to be mined is acquired by coal companies, gas companies did not need to acquire land (as subsurface resources in NSW are owned by the state), but they did need access to land in order to access those resources.

Clarification of the sources of authority, the substance of the social license, as well as the value of the social license changed people's attitude toward gas operations. The attitude changed from cautious openness, some conflict, and protest events to a mutual form of respect (Haines et al., 2022).

References

Baba, S., Hemissi, O., Berrahou, Z., & Traiki, C. (2021). The spatiotemporal dimension of the social license to operate: The case of a landfill facility in Algeria. *Management International – MI, 25*(4), 247–266.

Baer, M. D., Frank, E. L., Matta, F. K., Luciano, M. M., & Wellman, N. (2021). Untrusted, over-trusted, or just right? The fairness of (in)congruence between trust wanted and trust received. *Academy of Management Journal, 64*(1), 180–206.

Benson, M. L., & Simpson, S. S. (2018). *White-collar crime: An opportunity perspective* (3rd ed.). Routledge.

Bentzrød, S. B. (2022a). Jernbanen i Moss står bom fast i kvikkleire – For ett år siden fant Bane Nor mer kvikkleire i Moss sentrum enn de visste om (The railway in Moss is stuck in quick clay – A year ago, Bane Nor found more quick clay in the center of Moss than they knew about), daily Norwegian newspaper *Aftenposten*, Sunday, February 20, p. 1.

Bentzrød, S. B. (2022b). Aksjonsgruppe i Moss tapte ny rettssak – Lagmannsretten konkluderer med at vedtak som ble gjort om jernbaneutbygging i Moss var lovlig (Action group in Moss lost a new lawsuit – The court of appeal concludes that decisions made on railroad development in Moss were legal), daily Norwegian newspaper *Aftenposten*, Wednesday, February 23, p. 21.

Beukel, J., & Geuns, L. (2019). *Groningen gas: The loss of a social license to operate.* Hague Centre for Strategic Studies.

Bundy, J., & Pfarrer, M. D. (2015). A burden of responsibility: The role of social approval at the onset of a crisis. *Academy of Management Review, 40*(3), 345–369.

Chan, J., Logan, S., & Moses, L. B. (2020). Rules in information sharing for security. *Criminology & Criminal Justice.* Published online pages 1–19. https://doi.org/10.1177/1748895820960199

Chown, J. (2021). The unfolding of control mechanisms inside organizations: Pathways of customization and transmutation. *Administrative Science Quarterly, 66*(3), 711–752.

Demuijnck, G., & Fasterling, B. (2016). The social license to operate. *Journal of Business Ethics, 136*, 675–685.

Desai, V. M. (2016). Under the radar: Regulatory collaborations and their selective use to facilitate organizational compliance. *Academy of Management Journal, 59*(2), 636–657.

Direnzo, M. S., & Greenhaus, J. H. (2011). Job search and voluntary turnover in a boundaryless world: A control theory perspective. *Academy of Management Review, 36*(3), 567–589.

Durand, R., Hawn, O., & Ioannou, I. (2019). Willing and able: A general model of organizational responses to normative pressures. *Academy of Management Review, 44*(2), 299–320.

Eberl, P., Geiger, D., & Assländer, M. S. (2015). Repairing trust in an organization after integrity violations. The ambivalence of organizational rule adjustments. *Organization Studies, 36*(9), 1205–1235.

Fitzgibbon, W., & Lea, J. (2018). Privatization and coercion: The question of legitimacy. *Theoretical Criminology, 22*(4), 545–562.

Gill, M. J. (2019). The significance of suffering in organizations: Understanding variation in workers' responses to multiple modes of control. *Academy of Management Review, 44*(2), 377–404.

Gomulya, D., & Mishina, Y. (2017). Signaler credibility, signal susceptibility, and relative reliance on signals: How stakeholders change their evaluative processes after violation of expectations and rehabilitative efforts. *Academy of Management Journal, 60*(2), 554–583.

Gottschalk, P., & Benson, M. L. (2020). The evolution of corporate accounts of scandals from exposure to investigation. *British Journal of Criminology, 60*, 949–969.

Grønningsæter, F. (2022). Russlands svarte økonomi (Russia's black economy), Norwegian business magazine. *Kapital, 5*, 16–23.

Haines, F., Bice, S., Einfeld, C., & Sullivan, H. (2022). Countering corporate power through social control: What does a social licence offer? *The British Journal of Criminology, 62*, 184–199.

Hurst, B., Johnston, K. A., & Lane, A. B. (2020). Engaging for a social license to operate. *Public Relations Review, 40*. Published online https://doi.org/10.1016/j.pubrev.2020.101931

Jørgensen, G., & Mannsåker, H. (2022). Blir sjuk av støyen fra vindturbinene (Get sick from the noise from the wind turbines), Norwegian public broadcasting *NRK*, www.nrk.no, published February 21.

Kim, P. H., Dirks, K. T., & Cooper, C. D. (2009). The repair of trust: A dynamic bilateral perspective and multilevel conceptualization. *Academy of Management Review, 34*(3), 401–422.

König, A., Graf-Vlachy, L., Bundy, J., & Little, L. M. (2020). A blessing and a curse: How CEOs' trait empathy affects their management of organizational crisis. *Academy of Management Review, 45*(1), 130–153.

Kostova, T., Roth, K., & Dacin, M. T. (2008). Institutional theory in the study of multinational corporations: A critique and new directions. *Academy of Management Review, 33*(4), 994–1006.

Kownatzki, M., Walter, J., Floyd, S. W., & Lechner, C. (2013). Corporate control and the speed of strategic business unit decision making. *Academy of Management Journal, 56*(5), 1295–1324.

Lange, D., Bundy, J., & Park, E. (2022). The social nature of stakeholder utility. *Academy of Management Review, 47*(19), 9–30.

Mannucci, P. V., Orazi, D. C., & Valck, K. (2021). Developing improvisation skills: The influence of individual orientations. *Administrative Science Quarterly, 66*(3), 612–658.

Melé, D., & Armengou, J. (2016). Moral legitimacy in controversial projects and its relationships with social license to operate: A case study. *Journal of Business Ethics, 136*, 729–742.

Nason, R. S., Bacq, S., & Gras, D. (2018). A behavioral theory of social performance: Social identity and stakeholder expectations. *Academy of Management Review, 43*(2), 259–283.

Panda, S. S., & Sangle, S. (2019). An exploratory study to investigate the relationship between social license to operate and sustainable development strategies. *Sustainable Development, 27*, 1085–1095.

Paruchuri, S., Han, J. H., & Prakash, P. (2021). Salient expectations? Incongruence across capability and integrity signals and investor reactions to organizational misconduct. *Academy of Management Journal, 64*(2), 562–586.

Pillay, S., & Kluvers, R. (2014). An institutional theory perspective on corruption: The case of a developing democracy. *Financial Accountability & Management, 30*(1), 95–119.

Rooney, D., Leach, J., & Ashworth, P. (2014). Doing the social in social license. *Social Epistemology, 28*(3–4), 209–218.

Saenz, C. (2019). Building legitimacy and trust between a mining company and a community to earn social license to operate: A Peruvian case study. *Corporate Social Responsibility and Environmental Management, 26*(2), 296–306.

Sale, H. A. (2021). The corporate purpose of social license. *Sothern California Law Review, 94*(4), 785–842.

Shadnam, M., & Lawrence, T. B. (2011). Understanding widespread misconduct in organizations: An institutional theory of moral collapse. *Business Ethics Quarterly, 21*(3), 379–407.

Sonnenfeld, J. (2022a). The great business retreat matters in Russia today – Just as it mattered in 1986 South Africa, *Fortune*, www.fortune.com, published March 7.

Sonnenfeld, J. (2022b). Over 300 companies have withdrawn from Russia – But some remain, Yale School of Management, www.som.yale.edu, published March 10.

Sutherland, E. H. (1939). White-collar criminality. *American Sociological Review, 5*(1), 1–12.

Sutherland, E. H. (1983). *White collar crime – The uncut version*. Yale University Press.

Waheed, A., & Zhang, Q. (2022). Effect of CSR and ethical practices on sustainable competitive performance: A case of emerging markets from stakeholder theory perspective. *Journal of Business Ethics, 175*, 837–855.

Chapter 3
Cooperative Member Revolt

Obos is Norway's largest housing developer. Obos' vision is to build the society of the future and, in doing so, fulfill housing dreams. Obos is a member organization where residents and prospects pay an annual membership fee. Obos engages in the development and sale of homes and properties, banking and financial services, property management, real estate brokerage, and other forms of service production in the housing and property sector. The organization is a cooperative owned by its 502,527 members. The cooperative was established in 1929 to provide a solution to housing shortages for low-income families in the capital of Oslo. After World War II, Obos played an important role of building apartment blocks on the east side of Oslo. The rich people live on the west side of Oslo, while the less fortunate live on the east side of the city center. Apartments were affordable for poor families as Obos required minimal deposits and favorable loans. To be qualified to buy the most attractive Obos apartments, buyers had to document membership for several decades when moving into the 1960s and 1970s.

The case study in this chapter was presented to Obos management for contradiction, and the comments from the senior advisor for the member organization at Obos, Pettersen (2022), are included in the following text.

According to Holm (2021), Obos is both a member organization and a commercial enterprise:

> The reason lies in the history: The housing construction associations became the mainstay of the social democratic housing policy that really took hold after World War II. The idea was to operate without profit, build rationally, get affordable government loans, and pay a symbolic plot rent. The model worked effectively, and the housing construction associations built more than 200,000 homes during this period. Without Obos and the other housing associations, the Norwegian welfare society would have looked very different.

In the 1980s, a housing market existed where supply of and demand for apartments seemed more in an equilibrium state in Oslo where most people could afford housing on the open market. Then Obos transformed its business into more expensive construction projects with not only apartments with 60 or 70 square meters but also luxury apartments on the west side of Oslo of more than 100 square meters.

"Here you present reality as if it was OBOS that changed strategy, while in reality it was the external conditions that in the late 70s and 80s were dramatically changed. This is misleading to the reader. It was the state and the municipality that abolished the social housing policy and that no longer would pay for the construction of homes at below market price. You also present it as if OBOS is now mainly building expensive homes in Oslo west, which of course is not correct. OBOS does mainly not that" (Pettersen, 2022).

The housing market in Oslo went again out of balance after the year 2000. Obos dwellings in Oslo were 11.5 percent more expensive in the first quarter of 2016 compared to the same period the previous year (Oesterud, 2016). Social housing was in high demand. However, Obos seemed not ready anymore to take on the role of providing affordable housing for low-income families. Housing development was still the main activity carried out by Obos in the 2020s. The cooperative business expanded and combined residential construction in Norway, Sweden, and Denmark. Then a cooperative member revolt started where Obos management was accused of wrongdoing and fraud.

Challenging the Social License

The source of license authority among 502,527 individuals was their membership at Obos. They represented a bottom-up approach to compliance by the cooperative member revolt. While unstructured and poorly coordinated, they felt entitled to express their concerns both as members and as citizens in the community. They counted in authorizing or denying the company Obos their social license to operate.

In addition, various other stakeholders voiced their opinions in an outside-in approach. For example, in 2021, former mayor of Oslo, Fabian Stang, claimed that Obos was sabotaging its own social mission (Stang, 2021):

> The housing construction company Obos has had large profits. Bravo! But the profits are kept far away from the owners that are the members. The money is not spent on a careful price reduction on new apartments, which would result in a fall in prices throughout the market. They are used for constantly new activities, further and further away from the basic idea. Many members now see that Obos that they thought was theirs has turned into a profit seeker. Like when Obos offered an apartment at Majorstuen for NOK 95 million. Obos should first build ordinary homes for ordinary people before the upper part of the luxury market gets its share. And then there is the sale of an entire block at Ulven. Right in front of the nose of members waiting neatly in line, ready-to-move-in apartments were sold to a rental investor. The board let the sun be shining on them in a report they ordered, which said the sale did not violate the law or the statutes of the cooperative.

Two days later, Stang suggested in a newspaper interview that Daniel Siraj should resign from the CEO position at Obos. The argument was that Siraj was non-democratic. A vote at the general assembly meeting resulted in 105 delegates voting for the dismissal of Siraj, while 343 delegates voted in favor of him staying in the CEO position (Løtveit, 2021).

Holm (2021) phrased the question; is Obos the solution or the problem:

> There is revolt among Obos' members. They want democracy and a more social profile. For Obos' leadership, the time has come to examine own bowels. 502,000 Obos members who have been passive so far are starting to move themselves. More and more of them have noticed that they have neither power nor influence. Through various schemes, the members are represented at the annual general meeting, but as a member you get minimal information and, for example, membership votes, so-called primaries, are never held, as you have in many other associations. Obos has a board appointed by the general meeting, and in practice it is the board and the administration that have managed the housing association.

"Whether it is you who translates incorrectly or whether it is what Holm actually writes, I do not know, but it is incorrect. The general meeting does not elect the board of OBOS. The general meeting elects a supervisory board, and it is this supervisory board that elects the board" (Pettersen, 2022).

"Holm's next sentence, which you uncritically reproduce, more than suggests that it should not be the case that it is the board that rules. Both the law and the articles of association clearly state that this is the way it should be. The board is responsible and must make the strategic choices. This is well and thoroughly accounted for by Bråthen and Co." (Pettersen, 2022, referring to the democracy project described below).

Holm (2021) did not answer his own question; is Obos the solution or the problem. However, he suggested that Obos should get to its roots. He said how Obos can get back to its roots. First, members have to be empowered, while management power has to be reduced. Next, a home culture rather than a business culture should dominate the cooperative. Furthermore, architecture and landscaping should go hand in hand with apartment buildings. Finally, management should concentrate on social housing.

Hegtun (2021) phrased a similar question; has Obos lost its soul:

> Close down Obos! Kick out the leaders! Cut out the investments in Sweden! Reduce prices! In parts of the membership of the housing group Obos, the mood is now very low. In nine days, there may be a riot at the general meeting.

Fraud examiners from law firm KPMG (2021: 1) were hired to conduct a corporate investigation at Obos, based on the following mandate for the examination:

> On April 9, 2021, the board of directors at Obos commissioned KPMG Law to review relevant facts of the Ulven transaction and make associated legal assessments of these. The main purpose of the investigation is to assist the board in assessing whether irregularities or other matters worthy of criticism have occurred.
>
> The background for the assignment is that Obos on the occasion of the development at Ulven in Oslo sold two apartment blocks with a total of 182 apartments to the private rental company Quality Living Residential (QLR) for NOK 936 million. In retrospect, criticism has been leveled at Obos from various quarters. The criticism is mainly related to whether the sale fulfills Obos' purpose as a housing association and the members' interests as such. Furthermore, questions have been raised about the relationship between the CEO of Obos and the purchasing representative from QLR, as well as the relationship between the executive director of housing development and his uncle and cousin who invested in QLR.

Obos had sold 182 apartments at Ulven in Oslo to the real estate company Quality Living Residential for NOK 936 million. The homes were to be rented to the growing corporate market in the area (Jacobsen, 2020):

- Since the apartments we build at Ulven are primarily housing cooperatives, we welcome a rental concept with high quality in the area. The sale of Ulven West to one entrepreneur means that the project will be completed quickly, thus shortening the construction activity time for those who already live in the area, says CEO Daniel Kjørberg Siraj in Obos.

The project at Ulven will have park and squares in the immediate vicinity, underground parking, and car-free street gardens. According to the plan, the homes in Ulven West will be ready for occupancy in the spring of 2023. The general contractor is Team Veidekke, which is a construction company (Jacobsen, 2020):

- The plan is to rent out the homes to employees associated with the planned knowledge park Construction City and other knowledge organizations in the area, says Baard Schumann.

Schumann established QLR in 2018. The purpose of the company was to invest in rental projects. The equity in the company was provided by, among others, Oslo Pension Fund, the Baumann family, Wenaas Capital, and Eidissen Consult. Pareto Securities and the Swedish bank SEB assisted in structuring the transaction.

Motive Convenience Themes

Daniel Kjørberg Siraj was appointed chief executive officer at Obos in 2017. His predecessor Martin Mæland held the CEO position for 34 years since 1983. Mæland was a social democrat who had a loyal approach to the vision and mission of Obos as a construction cooperative building ordinary homes for ordinary people. Lars Buer, who held the board chair position, was a trade unionist also committed to the social democracy of Obos as a member organization for ordinary people.

After 4 years in the position of CEO at Obos, Daniel Kjørberg Siraj became the main target for a membership revolt exemplified by Stang's (2021) article. The revolt included demonstrations in front of Obos headquarters in Oslo with the demand from members stating on posters that Obos is "ours" (Sørgjeld, 2021).

The demonstration consisted of five people. Hardly the foremost sign of wide revolt (Pettersen, 2022).

In 2021, less than 20 percent of Obos' revenues came from housing. CEO Siraj did not think that was a problem. He was proud of all the large-scale prestige projects that he had launched. One of them was a giant construction effort to build a completely new city district. Some observers labeled it megalomania (Lundgaard & Sørgjeld, 2021).

CEO Siraj sold an entire block of apartments to an investor who was to make money on rental arrangements. This was in conflict with the basic idea of Obos to provide ownership of ordinary homes to ordinary people. The idea of home ownership is rooted in the Norwegian tradition where very few rent their homes. However, CEO Siraj preferred to sell the block to investor Baard Schumann with whom he had a comradely tone in the construction business (Lorch-Falch & Tomter, 2021a).

The main theme for motive convenience was corporate gain to make Obos even more profitable as illustrated in Fig. 3.1. In many organizations, ends justify means (Campbell & Göritz, 2014). If ends in terms of ambitions and goals are difficult to realize and achieve in normal ways, deviant means represent an alternative in many organizations (Jonnergård et al., 2010). Among most executives, it is an obvious necessity to achieve goals and objectives, while it is an obvious catastrophe failing to achieve goals and objectives. Welsh and Ordonez (2014) found that high-performance goals cause unethical behavior. Dodge (2009: 15) argued that it is tough rivalry making executives in the organization commit wrongdoing to attain goals:

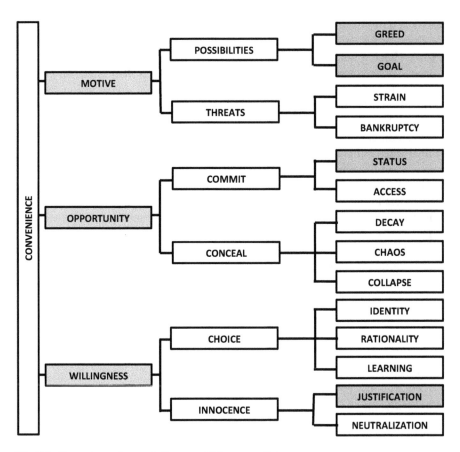

Fig. 3.1 Convenience themes in the case of Obos executives

The competitive environment generates pressures on the organization to violate the law in order to attain goals.

Individual executives would like to be successful, and they would like their workplace to be successful. Being associated with a successful business is important to the identity of many executives. They explore and exploit attractive corporate economic possibilities in both legal and illegal ways, so that their organizations can emerge just as successful, or as even more successful, than other organizations. Profit orientation becomes stronger in goal-oriented organizations whose aim tends to be an ambitious financial bottom line.

It seems that Siraj at the individual level wanted to climb in the hierarchy of needs into fame and admiration. Maslow (1943) developed a hierarchy of human needs where needs start at the bottom with physiological need, need for security, social need, and need for respect and self-realization. When basic needs such as food and shelter are satisfied, then the person moves up the pyramid to satisfy needs for safety and control over own life situation. Further up in the pyramid, the person strives for status, recognition, and self-respect. While street crime is often concerned with the lower levels, white-collar crime is often concerned with the upper levels in terms of status and success.

Concern for others is sometimes a motive for executive wrongdoing (Agnew, 2014). Helping others can be a self-interested, rational action that claims social concern (Paternoster et al., 2018). In a portrait interview with Siraj, he claimed concern for others in his membership in the Pentecostal congregation (Mauno, 2017). He might have satisfied his desire to help others as a social concern in his business decisions.

Accordingly, Agnew (2014) suggested that economic wrongdoing can be committed when individuals think more of others than of themselves. An entrepreneur can commit financial crime to ensure that all employees have a job where they can return. A trusted employee can pay bribes to make sure that the company will have new orders to survive in the future. An executive may commit embezzlement to be able to help his adult children to recover after personal bankruptcy. Agnew (2014) argued that social concern consists of four elements, namely, that 1) individuals care about the welfare of others, 2) they want close ties with others, 3) they are likely to follow moral guidelines such as innocent people should not suffer harm, and 4) they tend to seek confirmation through other people's actions and norms. That a person puts others before oneself will initially lead to less crime. However, economic crime may be committed where the welfare of others and their success is the motive.

Opportunity Convenience Themes

Several executives objected to the sale of the Ulven block to the investor Schumann who wanted to rent out apartment. One of them was chief housing officer Arne Baumann who looked at himself as a housing provider for members. But the housing director explained that he was loyal to the chief executive (Lorch-Falch & Tomter, 2021a):

> Housing director Arne Baumann sees himself as someone who builds homes for the members. According to KPMG, he said that it "tears in the heart of the home builder" to sell a plot in central Oslo to external investors who will rent out. But the director of housing also explained that he was loyal to the CEO. When the agreement was entered into in May last year, Schumann was given a deadline of October 1, 2020, to put money in place. The money did not appear within the deadline. At the time, both housing director Arne Baumann and director of commercial real estate, Nils Bøhler, thought that Obos should turn around to sell to members. Siraj instead gave an extended deadline to get the agreement realized.

Similarly, the board did not react to the Siraj deviance, and board chair Roar Engeland in his account expressed support for the decision, although it leads to fewer homes for members (Lorch-Falch & Tomter, 2021a):

> Like Siraj, he saw that the sale could provide almost one billion in cash. Money Siraj could spin to get plots for more homes than Schumann bought. However, in the short term, the sale means that there will be fewer homes for the members.

The status of CEO Siraj can explain his ignorance of negative reactions to his business model rather than membership model of the cooperative Obos. Status as a convenience theme in the organizational dimension is illustrated in Fig. 3.1. Status is an individual's social rank within a formal or informal hierarchy or the person's relative standing along a valued social dimension. Status is the extent to which an individual is respected and admired by others, and status is the outcome of a subjective assessment process (McClean et al., 2018). High-status individuals enjoy greater respect and deference from, as well as power and influence over, those who are positioned lower in the social hierarchy (Kakkar et al., 2020: 532):

> Status is a property that rests in the eyes of others and is conferred to individuals who are deemed to have a higher rank or social standing in a pecking order based on a mutually valued set of social attributes. Higher social status or rank grants its holder a host of tangible benefits in both professional and personal domains. For instance, high-status actors are sought by groups for advice, are paid higher, receive unsolicited help, and are credited disproportionately in joint tasks. In innumerable ways, our social ecosystem consistently rewards those with high status.

Especially individuals with high status based on prestige rather than dominance tend to be excused for whatever wrongdoing they commit. Individuals who attain and maintain high rank by behaving in ways that are assertive, controlling, and intimidating are characterized as dominant. Individuals who attain and maintain high rank by their set of skills, knowledge, expertise, and willingness to share these with others are characterized as prestigious (Kakkar et al., 2020).

Willingness Convenience Themes

CEO Siraj did not think that his business model deviates from the social model (Mauno, 2017):

- Do you ever get tired of being confronted with the glossy image of the old, social demo-cratic project Obos – those who built apartments for ordinary people in housing need?
- No, I'm never tired of that story. I think it's a proud story Obos has, and I still like to think that we take social responsibility by building as many homes as possible and start projects that we may not make as much money on, but that help young home buyers, says Siraj.

By the way, I was called "an anti-social housing shark" in an editorial in your newspaper. I still remember that. Ha-ha-ha! He laughs.

At the annual general meeting on June 22, 2021, CEO Siraj said he was sorry, as a response to a request that he should step down from the position of chief executive (Lorch-Falch et al., 2021):

Siraj addressed the congregation and presented the story of Obos. He reminded that the company makes money that goes to housing construction. Last year, the shovel was put in the ground for over 3000 homes. He apologized if members have perceived the leadership as arrogant. Although the general meeting does not have the power to replace the CEO, Jostein Starrfelt nevertheless proposed that the board of directors and the supervisory board should start work on replacing the CEO.

- Everyone gets to express their opinions. That's how member democracy works. As a top manager, you have to endure different views on the job you do, Siraj told us before the meeting.

Starrfelt took the floor and asked everyone to think about whether Siraj should continue to steer the ship.

- I do not believe that the CEO has the right expertise, or the deep-seated commitment needed to renew Obos to become a strong, member-driven organization that engages, listens, and delivers, he said.

The willingness to build for the rich and mighty seemed based on a belief that if Obos made money on the rich and mighty, then there would be even better funding for ordinary homes for ordinary people. In the annual report for Obos for 2020, CEO Siraj wrote that he would help young people into their own first homes by sharing space and saving money:

Obos is more than building homes and making money. One of the biggest innovations is the brand new home purchase model Bostart and Deleie, which open the way into the housing market for many who would otherwise be left out. An absolutely important task for Obos is the major social mission associated with contributing to life between the houses. NOK 567 million have been returned in the five-year period, both to members and living environments in the form of support for sports, culture, local activities, and social meeting places.

CEO Siraj justified his actions as illustrated as the convenience theme along the willingness dimension in Fig. 3.1. In a justification, the actor admits responsibility for the act in question but denies its pejorative and negative content. Justifications are different from denials, excuses, or admissions. In a denial, the actor either disavows that anything untoward happened or denies responsibility for whatever it is that happened. In an excuse, the actor admits the act in question is wrong, but denies having full responsibility for it. In an admission, reference is made to the wrongdoer by name as having engaged in the wrongdoing.

Investigation Report Outcome

Fraud examiners from KPMG (2021) found that there was a close relationship between CEO Siraj and QLR executive Schumann. The tone was comradely. They had extensive contact on various business matters. Siraj never conducted an assessment of his potential partiality because he through his relationship with Schumann to be exclusively business-like. The board of directors at Obos had no knowledge of the nature and extent of the relationship, but Siraj informed the board at its meeting in November 2018 that Schumann was the chairman of the board of a rental enterprise that was set up by a financial fund. Siraj and Schumann confirmed to the examiners that they have known each other as industry colleagues for about 10 years. They have been active in the housing policy debate in politics, participated together on municipal committees, and met each other in various industry contexts. On two occasions, they participated together in television programs by the Norwegian public broadcaster NRK. Siraj had used the terms "good friend" and "good buddy" about Schumann in social media. They had never visited each other privately, participated together in leisure activities, or been in social contact of a private nature. They had never done business together privately, exchanged gifts, or covered expenses among themselves or their respective family members. Siraj did not consider the relationship with Schumann to be a private friendship.

Based on these statements of facts as described by KPMG (2021), fraud examiners found that Siraj's impartiality was decent. They found no information that Siraj had acted in disfavor of Obos and in favor of Schumann and Quality Living Residential. They found no evidence of either infidelity or corruption. The relationship did not constitute a conflict of interest according to Obos' ethical guidelines. There were circumstances that could be perceived externally as the relationship also being of a private nature, but according to the ethical guidelines, examiners found that there was no evidence suitable for weakening the confidence in the CEO's impartiality.

The above conclusion relates to the part of the investigation mandate that was concerned with questions about the relationship between the CEO of Obos and the purchasing representative from QLR. The same part of the mandate also questioned the relationship between the executive director of housing development and his uncle and cousin who invested in QLR (KPMG, 2021: 5):

> Executive vice president housing development heads the housing development division and has been a board member of Ulven Housing in the period from November 22, 2017, to April 29, 2020. He is a board member of Obos New Homes and other Obos companies. During the period as a board member of Ulven Housing, the executive vice president was involved in the case processing of the Ulven transaction. KPMG has evidence that the executive vice president of housing development was contacted by telephone by his wealth advisor on September 4, 2020, in connection with the Ulven transaction. The wealth advisor is also an advisor to the family branch that invested in QLR. In the conversation, the executive vice president became aware that the investment company of the uncle and cousin was considering investing in QLR. (...) The audio log of this telephone conversation has been reviewed by the external auditor. KPMG is told that the content does not deal with information that was not otherwise publicly known.

As in the case of the CEO, fraud examiners draw the conclusion that they found no evidence telling that the housing executive acted in favor of any other but the employer Obos. The executive did not act in favor of the investor family or in favor of himself. There was no basis found for suggesting insider trading, infidelity, or corruption.

Another part of the investigation mandate was concerned with Obos on the occasion of the development at Ulven in Oslo that sold 2 apartment blocks with a total of 182 apartments to the private rental company Quality Living Residential (QLR) for NOK 936 million. In retrospect, criticism was leveled at Obos from various quarters. The criticism was mainly related to whether the sale fulfills Obos' purpose as a housing association and the members' interests as such. KPMG (2021) concluded that the transaction with QLR did not violate rules and regulations at Obos.

Violations of the Social License

Member allegations of social license violations by Obos management in their operations were concerned with four issues:

1. The mission and vision of Obos is to secure pleasant and affordable housing for members of the cooperative. They should build ordinary homes for ordinary people. It was a violation of the cooperative purpose to sell two complete residential buildings with many apartments to a landlord whose business purpose is to make money on renting the apartments to tenants.
2. The sales price achieved in the anti-purpose transaction was below market value as estimated by Norwegian kroner per square meter. Obos thus suffered a loss compared to selling each apartment separately to its members. The giveaway price and the following loss seemed caused in close personal relationships between individuals on the seller and the buyer sides, as exemplified below.
3. There was a close relationship and comradely tone between the CEO at Obos and the representative of QLR causing impartiality in connection with the sale of the apartment blocks. The two privileged persons communicated directly with each other about the transaction with minor involvement of governance bodies at Obos.
4. There was also a close relationship between the executive vice president in charge of housing development at Obos and the relevant family members who invested in the purchase of the apartment block. The vice president's impartiality was not at all trustworthy, and he was too late removed from his involvement in the transaction.

The second issue concerning pricing was confirmed by investigative journalists (Lorch-Falch & Tomter, 2021b: 10):

> Our calculations showed that Obos sold the homes 20 percent more expensive to the members than to QLR, even though the apartments in the price list for members were larger on average. We thought this was sensational as well. When KPMG later carried out an

investigation, the calculation was based on a similar procedure, but they used points in time that Obos management thought it was relevant. Then KPMG also found that the price to members was higher, but KPMG put in several large discounts and came to the conclusion that the price anyway was reasonable.

According to Solberg (2022), member-owned organizations over time tend to reduce and in practice partly deprive individual members of their influence:

> A member-owned organization is an organization where membership should provide influence and co-determination. It is crucial that one now actively enters into processes that upgrade the foundation through statutes of association and elected functions.

One of the community revolt leaders made a post on his blog why the social license was lost. He argued that the issues above illustrate that Obos is no longer a member-governed cooperative institution. He mentioned a number of incidents in addition to those listed above, such as favoring employees in the Obos organization at the expense of other members, demonstrating arrogant executive behavior, and granting hunting rights to privileged individuals. The revolt leader wrote that the members are the true owners of the cooperative (Larsen, 2021):

> Obos is owned by the members. The members exercise their corporate governance through the general assembly meeting and the elected general meeting representatives. Put at the forefront are the board and administration who are servants of the owners. More nuanced, we can state that the board and administration must ensure that they act in accordance with the owners' wishes. In this context, several of the above issues are relevant: The reason why they have created attention and engagement is obviously that they are perceived as controversial. It could have been okay if the positions taken were rooted in the members, but they were not.

As quoted earlier, the former mayor of Oslo claimed that Obos was sabotaging its own social mission. This critique is in line with the first violation issue. Obos should build ordinary homes for ordinary people before the upper part of the luxury market gets its share. There is still a significant shortage of apartments for ordinary people, while Obos in recent years has built apartment blocks where the top floors are reserved for rich people in demand for luxury apartments (Stang, 2021).

Similarly, Holm (2021) referred to the revolt where members requested Obos to return to the corporate social profile. In addition, as the quote from Larsen (2021) indicates, they wanted democracy. More and more of the members had noticed that they have neither power nor influence. Hegtun (2021) asked whether Obos had lost its soul. Some protesters suggested that executives suffered from megalomania that refers to a mental disorder characterized by an excessive increase in attention to one's own person (Lundgaard & Sørgjeld, 2021). Protesters disliked the comradely tone between elite members who supposedly negotiated directly and secretly with each other (Lorch-Falch & Tomter, 2021a). The revolt included demonstrations in front of Obos headquarters with the demand from members stating on posters that Obos belongs to the members (Sørgjeld, 2021).

A new scandal emerged as an Obos subsidiary was fined by the Norwegian financial supervisory authority in 2022 (Mjelde, 2022: 31):

Obos the company receives harsh criticism and fines after the Financial Supervisory Authority of Norway uncovered several serious violations of the Money Laundering Act.

This was yet another violation of the main purpose of Obos, which is to build ordinary housing for ordinary people rather than to operate as a financial institution handling other people's money.

"If you had made an effort to read the articles of association of OBOS, you would easily have discovered that banking and real estate are among the purposes of OBOS. Managing savings of members and lending to individual members and housing associations have been a purpose for OBOS since its inception in 1929. From OBOS Articles of Association §2: 'the association further aims to: 1. Receive savings for management, as well as to conduct lending activities 2. Subscribe for parts or shares in limited liability companies that conduct activities of significance to the housing cooperative 3. Undertake the construction and/or management of buildings on behalf of others than the cooperative owners 4. Operate real estate business'" (Pettersen, 2022).

Law professor Beate Sjåfjell at the University of Oslo was surprised to learn that Obos management had entered wrong names into protocol minutes of meetings and even been reluctant to correct the error in the aftermath. According to the law professor, this was a violation of the Norwegian Business Register Act by CEO Siraj (Lorch-Falch & Tomter, 2021b: 15): "Siraj's explanation meant a clear violation of the Business Registration Act, according to her."

Pettersen, the then director of communications at Obos, attempted to stop investigative journalists Lorch-Falch and Tomter (2021b: 15) at the Norwegian public broadcasting corporation (NRK) from publishing their findings:

While we were working on completing the story about the housing director's connections, it turned out that Obos had contacted the well-known attorney Cato Schiøtz. The director of communications wrote on Thursday, March 25, 2021: "After a thorough review of the case with him (Schiøtz), the conclusion is that there are no serious, reprehensible matters regarding impartiality and other formalities on the part of OBOS in the case." We immediately noticed the wording "serious, reprehensible matters." The language of the attorney could be interpreted as being conditions worthy of criticism, but not serious. Furthermore, it said: "Immediately after Easter, attorney Cato Schiøtz will come back to you with a summary of the case, including the assessment in relation to the journalism charter." We informed that a reply had to come as soon as possible, because we planned to publish before Easter. The deadline for submitting proposals to the general meeting was Maundy Thursday, April 1. We thought that our article was more relevant to members and the general meeting if it could be published as planned, before Easter. Then we got a new answer, directly from Schiøtz on March 26. He wrote to us that the information we wanted to publish together with the comments was "completely taken out of thin air and is an insulting and unfounded speculation," and further: "It is completely impossible to see that there are any kind of irregularities in this process. In my opinion, no criticism can be leveled at the proceedings in general or at the issue of the handling of any questions of impartiality in particular." He further questioned "what factual basis NRK has presented its sources in advance of their statements."

Now it was useful for us to have applied a timeline and role maps, because then we could quickly check that we had coverage for our information. He also claimed that NRK could be in the process of violating the journalism charter, section 4.1, "Emphasize objectivity and consideration in content and presentation." After an ethics meeting, the management replied that NRK publishes the case. We did not have a TV interview, but were able to publish an online news case on March 28, 2021: "The family of the housing director in Obos became a rental investor at Ulven. CEO Daniel Siraj told NRK that the housing director was out of the board when his family joined the investor side at Ulven. According to official documents, he was still on the board of Ulven Housing."

Since then, we have not heard anything more from Schiøtz.

It is interesting to notice the number of attorneys (e.g., Schiøtz) and law professors (e.g., Bråthen) that Obos management has paid to defend the legal license to operate.

Regaining the Social License

It seemed quite obvious that Obos management intended never again to repeat the criticized transaction. Furthermore, member involvement was enhanced by establishing a new organizational structure that would give members a real chance of influence.

Furthermore, company representatives learned that an a priori assertion of their legal right to manage properties freely would be met by anger and defiance. Relying on their legal rights was seen as arrogant and likely to lead to another member uproar.

At the general assembly meeting on June 21, 2021, a democracy project was launched. A record number of delegates – 568 cooperative members – participated at the meeting that voted in favor of the project. The mandate for the democracy project was to study legal and economic preconditions and provide professionally based advice for increased democratic influence at Obos. The mandate stated that the purpose was to produce a robust and future-oriented management structure for a large cooperative with broad membership. It should include an analysis of how the current governing and controlling bodies are composed and function. The project should look at relevant legislation, articles of association, and other relevant cooperatives, consideration of Obos' main purpose, as well as representation from various groups of members, electoral arrangements, and participation.

The project was set up to work independently, freely, and holistically with professional issues. The project was to be carried out by external management, external professional resources, Obos members, and employees. The entire breath of Obos' membership was to be involved through a reference group. The democracy committee was to conclude its work within half a year. It was decided that the committee's recommendations should be published when their report was to be handed over to the Obos board, so that stakeholders and others interested would have the same basis for making up their minds in various discussion forums.

To offer ordinary homes to ordinary people while the prices in the capital Oslo were still very high and often a barrier to entry, Obos introduced a new financial model caused by the member revolt. According to the new model, Obos offered members the option of buying half of the apartment and rent the other half from Obos. Over time, the member then has the option of increasing ownership share from 50 percent by down payments to Obos at the discretion of the owner's financial situation (Lundgaard, 2022: 6):

Obos has received criticism for not helping people without a lot of money to buy an apartment. Now the housing giant is making an effort.

- This was the rescue for me. Without this opportunity, I would not have been able to buy an apartment at all, says Josefin Ingvardsson (40) who is standing outside a construction site at Løren with her sons Leo (7) and Noa (12). Behind high fences, the block they are to move into next year is about to rise. There is the apartment of 68 square meters they will eventually own themselves.
- I have a good salary. But it would take many years to save up equity. It is quite despairing, says the divorced mother of two. The 'rescue' for her is an Obos apartment with a so-called co-ownership model. She has bought half of the apartment. The rest she rents from Obos. Thus, the requirement for capital was greatly reduced. She can spend what she saves on more and more of the half she rents. Obos listened to the rebels.

"OBOS Housing Start was launched in May 2018 and OBOS Part Ownership was launched in February 2020, that is more than a year before the membership uprising. Perhaps an academic publication should rely on somewhat more reliable sources than editorial media?" (Pettersen, 2022).

The described two measures of democracy project and co-ownership were introduced in an attempt to regain the social license to operate. While critical members and revolt leaders were waiting for positive outcomes of both initiatives, Obos management was planning for the next general assembly meeting in June 2022.

The attempts to regain the social license by Obos management can be studied in terms of factors that are needed to earn the license as suggested by Saenz (2019) and Sale (2021) as illustrated in Table 3.1.

The report from the democracy project was published in February 2022 by the review committee (Bråthen et al., 2022). Unfortunately, it was a legal document mainly written by lawyers. An example might illustrate the lack of focus on the social license to operate. The general assembly meeting was dominated by individuals who are both members of Obos and employees at Obos. The revolt leader

Table 3.1 Attempts to regain the social license by Obos executives

Social legitimacy	Violation	Correction
Pragmatic legitimacy	Less business of ordinary housing for ordinary people	Strengthen business of ordinary housing for ordinary people by co-ownership model
Moral legitimacy	Management procedures ignoring membership criticism	Democracy project involving membership representatives by information sharing
Cognitive legitimacy	Deviant actions considered violations of company guidelines	Investigation report found actions only legally legitimate where correction is still missing
Trust vulnerability	**Violation**	**Correction**
Risk tolerance	Executives taking too much risk in non-core business sectors	Return to core business of ordinary housing for ordinary people
Adjustment level	Executives belonged to the elite distant from the members	Democracy project to close gap of management versus members
Relative power	Members had no power and left the position of being trustors	A representative democracy was suggested

suggested that the fraction of employees having voting rights should be restricted so that the broader membership would gain more influence. However, Bråthen et al. (2022) made it into a legal issue where they claim that such a restriction on voting rights for Obos employees would represent a violation of a law regarding housing cooperatives. The revolt leader will probably be able to find numerous legal experts that will disagree with the Bråthen committee and argue that restrictions in voting rights can be legitimate to avoid double roles of employees in the general assembly as members.

> The fact is that 'the revolt leader' hired what according to him was Norway's foremost expert on the subject, Christian Fr. Wyller. Wyller concluded, as I assume you know, similar to the committee. Wyller believes that such a restriction, that is to limit the membership rights of members employed at OBOS, is illegal. Also Andreas Mellbye at law firm Wiersholm and Professor Filip Truyen at the University in Bergen and the Norwegian School of Economics conclude similar to Wyller. Your claim that it will be easy to find experts who conclude differently thus appears to be highly speculative (Pettersen, 2022).

Discussions continued after the democracy project report was published. It was argued that the term "member revolt" was misleading because a very small fraction of members had actually involved themselves in the criticism of the Obos management and in issues related to the social license to operate. Furthermore, the statement that Obos "should build ordinary homes for ordinary people" is not founded in any legal documents or other authoritative sources, but only in the historical perception and understanding of the mission and vision of the cooperative business of Obos. Also, the following statement was criticized for lacking foundation in any source of authority: "It was a violation of the cooperative purpose to sell two complete residential buildings with many apartments to a landlord whose business purpose is to make money on renting the apartments to tenants."

"The sales price … was below market value …" is yet another statement that has been criticized for lacking evidence. Since the alternative of offering apartments to individual members never was assessed in terms of price, it is indeed difficult to substantialize the statement.

"Unfortunately, it was a legal document mainly written by lawyers" is a statement that might seem unfair since the general assembly defined the mandate for the democracy project. However, Bråthen and his team could have rejected the mandate in case they found it not suited in light of the member revolt. Generally, fraud examiners are never obliged to accept an assignment where they disagree with the mandate.

"The general assembly meeting was dominated by individuals who are both members of Obos as well as employees at Obos" is yet another statement questioned in the aftermath. Domination might relate to both participation fraction and involvement fraction, where participation is the number of employees in relation to the number of non-employees, while involvement is the talking in the meeting by employees compared to non-employees.

Finally, the following statement was disliked by a lawyer on the democracy project: "The revolt leader will probably be able to find numerous legal experts that will disagree with the Bråthen committee and argue that restrictions in voting rights can be legitimate to avoid double roles of employees in the general meeting as members."

References

Agnew, R. (2014). Social concern and crime: Moving beyond the assumption of simple self-interest. *Criminology, 52*(1), 1–32.

Bråthen, T., Fjørtoft, T., Refsholt, H., Minde, S. W., Kronborg, A. K., Allgot, B., & Boye, E. (2022, February 15). Demokratiutvalgets innstilling (the democracy Committee's recommendations). Obos, www.obos.no, Oslo.

Campbell, J. L., & Göritz, A. S. (2014). Culture corrupts! A qualitative study of organizational culture in corrupt organizations. *Journal of Business Ethics, 120*(3), 291–311.

Dodge, M. (2009). *Women and white-collar crime*. Prentice Hall.

Hegtun, H. (2021). Granskere har gått inn i PC-en og telefonen hans. «Helt greit», sier presset Obos-sjef (investigators have entered the PC and his phone. "Quit all right", says the Obos boss, weekly magazine. *A-magasinet*, www.aftenposten.no, published June 12.

Holm, E. D. (2021). Er Obos løsningen eller problemet? (Is Obos the solution or the problem?), daily Norwegian newspaper. *Aftenposten*, www.aftenposten.no, published June 21.

Jacobsen, S. (2020). Har solgt 182 leiligheter for 936 millioner (Have sold 182 apartments for 936 million), daily Norwegian business newspaper. *Finansavisen*, www.finansavisen.no, published December 3.

Jonnergård, K., Stafsudd, A., & Elg, U. (2010). Performance evaluations as gender barriers in professional organizations: A study of auditing firms. *Gender, Work and Organization, 17 /6*, 721–747.

Kakkar, H., Sivanathan, N., & Globel, M. S. (2020). Fall from grace: The role of dominance and prestige in punishment of high-status actors. *Academy of Management Journal, 63*(2), 530–553.

KPMG. (2021). *Ulven-transaksjonen – Granskingsrapport til styret i Obos (the Ulven transaction – Investigation report to the board at Obos)* (p. 34). Law firm KPMG.

Larsen, B. E. (2021). Noen betraktninger før Obos' generalforsamling 2021 (Some considerations before Obos' general assembly 2021). *Benjamin E. Larsen's blog*, www.benjaminlarsen.net, posted June 19.

Lorch-Falch, S., & Tomter, L. (2021a). Slaget om Obos (the battle of Obos), public Norwegian broadcasting corporation. *NRK*, www.nrk.no, published June 22.

Lorch-Falch, S., & Tomter, L. (2021b). *Obos-avsløringene (the Obos revelations)*, Report to the Norwegian consortium for investigative journalists that is a member of the Global Investigative Journalism Network, July 2021.

Lorch-Falch, S., Tomter, L., & Engebretsen, D. K. (2021). Obos-opprøret tapte kamp om maktseter (the Obos uprising lost the battle for seats), Norwegian public broadcasting. *NRK*, www.nrk.no, published June 22.

Løtveit, H. (2021). Ber Siraj gå: -Selv Putin får ikke så mange stemmer mot seg (Asks Siraj to leave: -Even Putin does not get that many votes against him), daily Norwegian financial newspaper. *Finansavisen*, www.finansavisen.no, published June 23.

Lundgaard, H. (2022). Hun hadde ikke sjanse til å kjøpe leilighet. Nå skal flere tusen få samme muligheten (she had no chance of buying an apartment. Now several thousand will have the same opportunity), daily Norwegian newspaper. *Aftenposten*, Thursday, February 24, page 6.

Lundgaard, H. and Sørgjeld, C. (2021). Milliardene renner inn i Obos-kassen. Men mer enn 80 prosent kommer ikke fra boligbygging (The billions are floating into the Obos cash register. But more than 80 percent do not come from housing construction), daily Norwegian newspaper. *Aftenposten*, www.aftenposten.no, published June 21.

Maslow, A. H. (1943). A theory of human motivation. *Psychological Review, 50*(4), 370–396.

Mauno, H. (2017). Han er pinsevenn og BMW-eier. Men ikke si at han er fra Flekkefjord (He is a Pentecostal friend and BMW owner. But do not say that he is from Flekkefjord), daily Norwegian newspaper. *Dagsavisen*, www.dagsavisen.no, published June 25.

McClean, E. J., Martin, S. R., Emich, K. J., & Woodruff, T. (2018). The social consequences of voice: An examination of voice type and gender on status and subsequent leader emergence. *Academy of Management Journal, 61*(5), 1869–1891.

Mjelde, K. N. (2022). Obos-selskap får krass kritikk og bot (Obos company receives harsh criticism and fine), daily Norwegian business newspaper. *Dagens Næringsliv*, Friday, February 25, p. 31.

Oesterud, T. I. (2016). The prices for OBOS housing in Oslo increased by 11.5 percent. *Norway today*, www.norwaytoday.info, published April 1.

Paternoster, R., Jaynes, C. M., & Wilson, T. (2018). Rational choice theory and interest in the "fortune of others". *Journal of Research in Crime and Delinquency, 54*(6), 847–868.

Pettersen, Å. (2022). *Thank you for sending the book manuscript. In the attached file, I allow myself to point out some pure factual errors, as well as statements that in the context lead the reader on wild paths. I take it for granted that these will be changed before the manuscript is published*, email communication, Monday, May 2, at 4pm.

Saenz, C. (2019). Building legitimacy and trust between a mining company and a community to earn social license to operate: A Peruvian case study. *Corporate Social Responsibility and Environmental Management, 26*(2), 296–306.

Sale, H. A. (2021). The corporate purpose of social license. *Sothern California Law Review, 94*(4), 785–842.

Solberg, F. (2022). Rydd Opp i våre medlemseide organisasjoner som eksempelvis coop og Tobb (clean up our member-owned organizations such as coop and Tobb), web-based discussion forum. *Trønderdebatt*, www.tronderdebatt.no, published March 29.

Sørgjeld, C. (2021). På utsiden demonstrerte Obos-opprøret. På innsiden ble de nedstemt (on the outside, the Obos demonstration revolted. On the inside, they were voted down), daily Norwegian newspaper. *Aftenposten*, www.aftenposten.no, published June 22.

Stang, F. (2021). Obos saboterer sitt eget samfunnsoppdrag (Obos sabotages its own social mission), daily Norwegian newspaper. *Aftenposten*, www.aftenposten.no, published June 21.

Welsh, D. T., & Ordonez, L. D. (2014). The dark side of consecutive high performance goals: Linking goal setting, depletion, and unethical behavior. *Organizational Behavior and Human Decision Processes, 123*, 79–89.

Chapter 4
Police Deviance and Criminality

The legal license to operate for a police force is based on the nation's empowerment of the police to use force against citizens in the country if considered necessary. While armed forces are supposed to defend the country against external threats, police forces are supposed to defend the country against internal threats. Internal threats include crime such as murder, rape, and fraud. The legal license implies that police forces are equipped to prevent and detect crime and bring offenders to justice. The police are a body sanctioned by local, state, or national government to enforce laws and apprehend those who break them. The primary motive of the police is service to the public (Brooks & Button, 2011).

The social license to operate for a police force is based on the perceived integrity and accountability of police units in the community (Davidson & Gottschalk, 2012). Integrity refers to the quality of being honest and morally upright. Integrity is the quality of acting in accordance with the moral values, norms, and rules that are considered valid and relevant within the context in which the actor operates (Loyens et al., 2021). Practices that impugn the integrity of the police range from obtaining evidence without following proper procedure to involvement in criminal acts. Accountability refers to situations in which someone is required or expected to justify actions or decisions. It also refers to situations where an officer or a unit bears the responsibility to someone or for some activity. However, many organizations lack effective and efficient accountability mechanisms (Desmond et al., 2022).

Violations of the social license to operate can cause citizens to be reluctant to cooperate with police officers. Citizens simply do not trust the police and therefore do not want to get involved as witnesses, informants, or other cooperative roles. Without access to information from witnesses or informants, the police capability to protect the society against threats and detect, stop, and pursue crime is reduced and sometimes eliminated. Furthermore, social license violations can cause citizens to fight the police force rather than cooperate with it. Police officers can be harassed, and police stations can be put on fire as happened in the United States (Paybarah, 2021):

P. Gottschalk, *Financial Crime Issues*,
https://doi.org/10.1007/978-3-031-11213-3_4

Three days after George Floyd was killed in police custody in Minneapolis last year, the city's third precinct police building was set on fire. Thousands of protesters surrounded the building as it burned, sending giant orange flames and tall black clouds of smoke in the sky.

This chapter tells the story of a trusted police officer who was engaged in fighting serious organized crime. He was convicted of receiving bribes from organized criminals. As a consequence of his public trial and the public perception that he was not a single rotten apple in the force, the police lost many of their trusted witnesses and informants, in both the upper world and the underworld. Without such sources of information, the police force suffered a serious setback in fighting organized criminals.

Opportunistic Officer Behavior

Whereas the criminal justice system is designed to determine whether a deviant police officer as an offender is guilty or innocent, the principal-agent model of policing can provide insights into police officer behavior in law enforcement. The interests of principal and agent tend to diverge, they may have different risk willingness or risk aversion, there is knowledge asymmetry between the two parties, and the principal has imperfect information about the agent's contribution (Bosse & Phillips, 2016). Agency theory suggests that the chief as a principal and the field officer as an agent may have different preferences in policing tasks, varying knowledge levels of relevant policing issues, and opposite or diverging risk willingness when it comes to policing. In addition, the principal lacks information about activities of the agent. For instance, goals may justify means for a field officer in a critical situation. In this chapter, the opportunistic behavior of a convicted police officer in Norway is discussed based on principal-agent theory.

The police are agents of the government, whereas field officers are agents of police chiefs (Gottschalk, 2018). A relationship of agency implies that an agent is acting on behalf of a principal. This relationship can be challenging when a police officer is tasked with special assignments such as dialogue with criminal biker gangs, drug dealers, and informants in the shadow economy. The rule of the game can be very different in undercover operations and in dealing with transnational organized criminals. The convicted field officer in Norway illustrates dilemmas found in the principal-agent model of policing (Zondag et al., 2021), where the issue is police deviance and criminality (Davidson & Gottschalk, 2012). Explicitly, if one applies principal-agent theory to undercover policing, it provides a framework to gain insights into why police officers might violate laws, guidelines, and social license.

The conviction after a 4-month trial was appealed from Oslo District Court in 2017. Borgarting Court of Appeal in Oslo had its hearing in 2019. The verdict of 21 years' imprisonment for the police officer was confirmed. The Supreme Court of Norway denied case access to review the matter. Therefore, the trusted police officer was sentenced to the longest prison sentence possible according to Norwegian law.

He was convicted for aiding a drug smuggler for many years and taking bribes from the smuggler. The case captivated a nation accustomed to clean law enforcement. The field officer was once in charge of combating Oslo's criminal gangs such as the Hells Angels and other biker gangs. He denied the accusations against him (Gottschalk, 2018).

During the 4-month trial in spring 2017, prosecutors accused the former police officer of aiding a smuggling ring for more than a decade by providing information on police and customs staffing, much of it via hundreds of cryptic mobile phone text messages, in return for illegal bribing payments.

The police officer's co-defendant was a cannabis smuggler who admitted organizing the import of tons of hashish. The cannabis smuggler was the prosecution's key witness against the police officer and was sentenced to 15 years in prison. Many observers were surprised that the organized criminal was sentenced less severely than the deviant police officer. People were surprised that the judge had more trust in statements from the hashish smuggler than the former police officer, where the smuggler received a rebate in his sentence because he blew the whistle on the officer.

"This case is unique in Norwegian legal history," the judge said as he read the unanimous verdicts against the police officer and the drug smuggler; the police officer "has actively and deliberately contributed to a well-organized and extensive import of hashish," he said (Solsvik, 2017). Such cases are indeed rare in Norway as it is ranked the fourth-least corrupt country on Transparency International's corruption index. As one of the few countries in the world, Norway has a practice of unarmed police officers who only are allowed to carry guns in special operations.

The defense attorneys argued during the trial that the evidence of contact with criminals was merely a result of normal police work intended to extract information, partly in undercover operations, and that the former officer had not received any money or gifts. He had simply done his job in fighting organized crime. The court had to understand, argued the defense that successfully combatting serious and transnational organized crime requires measures and behaviors that are different from street patrolling and other regular police work. However, as evidenced by the prosecution, the officer had indeed received favors that represented substantial financial assets from the smuggler.

The former Norwegian police officer now convicted had written a book chapter on how his team successfully disarmed criminal gangs in Oslo. The chapter appeared in the Stockholm gang model book in Sweden edited by Leinfelt and Rostami (2012). The former officer headed the Oslo gang project as it was established in 2006. The project was initiated after a massive shoot-out among rival gangs in Norway's capital Oslo. Gang warfare had reached the central areas of the city, and there were innocent victims. Residents of the capital felt unsafe in the midst of new violent settlements between gangs. The former police officer implemented a dialogue strategy toward the gangs, where he and his team met gang leaders on a regular basis to trade information (Gottschalk, 2018).

For example, when a chapter of the Hells Angels was planning its 15th anniversary in Oslo, dialogue with the police officer occurred. The Hells Angels leader was able to rent a hotel in Oslo based on a recommendation from the police officer, and the motorcycle gang had an international party in their club house where everything was allowed. In return, the Hells Angels promised not to turn up in public places or bars where people might become worried and scared.

Principal-Agent Perspective

Principal-agent theory is a dominant perspective addressing management challenges in organizations. The agency problem arises whenever one party (a principal) employs another (an agent) to do work that the principal for some reason does not do. The interests of the principal and agent diverge, and the principal has imperfect information about the agent's contribution. Agency theory is based on the assumption of narrow self-interest (Bosse & Phillips, 2016), mainly on the side of the agent.

While the chief of police can be defined as the principal who needs a field officer's policing work, the field officer can be defined as the agent carrying out law enforcement work on behalf of the police unit. In this perspective, the relationship between officer and chief can be studied in terms of agency theory with principal and agent. The seemingly cooperating parties are engaged in an agency relationship defined as an employment contract under which one person engages another person to perform some service on their behalf and delegate some decision-making authority to the agent to enable the agent to perform the service.

Principals expect agents to make decisions in the best interest of the principals. However, due to agency problems, agents may not make decisions in the best interest of superiors. On the contrary, agents may be succumbed to self-interest, opportunistic behavior, and ignorance of both reasonable and unreasonable requests from principals. Generally, corruption and other forms of economic crime are in agency theory considered the consequence of the principal's inability to control and prevent the agent from abusing his or her position for personal gain (Li & Ouyang, 2007).

Agency theory is a management theory often applied to crime, where normally the agent, rather than the principal, is in danger of committing crime. White-collar crime is thus illegal and unethical actions usually by agents of organizations (Vadera & Aguilera, 2015). There is an opportunity for the white-collar offender to carry out the regular job at the same time as crime is committed, because the principal is unable to monitor what the agent is doing, what knowledge the agent applies, and what risk the agent is willing to take (Chrisman et al., 2007; Li & Ouyang, 2007; Williams, 2008). Agency theory argues that the principal is unable to control the agent because of lack of insight and access to activities performed by the agent in roles such as mayor (by the city council), chairperson (by shareholders), or CEO (by the board) in hierarchical organizations (Eisenhardt, 1989; Garoupa, 2007).

Agency theory describes the relationship between the two parties using the metaphor of a contract that is more than employment. According to social contract theory, transactions can involve actors whose ability to comprehend their moral implications is inherently limited. A formal contract, guidelines, and regulations have the potential of preventing negative behavior, but they do not have the potential of causing any positive efforts on the part of the agent. Therefore, according to contract theory, arrangements can prevent certain negative outcomes, but not necessarily all, while they may encourage but not secure certain positive outcomes. Some employment arrangements can encourage opportunistic behavior by exploitation of weaknesses in organizational systems, sometimes to restore the perception of equity and equality (Leigh et al., 2010).

Agency theory specifically addresses which issues affect the relationship. Let us apply this to the relationship between the officer and the chief. Agency theory is primarily used for situations where two parties enter into a contract, but the reasoning of the theory is also relevant when no formal contract is signed or what might be more relevant, the contract does not deal with the issues brought forward by agency theory. An agency relationship arises whenever an individual or organization is authorized to act for or on behalf of another individual or organization (Benson & Simpson, 2018).

The chief as a principal expects the agent to make decisions in the best interests of the principal. The convicted police officer was running undercover policing for the police district. The chief of the police district is defined as the principal, whereas the officer is an agent in charge of dialogue and undercover operations. The principal-agent model of policing argues that the agent must act with the knowledge and skills at his or her disposal for the principal's goal, without regard to any other goals that may bear in his or her relations with the principal, including any self-goals. The field officer as an agent is a fiduciary who holds a legal as well as ethical relationship of trust with his or her principal (Mitnick, 1975: 28):

> The agent holding the fiduciary norm must act diligently, with the skills at his disposal, for the principal's goal, without regard for any other goals that may bear on his relation with the principal, including any self-goals. The norm may be expected in contractual discretionary agency, typically under conditions of trust, under principal dependency, or under agent domination of the principal's interests.

At the most general level, police work is the application of a set of legally sanctioned practices designed to maintain public order by imposing the rule of law on people who live in or travel through a given place which is internationally recognized as a geographically defined territory under the control of a particular national state (Sheptycki, 2007). The set of policing practices covers core issues like law enforcement through crime investigation and crime prevention, security issues involving mainly surveillance and counter-terrorism on a population, and jurisdictional issues in relation to having the legal authority to act in a particular place and under what legal framework and conditions. The police are given the power to use force legitimately in the course of fulfillment of their tasks (Ivkovic, 2009).

Policing organized crime remains problematic also because of its transnational nature (Gottschalk & Markovic, 2016). In the United Kingdom, Harfield (2008) argued that organized crime challenges long-held paradigms about police management and operations. He suggested that organized crime has developed to become an issue beyond the competence of conventional policing. In the United States and Canada, Beare and Martens (1998) made the same observation. Harfield (2008: 72) found that government "response will be based on trying to adapt a policing infrastructure intended for other policing functions rather than dealing with the problem of organized crime itself."

The convicted police officer certainly operated very non-traditional in his approach of communicating with serious criminal gangs and outlaw motorcycle clubs. He did not try to adapt to conventional policing as he worked with informants. Therefore, some argued that he should have been acquitted (Madshus & Hageskal, 2019) and that the verdict was a miscarriage of justice (Fjeld, 2020). The critics of the verdict suggested that the corruption was not at all obvious as it was rather favors as part of a pretended cooperation with criminals. Furthermore, the convicted officer belonged to a special task force within the police that involved other officers who were never prosecuted. In the principal-agent perspective, critics argued that dialogue and communication with organized criminals as well as management of undercover operations among the organized criminals require independence from the conventional police management to succeed and to stay personally safe. Because of the implicit independence and required empowerment of those officers and units involved, it was obvious that agency problems could easily occur and that such problems might not be solved by tighter management oversight and controls. The field officer simply found his own ways of dealing with the problem of organized crime while securing self-protection and potentially benefitting from his work without involving any of his superiors.

An important element in policing organized crime lies in dealing with the interface between organized crime groups and the legitimate environment, which are of vital importance to the existence of this type of criminal activity. Contacts, relationships, and exchanges between organized criminals and field officers are a threat to the legitimate environment, but they offer opportunities for organized crime prevention and detection. In the Netherlands, Bunt and Schoot (2003) identified three types of interfaces between organized crime groups and the legitimate environment. First, the demand from the licit environment for illegal products and services forms a breeding ground for organized crime groups. A typical example is drugs. Second, persons whose knowledge and skills enable organized crime groups to carry out their criminal activities. A typical example is deviant attorneys. Third, criminal groups make use of other opportunities or tools present in the licit environment. A typical example is the communication infrastructure in society.

In the principal-agent perspective, there is an opportunity for offenders to carry out their regular job at the same time as wrongdoing occurs. As illustrated by the secrecy and independence related to management of undercover operations and other non-traditional police work combatting organized transnational crime, the opportunity structure for deviance is greater than in traditional police service. The secrecy is emphasized in the metaphor labeled the "blue code of silence" that refers to an unspoken policy of concealment by police regarding the wrongdoing or illicit activity of other officers.

There was no doubt that the convicted police officer and his group were successful in combatting gangs and other organized criminals in Oslo for more than a decade. He was in fact labeled a wonderboy (Eggen et al., 2016). Given the achievements of these goals, he may have perceived that his means were also acceptable to others. Leaking information to one criminal in exchange for information on others was one of his means. Exchanging friendly favors and gifts with criminals was another means applied by him (Gottschalk, 2018).

Rotten Apple or Basket Metaphor

While the Norwegian public was surprised to learn about the police scandal as it was portrayed in the media, and important informants were reluctant to continue their cooperation with the police because of the revelation of the field officer's contacts and procedures, the field officer and professionals who are in the business of combatting serious transnational organized crime were, on the other hand, surprised that the somewhat deviant behavior had become an issue and resulted in a prison sentence of 21 years. Among the surprised professionals were agents at the Federal Bureau of Investigation (FBI) in the United States, who expressed in confidentiality that the police officer's way of dealing with the problem of organized crime was completely within normal practice. International experts in the field of combatting the mafia and other transnational criminals expressed surprise that the Norwegian authority for police oversight had charged the police officer. Police oversight authorities are citizens' watchdog bodies designed to ensure that police officers are operating with integrity and accountability (Prenzler & Lewis, 2005).

Norwegian police suffered from loss of informants as well as from harm to their social license to operate. They chose not to communicate that the way the police officer had been operating was indeed not that deviant given his special assignments in the task force to fight serious crime. Because of the strong final verdict from the court of appeals, the police management instead attempted to communicate that the convicted officer was a rotten apple where such occurrences should indeed be prevented in the future. The rotten apple metaphor basically suggests that by removing one single deviant individual from the police is sufficient action, and then there will be no problems anymore.

A single, standalone offender can be described as a rotten apple, but when several are involved in deviance, and organizational culture virtually stimulates offenses, then it is more appropriate to describe the phenomenon as a basket of rotten apples or as a rotten apple barrel or orchard, like Punch (2003: 172) defined them:

> The metaphor of 'rotten orchards' indicate(s) that it is sometimes not the apple, or even the barrel that is rotten but the *system* (or significant parts of the system).

Ashforth et al. (2008) argued that it is comforting to assume that one bad apple or renegade faction within an organization is somewhat responsible for offenses that we too often observe. The rotten apple view is a comfortable perspective to adopt for organizations like the police as it allows them to look no further than the suspected individual.

However, organizations are important to our understanding of deviance because organizations influence the actions of their members. Therefore, both micro and macro views are important to understand wrongdoing. It is when other forms of group and/or systemic deviance erupt upon an organization that a more critical look is taken on criminality (Gottschalk, 2012).

As stated in the introduction to this chapter, the public perception was that the officer was not a single rotten apple in the force. Rather, people thought there was a rotten basket in the police. Therefore, police management had to initiate an investigation that went beyond own attempted account of only one rotten apple. It was a case that "was apt to harm police confidence in society" as the investigation report phrased it (Borgerud et al., 2021: 7), where a violation of the social license to operate had occurred.

Officer Convenience Themes

Assuming that the allegations that led to conviction were correct, it is possible to identify convenience themes for the offender as illustrated in Fig. 4.1. The possibility was to receive bribes from organized criminals in return for favors related to information about smuggling routes. The police officer's status as a wonderboy combined with the blue code of silence enabled him to be an attractive official for corruption. The lack of oversight and guardianship derived from principal-agent shortcomings as well as from leadership reluctance to intervene that caused chaos where corrupt activities could conveniently be concealed.

The offender denied wrongdoing and claimed that preventing and detecting organized crime requires very different skills and behaviors compared to regular policing. Therefore, he could justify his actions by arguing that communicating with the underworld implied that he had to involve himself in actions and transactions that for outsiders might look like corruption. In a justification, the actor admits responsibility for the act in question, but denies its pejorative and negative content (Schoen et al., 2021). In addition to his justification, he could also neutralize potential guilt feeling by arguing that what he did was quite normal in special assignments in the police force. Maybe he sometimes felt a dilemma of sticking to procedures versus making the most successful approach in policing. The offender could argue that a dilemma arose whereby he made a reasonable tradeoff before committing the deviant act. A dilemma represents a state of mind in which it is not obvious for an offender what is right and what is wrong to do (Jordanoska, 2018).

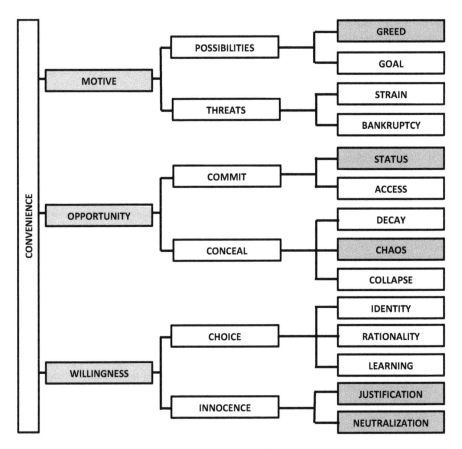

Fig. 4.1 Convenience themes in the case of the police officer

The Fraud Investigation Report

So far in this chapter, a number of issues have been discussed that can influence the police social license to operate. In the principal-agent perspective, it is a matter of the principal's very limited opportunity and ability to control what the agent is doing (Gottschalk, 2018). In the organizational perspective, it is a matter of a rotten apple versus a rotten barrel of deviant police officers (Gottschalk, 2012). Therefore, it is interesting to review how investigators appointed by the head of police would approach the topic of examining the case where one of their trusted officers, at one point perceived as a wonderboy (Eggen et al., 2016), was convicted of corruption to 21 years in prison.

One important topic for the fraud examiners was how whistleblowing messages concerned with the police officer had been handled by police management. Whistleblowing refers to the disclosure by an individual in an organization of deviant practices to someone who can do something about it. Whistleblowing is an action by an individual who believes that a colleague is involved in misconduct, causes unnecessary harm, or contributes to otherwise immoral offenses (Mpho, 2017). The mandate for the investigation of police misconduct after the verdict was phrased in terms of questions regarding whistleblowing (Borgerud et al., 2021: 7):

(a) Were messages of concern/feedback/reports about the convicted officer given in the period 1993–2013 and with special emphasis on the period 2004 and up to the arrest? In what form were these possibly given, and who was the recipient?
(b) How were these eventually followed up and with what result?
(c) Why were these eventually not followed up?

These questions seem to fit our perspective above concerned with principal-agent problems generally and the blue code of silence specifically. When studying police corruption, Skolnick (2002) found that the blue code of silence – sometimes called a blue wall, curtain, or cocoon of silence – is embedded in police culture. The feelings of loyalty and brotherhood may protect police officers against threats to safety and well-being when combatting criminal organizations and thereby prevent whistleblowing at observations of misconduct.

The investigation report by Borgerud et al. (2021: 39) discussed the issue of one rotten apple versus a basket of rotten apples, where they warned against the single apple approach:

> Both inquiry commissions and research on police corruption warn against the rotten apple theory and claim that it is directly detrimental to the prevention and fight against corruption and unethical police behavior. This was pointed out as early as in the 1970s. The rotten apple theory firstly narrows the focus and "acquits" the police organization and its leaders. Secondly, the theory assumes that the conditions in the rest of the organization are impeccable, but that is rarely the case. Third, the theory requires no more than that the rotten apple be punished and removed.

Therefore, the fraud investigators chose an organizational leadership perspective rather than a single rotten apple perspective. They chose a main perspective of leaders' monitoring of subordinates, where issues such as leadership failure and organizational culture were emphasized. However, the investigators failed in identifying the specific cause of management failure regarding the convicted police officer.

The investigators approached several information sources. They retrieved documents, instructions, and circulars. They held seminars with researchers and professionals. They interviewed police leaders and police employees. They had meetings with key personnel, and they had meetings with police union leaders and chief safety representatives within the police. They also systematized research and studies especially on police corruption and culture, attitudes, leadership, and learning in the police.

The fraud examiners identified a number of situations where whistleblowing potentially had occurred against the later convicted officer. However, when interviewing people, those who claimed they had blown the whistle were not supported by those who allegedly had received the notices. Most alleged receivers denied having heard or read about wrongdoing. These are some examples (Borgerud et al., 2021: 70):

At one point in time, a colleague of Jensen contacted the new section leader, and told that an informant had stated that Jensen sold intelligence information in the criminal environment. It was considered whether to follow up the suspicion, but for the sake of the informant's safety, no further investigations were initiated. The same official had a few years earlier suspected that Jensen, prior to a planned search that the official was to carry out, had warned one of the suspects, who was a close friend of Jensen. On another occasion, Jensen and a section leader decided not to pursue a tip against the same suspect. This led the official instead to notify the Swedish customs authorities, and then a large seizure of drugs was successfully made.

While the convicted police officer worked in the Oslo Police District, the National Criminal Investigation Services (Kripos) had been skeptical toward the dialogue model that the police district pursued (Borgerud et al., 2021: 70):

As mentioned above, the management of Kripos was for many years strongly critical of the Oslo Police District's approach to, and method for, combating MC crime, where the dialogue model deviated from the strategy that was agreed and practiced in the police in general. Eirik Jensen was central in this work. From Kripos' side, the criticism was repeatedly raised with the management in the Oslo Police District, also formulated as a question of whether Jensen's various roles as a police officer, informant handler and member of an MC club, were compatible with this work.

Kripos was also critical of the motorcycle club Iron Pigs, which was established in 2001 as a Norwegian branch of the American MC club Iron Pigs. The club was created by and for police officers and firefighters with an interest in Harley Davidson. Several employees in the section for organized crime were members, including Jensen. According to a key member, the section leader did not mind that employees in the section were members, as long as they behaved as police officers should. The club, however, was controversial in the police. Iron Pigs had a club room where both the legality of using the premises and serving of alcohol were questioned in the public. The club was a so-called 3 patch club. Membership was incompatible with work at Kripos, but not in the Oslo Police District. Kripos had raised this issue several times with the management in Oslo. In connection with national seminars on MC crime at Kripos in 2003 and 2004, foreign speakers, who were experts on MC crime, refused to let Jensen and other police officers in who were members of Iron Pigs. Kripos notified the Oslo Police District of the incidents.

The fraud investigation report by Borgerud et al. (2021) concluded that the corruption case was typical for police corruption risk factors: The convicted officer was involved in intelligence and use of covert police methods, and individual officers have to behave autonomously based on trust from superiors.

Regaining the Social License

The fraud examiners made a number of recommendations in the report that can have the potential of regaining the social license to operate policing against organized criminals. The first recommendation was concerned with the acknowledgement of the corruption risk in the police force. There had been an assumption that there is little or no corruption among police officers in Norway. Compared to other nations, Norwegian police might have a lower corruption rate, but it still exists. Police officers can be an attractive target for bribes, where some officers are not able to resist the temptation of accepting bribes. While there are little or no complaints regarding salaries among employees in the Norwegian police force, it is still attractive to some employees to earn a little extra (Borgerud et al., 2021: 88):

> Risk recognition is a prerequisite for active prevention of corruption in the police. The likelihood of corruption may seem small, but the consequences are great when it happens. It is necessary to strengthen the recognition and acknowledgement that the risk of corruption within the police is real. Risk recognition presupposes knowledge and sets requirements for leadership, both in terms of focus and involvement of employees. It is a manager's responsibility to ensure that police officers have the necessary professional ethical standard, integrity and professionalism in their policing practice.

The second recommendation was concerned with professional handling of worries and notifications from whistleblowers regarding deviance, misconduct, and potential crime (Borgerud et al., 2021: 88):

> The committee has learned that the reports of concern that employees and others made to Jensen's managers about possible breaches of instructions were to a little extent followed up. The reports of concern were mainly given orally. It was not recorded what was said, what was done, who was informed and why the leaders did not proceed with the case. It is a leadership responsibility to ensure that information about possible breaches of instructions is handled in a responsible and documentable manner.

The subsequent recommendations were concerned with strengthening internal controls (recommendation #3), facilitating a safe climate of expression (#4), professionalizing informant cooperation (#5), introducing informant reviews (#6), and securing professional training in informant work (#7). Recommendation #8 said that one might consider making parts of the informant regulations available to the public (Borgerud et al., 2021: 90):

> The police directorate's normal instructions from 2003 were originally publicly available, but was exempted from public access after a few years. Both the current normal instructions of 2019 and the informant instructions in the Oslo Police District are currently exempt from public access. The specific use and working methods must be exempt from public view for the sake of the safety of those involved and to ensure that the police are able to use the methods both in connection with investigation and prevention. The question, however, is whether the exemption from public access is too extensive. As a starting point, the police's instructions and regulations should be open. Transparency instills trust and ensures a real opportunity for democratic control.

The final recommendations #9, #10, and #11 were concerned with leadership, learning, knowledge, and research regarding corruption in the police. Borgerud et al. (2021) argued that while there is international research regarding police corruption, little has empirically been studied in Norway.

Unfortunately, the fraud examiners avoided the core issue of principal-agent problems in combatting serious and transnational organized crime, including undercover operations. The autonomy and independence of field officers obviously need to be balanced with controls and reviews, but this dilemma was not addressed by the fraud examiners. The report simply states that everything is leadership responsibility without addressing the problematic role of a leader as the principal in a

Table 4.1 Attempts to regain the social license by police management

Social legitimacy	Violation	Correction
Pragmatic legitimacy	Police officers helping organized criminals	Monitoring police officers when combatting organized crime in their information exchanges
Moral legitimacy	Police officers receiving bribes from organized criminals	Zero tolerance toward police corruption, even when favors are exchanged
Cognitive legitimacy	Unexpected deviance in the police force	Explain how police management and oversight works in a hierarchical structure
Trust vulnerability	**Violation**	**Correction**
Risk tolerance	Undercover and other risky activities with their own rules	Oversight and guardianship against police deviance
Adjustment level	Special task officers too autonomous and independent	Registration of informants and other sources of information
Relative power	Police management was not in control	Police management in charge by requiring written documentation

principal-agent relationship with an officer who infiltrates national and transnational criminal groups.

The attempts to regain the social license by police management can be studied in terms of factors that are needed to earn the license as suggested by Saenz (2019) and Sale (2021) as illustrated in Table 4.1.

References

Ashforth, B. E., Gioia, D. A., Robinson, S. L., & Trevino, L. K. (2008). Re-reviewing organizational corruption. *Academy of Management Review, 33*(3), 670–684.

Beare, M. E., & Martens, F. T. (1998). Policing organized crime. *Journal of Contemporary Criminal Justice, 14*(4), 398–427.

Benson, M. L., & Simpson, S. S. (2018). *White-collar crime: An opportunity perspective* (3rd ed.). Routledge.

Borgerud, I. M., Christensen, E., Finstad, L., Kassman, A., & Nylund, M. H. (2021, May 26). *Politikorrupsjon – Lederskap, risikoerkjennelse og læring* [Police corruption – Leadership, risk assessment and learning]. Report by the Evaluation Committee, Oslo, Norway.

Bosse, D. A., & Phillips, R. A. (2016). Agency theory and bounded self-interest. *Academy of Management Review, 41*(2), 276–297.

Brooks, G., & Button, M. (2011). The police and fraud investigation and the case for a nationalized solution in the United Kingdom. *The Police Journal, 84*, 305–319.

Bunt, H. G., & Schoot, C. R. A. (2003). *Prevention of organised crime – A situational approach.* Willan Publishing.

Chrisman, J. J., Chua, J. H., Kellermanns, F. W., & Chang, E. P. C. (2007). Are family managers agents or stewards? An exploratory study in privately held family firms. *Journal of Business Research, 60*(10), 1030–1038.

Davidson, J., & Gottschalk, P. (2012). *Police deviance and criminality – Managing integrity and accountability.* Nova Science Publishers.

Desmond, S. A., Rorie, M., & Sohoni, T. (2022). Working for God: Religion and occupational crime and deviance. *Deviant Behavior.* Published online https://doi.org/10.1080/01639625.2021.2022968.

Eggen, S., Andersen, G., Tommelstad, B., Widerøe, R. J., Hengingeng, T., & Hopperstad, M. S. (2016). Han var politiets 'wonderboy' – Nå er Eirik Jensen korrupsjonssiktet (He was the police 'wonderboy' – Now Eirik Jensen is charged with corruption). Daily Norwegian newspaper *VG.* www.vg.no, published February 12.

Eisenhardt, K. M. (1989). Agency theory: An assessment and review. *Academy of Management Review, 14*(1), 57–74.

Fjeld, J. T. (2020). BI-professor: -Justismord [BI professor: -miscarriage of justice]. Daily Norwegian newspaper *Dagbladet.* www.dagbladet.no, published June 19.

Garoupa, N. (2007). Optimal law enforcement and criminal organization. *Journal of Economic Behaviour & Organization, 63*, 461–474.

Gottschalk, P. (2012). White-collar crime and police crime: Rotten apples or rotten barrels? *Critical Criminology, 20*(2), 169–182.

Gottschalk, P. (2018). Opportunistic behavior in the principal-agent model of policing: The case of a convicted field officer in Norway. *International Journal of Police Science & Management, 20*(2), 109–115.

Gottschalk, P., & Markovic, V. (2016). Transnational criminal organizations (TCOs). The case of combating criminal biker gangs. *International Journal of Criminal Justice Sciences, 11*(1), 30–44.

Harfield, C. (2008). Paradigms, pathologies, and practicalities – Policing organized crime in England and Wales. *Policing, 2*(1), 63–73.

Ivkovic, S. K. (2009). The Croatian police, police integrity, and transition toward democratic policing. *Policing, 32*(3), 459–488.

Jordanoska, A. (2018). The social ecology of white-collar crime: Applying situational action theory to white-collar offending. *Deviant Behavior, 39*(11), 1427–1449.

Leigh, A. C., Foote, D. A., Clark, W. R., & Lewis, J. L. (2010). Equity sensitivity: A triadic measure and outcome/input perspectives. *Journal of Managerial Issues, 22*(3), 286–305.

Leinfelt, F., & Rostami, A. (2012). *The Stockholm gang model – Panther – Stockholm gang intervention and prevention project.* Stockholm County Police.

Li, S., & Ouyang, M. (2007). A dynamic model to explain the bribery behavior of firms. *International Journal of Management, 24*(3), 605–618.

Loyens, K., Claringbould, I., Heres-van Rossem, L., & van Eekeren, F. (2021). The social construction of integrity: A qualitative case study in Dutch football. *Sports in Society.* Published online https://doi.org/10.1080/17430437.2021.1877661.

Madshus, K., & Hageskal, A. (2019). Langer ut mot politiet etter Jensen-saken. Daily Norwegian newspaper *Dagbladet.* www.dagbladet.no, published January 30.

Mitnick, B. M. (1975). The theory of agency: The policing 'paradox' and regulatory behavior. *Public Choice, 24*(1), 27–42.

Mpho, B. (2017). Whistleblowing: What do contemporary ethical theories say? *Studies in Business and Economics, 12*(1), 19–28.

Paybarah, A. (2021). Burning of police station after George Floyd's death draws 4-year sentence. *The New York Times.* www.nytimes.com, published April 28.

Prenzler, T., & Lewis, C. (2005). Performance indicators for police oversight. *Australian Journal of Public Administration, 64*(2), 77–83.

Punch, M. (2003). Rotten orchards. «Pestilence», police misconduct and system failure. *Policing and Society, 13*(2), 171–196.

Saenz, C. (2019). Building legitimacy and trust between a mining company and a community to earn social license to operate: A Peruvian case study. *Corporate Social Responsibility and Environmental Management, 26*(2), 296–306.

Sale, H. A. (2021). The corporate purpose of social license. *Sothern California Law Review, 94*(4), 785–842.

Schoen, J. L., DeSimone, J. A., Meyer, R. D., Schnure, K. A., & LeBreton, J. M. (2021). Identifying, defining, and measuring justification mechanisms: The implicit biases underlying individual differences. *Journal of Management, 47*(3), 716–744.

Sheptycki, J. (2007). Police ethnography in the house of serious and organized crime. In A. Henry & D. J. Smith (Eds.), *Transformations of policing* (pp. 51–77). Ashgate.

Skolnick, J. H. (2002). Corruption and the blue code of silence. *Police Practice & Research, 3*(1), 7–19.

Solsvik, T. (2017, September 18). Norwegian policeman jailed for 21 years in drugs case. *Reuters.* www.reuters.com

Vadera, A. K., & Aguilera, R. V. (2015). The evolution of vocabularies and its relation to investigation of white-collar crimes: An institutional work perspective. *Journal of Business Ethics, 128*, 21–38.

Williams, J. W. (2008). The lessons of 'Enron' – Media accounts, corporate crimes, and financial markets. *Theoretical Criminology, 12*(4), 471–499.

Zondag, M. H. W., Brekke, A., Aasen, K. R., & Holm-Nilsen, S. (2021). Knallhard kritikk av Oslo-politiet etter Jensen-saken: Grunnleggende svikt i ledelsen [Strong criticism of the Oslo police after the Jensen case: Basic failure in management]. Norwegian public broadcasting *NRK*, www.nrk.no, published May 26.

Chapter 5
Military Regime Cooperation

The Danish law firm Offersen Christoffersen was commissioned to assess whether the company Bestseller had economic relations with the military junta in Myanmar in violation of the Danish Ministry of Foreign Affairs' or the EU's guidelines and rules for sanctions. The law firm should also assess whether Bestseller's due diligence in Myanmar lived up to international standards for corporate social responsibility (Christoffersen & Mikkelsen, 2021).

Bestseller had 2700 branded chain stores across 38 markets worldwide, and their products were sold in 15,000 multi-brand and department stores. Bestseller seemed to violate its social license to operate when it placed orders in Myanmar after the military coup in the country (Reed, 2022):

> In garments, multinational companies such as H&M, Bestseller and Primark brought in supply-chain investors and created jobs, mostly women, during Myanmar's decade of democratic transition, which ended with a coup. While some have suspended their Myanmar operations, others are quietly still buying.

Bestseller faced serious criticism (Einarsdottir, 2021; Thomsen, 2021), including negative comments from the Danish foreign minister (Rizau, 2021) and the fashion industry (Einarsdottir, 2021). A report by the United Nations showed that companies producing clothes in Myanmar had financial relations to the military.

The military in Myanmar carried out a coup on February 1, 2021, and established a junta of generals to rule the country. The European Union introduced sanctions against the junta on March 22 and April 19, 2021. Sanctions were implemented to harm military financial interests in the country, and the sanctions were targeted at companies with financial relations to the junta. Bestseller had since 2014 produced clothes at several factories in Myanmar.

Challenging the Social License

The foreign minister in Denmark, Jeppe Kofod, was upset over Bestseller's use of factories in Myanmar (Ritzau, 2021):

> The military is in power in Myanmar. According to the UN report, factories that Bestseller uses are effectively owned by the military. Two of the factories used by Danish clothing giant Bestseller in Myanmar in recent years are cooperating with the military in the country, according to a UN report. And this could have consequences, Denmark's foreign minister Jeppe Kofod told the newspaper. He is greatly exasperated by the cooperation.
>
> – I would like to make it quite clear that I think it is highly problematic if Bestseller chooses to have clothes produced in factories controlled by the military dictatorship in Myanmar, according to the UN, he told the newspaper.

Bestseller faced serious criticism from the clothing and fashion industry that could harm the company's outlets and their brands (Einarsdottir, 2021):

> Bestseller receives criticism for alleged military connections in crisis-stricken Myanmar. The Danish fashion giant Bestseller is once again in bad weather. This time it is due to their connections in crisis-hit Myanmar. Bestseller, which owns about twenty fashion brands such as Vero Moda, Only and Jack & Jones, produces at three factories in the industrial zone Ngwe Pinlae outside the city of Yangon. A report from 2019 to the UN Human Rights Council points out that the zone is controlled by the industrial conglomerate Myanmar Economic Holdings Limited (MEHL). Their owners consist of the military and individuals in the military leadership, among them chief of staff Min Aung Hlaing who is mainly responsible for the recent bloody attacks on civilians in the country where over 700 people have been killed, writes Fashion Forum.

Because of the criticism, Bestseller was "among the companies that froze orders from the south-east Asian country because of human rights concerns and civil unrest" (Reed & Nilsson, 2021). The European Union (EU) targeted Myanmar's lucrative energy sector in sanctions and put companies under pressure to divest from the country and cut off indirect funding for the junta. The EU imposed "sanctions against almost two dozen Myanmar government and military officials as well as a state-backed oil and gas group" (Meixler & Creery, 2022). Nevertheless, the Danish company wanted to resume its business in Myanmar again (Reed & Nilsson, 2021):

> Bestseller, which describes itself as a champion of sustainable development and whose Myanmar suppliers have about 48,000 workers, concluded that the three factories were not on military-owned land, and it had not violated EU sanctions. The Danish group also said it had 'started to resume business in Myanmar again'.

To legitimate a resumption of its business in Myanmar again, Bestseller argued that their business did not benefit the military junta (Reed & Nilsson, 2021):

> Proceeds from the garment industry for the most part do not directly benefit the country's military, unlike industries such as gemstones, timber, and oil and gas. However, Bestseller commissioned an independent investigation into its business in the country to investigate the status of three of its factories in an industrial zone linked to Myanmar Economic Holdings, a military-controlled conglomerate that has been placed under sanctions by the US, EU and UK since the coup.

Surprisingly, Bestseller's response to the threat of losing the company's social license to operate was to commission an investigation primarily into the legal license to operate by lawyers as examiners.

Bestseller's Convenience Themes

Assuming that the allegations against the company were correct, it is possible to identify convenience themes for the offender as illustrated in Fig. 5.1. There was a corporate threat against supply of quality goods at low prices from Myanmar. At the same time, the possibility of continued supply would ensure more profits. The company had access to resources to continue their business in Myanmar, and the lack of oversight and guardianship by the international community created a chaotic situation. It was a rational choice for the company to continue its business in Myanmar that they justified by the employment they provided to thousands of poor people in the country.

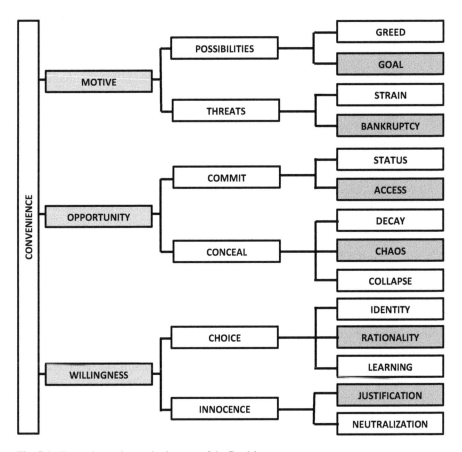

Fig. 5.1 Convenience themes in the case of the Danish company

The founder of Bestseller was Troels Holch Povlsen, and his son Anders Holch Povlsen developed the business into 2700 retail stores and 15,000 retail customers. The number of employees was 17,000 at Bestseller headquartered in Brande in Denmark. The son became a billionaire and remained the CEO and sole owner of the international retail clothing chain as a privately held and family-owned clothing company. In a statement, Anders Holch Povlsen said that "we cannot imagine anything worse than if our company, in any way possible, should contribute to the situation Myanmar now finds itself in. Our work in the country to date has been about the exact opposite – contributing positively to the country's development, both economically and politically" (Larsen, 2021). He argued that continuing operations in Myanmar would help poor people, where almost half of the population lives below the poverty line. He claimed that it would cause serious harm to the population if international businesses had to withdraw from Myanmar. He argued that corporate social responsibility implies staying in Myanmar, while critics argued that the only responsible thing to do would be to close down business in Myanmar as long as a military clique was in power in the country.

This CEO reasoning is in line with the motive of social concern for others. Agnew (2014) introduced the motive of social concern for wrongdoing, where there is a desire to help others, and thus moving beyond the assumption of simple self-interest. However, as argued by Paternoster et al. (2018), helping others can be a self-interested, rational action that claims social concern.

The CEO reasoning for the motive of corporate possibilities might also be founded in the historical tradition of reputation benefits from being an employer in Myanmar. When the previous military dictatorship collapsed, and Aung San Suu Kyi was elected president in the country, being an employer of workers caused a corporate reputation improvement by the Myanmar "fairytale" (Mortensen et al., 2019). With the Nobel Peace Prize winner Kyi in front as president of Myanmar, Bestseller and other companies contributed to raising the standard of living in the country. By establishing factories in Myanmar with very low wages for employees, Bestseller and others could claim that they contributed to the adventurous improvements for local people. At the same time, the companies were making substantial profits from sale of the garments on markets in Europe. If withdrawing from production in Myanmar, Bestseller faced the threat of significant reduction in profits and possible economic losses in the clothing business as indicated in Fig. 5.1.

In the opportunity structure, Bestseller management had access to resources to continue operations in Myanmar as indicated in Fig. 5.1. The company had also an opportunity to conceal potential links to the junta by avoiding direct trade with garment factories. Instead, Bestseller did business with local vendors that had links to the factories. In the principal-agent perspective of detachment (Bosse & Phillips, 2016), Bestseller as a principal appeared detached from factories as agents that were producing clothes for the company.

The innocent justification might rely on an argument that many other foreign companies operated the same business structure as Bestseller in Myanmar. Furthermore, the employment argument of securing a minimum standard of living among workers could also be used to justify continued operations in Myanmar despite junta dictatorship in the country.

The Fraud Investigation Report

The mandate for the examiners asked them to conduct a review of whether Bestseller had lived up to the highest, international standards for corporate social responsibility, inclusive the United Nation's guidelines for human rights and business and OECD's guidelines for multinational enterprises. The other part of the mandate asked examiners to review whether Bestseller had economic relationships with the military and thus had acted in violation of the rules from the Danish foreign ministry and the European Union.

Examiners argued that discontinuing activities in Myanmar would be a breach of Bestseller's corporate social responsibility (Christoffersen & Mikkelsen, 2021: 120):

> Myanmar's situation is bleak, not just politically but also economically. In case many international companies decide to halt their activities in Myanmar, it would cause an economic meltdown and lead to widespread and serious poverty and famine. It is therefore, in our view, in clear breach of Bestseller's corporate social responsibility, should they decide not to continue with their economic and social activities in Myanmar. It is therefore our recommendation, that Bestseller as quickly as possible resume their activities in Myanmar.

One main question that examiners were commissioned to answer was whether Bestseller had economic relations with the military in Myanmar as a result of 3 of the 30 factories, from which Bestseller sourced products, were placed in the Ngwe Pinlae industrial zone. Based on the review, examiners did not believe that there were reasonable grounds to assume that the three factories were located on plots of land that were owned, directly or indirectly, by the military. Neither did examiners believe that there were reasonable grounds to assume that the three factories had paid administration fees, directly or indirectly, to the military. Based on the volatile situation in Myanmar, examiners recommended that Bestseller should continue to exercise considerable due diligence in order to avoid breaching the EU sanctions.

Another main question addressed by the examiners was whether Bestseller had acceptable standard in its corporate social responsibility (Christoffersen & Mikkelsen, 2021: 121):

> We are clearly of the opinion that there is no doubt that Bestseller lived up to their corporate social responsibility in accordance with the highest international standards in relation to their activities in Myanmar.

A third main question was whether Bestseller, in case of economic relations with the military, was in breach of Danish or EU guidelines and rules. Examiners found that there were no reasonable grounds to assume that Bestseller had any economic relations with the military in Myanmar as a result of their activities in the Ngwe Pinlae industrial zone. They found no evidence of breaches of the sanctions from the EU.

The conclusions drawn by examiners were based on various documents from Bestseller including emails, minutes of meetings, and contracts. They interviewed a number of people where some interviewees had to remain anonymous because of safety issues. Some relevant information sources never responded to requests from the examiners.

Regaining the Social License

The investigation by Christoffersen and Mikkelsen (2021) was an attempt to regain not only the legal license to operate but also the social license to operate in Myanmar. The main argument for continuing Bestseller business in the country that had been occupied by a military dictatorship was concerned with avoidance of poverty. The firm claimed that 48,000 persons in Myanmar were dependent on new orders of clothing from Bestseller. The story was told that not only employees would suffer but also their families. Furthermore, the firm claimed that their continued business activities in Myanmar in no way would benefit the military junta. Investigators strongly recommended Bestseller to place new orders when their report was released on May 10, 2021.

However, on August 27, 2021, Bestseller announced that they had stopped their business in Myanmar already and that they would place no new orders (Bestseller, 2021):

> Following the announcement from IndustriALL Global Union and their Myanmar affiliate, the Industrial Workers Federation of Myanmar (IWFM), Bestseller will not place new orders in the country until an impact assessment and dialogue with experts, NGOs, trade unions and other relevant stakeholders with a clear focus on the wellbeing of garment workers in Myanmar has been conducted.

The report by Christoffersen and Mikkelsen (2021) was obviously not sufficient to regain the social license since global and local unions were still skeptical to business activities in Myanmar. The only relevant attempt to regain the license seemed to be by not placing new orders in Myanmar. The argument that poor workers and their families would suffer income loss was contradicted by the argument that the wellbeing of garment workers in the country was not guaranteed and that the military junta would benefit from Bestseller business in the country (Thomsen, 2021).

Furthermore, while stakeholders felt sorry for citizens in Myanmar who suffered under the boycott, stakeholders also knew that there are always innocent victims of various sanctions. For example, when hospital employees go on strike to gain higher wages, then patients waiting in line for treatment become innocent victims. Therefore, it may not come as a surprise that the innocent-victim approach suggested by the investigators did not work for Bestseller to regain the social license to operate in Myanmar.

The attempts to regain the social license by Bestseller management can be studied in terms of factors that are needed to earn the license as suggested by Saenz (2019) and Sale (2021) as illustrated in Table 5.1.

Table 5.1 Attempts to regain the social license by Bestseller executives

Social legitimacy	Violation	Correction
Pragmatic legitimacy	Supporting business benefitting military junta	Withdraw from further business that could benefit the military junta in Myanmar
Moral legitimacy	Military junta hurting innocent civilians	Keep readiness to return to business in Myanmar if social license from local unions
Cognitive legitimacy	Profiting from poor people in the country	Keep readiness to return to business in Myanmar if acceptable to garment industry
Trust vulnerability	**Violation**	**Correction**
Risk tolerance	Ignorance of transition from democracy to dictatorship	Alignment with other corporations and national guidelines
Adjustment level	Military junta's power regulation of business conduct	Home country's guidelines for business abroad
Relative power	Retail customers in chain stores reacted to misconduct	Avoidance of garments marked "made in Myanmar"

References

Agnew, R. (2014). Social concern and crime: Moving beyond the assumption of simple self-interest. *Criminology, 52*(1), 1–32.

Bestseller. (2021). Not placing new orders in Myanmar, Bestseller, www.bestseller.com, published August 27.

Bosse, D. A., & Phillips, R. A. (2016). Agency theory and bounded self-interest. *Academy of Management Review, 41*(2), 276–297.

Christoffersen, J., & Mikkelsen, M. S. (2021 May 10). *Redegjørelse: Bestseller A/S' samfundsansvar i Myanmar (Statement: Bestseller Ltd.'s Social Responsibility in Myanmar)*, law firm Offersen Christoffersen, Copenhagen, Denmark, p. 122.

Einarsdottir, I. E. (2021). Bestseller får kritikk for påståtte militærforbindelser i kriserammede Myanmar (bestseller receives criticism for alleged military connections in crisis-stricken Myanmar), fashion industry magazine. *Melk & Honning*, www.melkoghonning.no, published April 20.

Larsen, M. (2021). Danish company bestseller urges EU to take action on Myanmar. *ScandAsia*, Nordic News and Business Promotion in Asia, www.scandasia.com, published April 21.

Meixler, E. & Creery, J. (2022). EU targets Myanmar's lucrative energy sector in latest sanctions. Financial Times, www.ft.com, published February 22.

Mortensen, N. H., Danwatch, K. L. H., Myanmar Now, Cha, P. T., & Frontier. (2019). Baksiden av eventyret om "made in Myanmar" (the flip side of the fairytale about "made in Myanmar"), Norwegian foreign aid magazine. *Bistandsaktuelt,* www.bistandsaktuelt.no, published April 29.

Paternoster, R., Jaynes, C. M., & Wilson, T. (2018). Rational choice theory and interest in the "fortune of others". *Journal of Research in Crime and Delinquency, 54*(6), 847–868.

Reed, J. (2022). Stay or go: The dilemma for multinationals in Myanmar. *Financial Times*, www.ft.com, published January 25.

Reed, J., & Nilsson, P. (2021). H&M and Primark resume Myanmar orders for first time since coup. *Financial Times*, www.ft.com, published May 21.

Ritzau. (2021). Kofod fortørnet over Bestsellers brug af fabrikker i Myanmar (Kofod upset over Bestseller's use of factories in Myanmar), Danish broadcasting. *TV2*, www.nyheder.tv2.dk, published April 18.

Saenz, C. (2019). Building legitimacy and trust between a mining company and a community to earn social license to operate: A Peruvian case study. *Corporate Social Responsibility and Environmental Management, 26*(2), 296–306.

Sale, H. A. (2021). The corporate purpose of social license. *Sothern California Law Review, 94*(4), 785–842.

Thomsen, C. B. (2021). Dansk tøjgigant vil ikke støtte brutalt militær og trækker sig ud af Myanmar – i hvert fald for en periode, Danish daily newspaper. *Politiken*, www.politiken.dk, published September 16.

Chapter 6
Whistleblowing Failure

One kind of violation of the social license to operate is ignorance toward messages, notices, and warnings from whistleblowers. Whistleblowers are individuals internally or externally who notice something that seems suspicious, and thus they suspect wrongdoing. Whistleblowers report their observations to someone who potentially can do something about the matter (Mpho, 2017). As illustrated in the police case study earlier in this book, Norwegian police attempted to regain their social license to operate by strengthening whistleblowing procedures as well as emphasizing management responsibility for oversight and control (Borgerud et al., 2021).

Challenging the Social License

Similarly, the case study in this chapter is concerned with alleged ignorance toward whistleblowing in a municipality in Norway. When the investigation report by Ernst and Young (2022) was presented, the media wrote about management failure at the top levels (Håkensbakken, 2022):

> There are many questions in this case. The consultants at Ernst & Young have been hired to answer some of them. In their report, they conclude that the municipality has handled messages of concern and notifications regarding the home care service in line with the Working Environment Act's rules for notification. The report must nevertheless be read thoroughly by the municipal council, as the municipality's highest body. They can hardly say they are satisfied with the fact that 36 percent of municipal employees in a survey answer that there is no justifiable culture of free expression in the municipality, while 12 percent answer "do not know." It is first and foremost employees in the home care service who experience a "deficient culture of expression." The reviews clearly show that one is not in line concerning improvements of the home care service. This is not about who said what and when. Nor about what they do in other municipalities. For Vestre Toten municipality, it is about providing sufficient resources and good enough follow-up to provide a sound offer to its own

65
P. Gottschalk, *Financial Crime Issues*,
https://doi.org/10.1007/978-3-031-11213-3_6

residents who need it, and at the same time be an attractive workplace in the competition for health care workers.

Similar to the Obos case (KPMG, 2021), investigators from Ernst and Young (2022) concluded that there was no violation in the municipality of the legal license to operate. The observed deficient culture of expression was perceived as a violation of the social license to operate since disabled and older citizens were the recipients of services from the municipal home care unit. It was a violation of the social license to operate also visible by the fact that qualified healthcare workers became reluctant to work in the municipality.

The sources of license authority included the older and disabled care recipients, healthcare workers, citizens having family members in municipal care, and the media. One local newspaper in particular was emphasized as a media channel for expression of concerns, as described by the investigators (Ernst & Young, 2022: 30):

> The statement that a new head of the home care service should have made – "Those who go to the media harm the home care service" – will, if the statement is correct, be able to reinforce an experience of a continuation of an already established culture of fear in the entity (…) The perceived culture of fear must also have meant that leaders are anxious to say or make mistakes, and thus risk being named in the media, for example in Oppland Arbeiderblad (OA), which has been active in producing negatively angled articles about the municipality (…) According to the former head of the home care service, the incident has been presented in the media as her ordering an employee on 100% sick leave to work, which she has denied.

The municipal home care is an arrangement with the objective of having people stay in their private homes – houses or apartments – as long as possible. The motive is to secure a standard of living for the service recipients where their former lifestyle can continue as much as possible despite emerging problems. The motive is also to save costs in nursing homes, where the costs for one nursing home resident far exceed the costs of visiting a private home resident several times around the clock every day. It was estimated that eight home visits in a 24-hour cycle is much cheaper for the municipality than having the person in a municipal old-age home or nursing home.

The substance of social license to operate in this home care case relates to the trust that relatives and recipients place in the municipal service. Trust refers to an acceptance of vulnerability to another's action (Baer et al., 2021). Trust implies that vulnerability is accepted based upon positive expectations of the motives and actions of another. Trust is associated with dependence and risk (Chan et al., 2020). When a 95-year-old in a wheelchair living at home opens the door to a stranger from the municipality, the person makes herself or himself vulnerable to mistakes by the service provider, including potentially wrong medication.

The value of social license might be found in the efficiency of service provision as well as the quality of the workforce. If there is not only a trusted relationship between provider and receiver of health services at home but also a trusted relationship between the municipality and the community, then there is a foundation for efficient service provision. If there is a culture of free speech among municipal employees, then there is a foundation for recruiting and keeping a qualified workforce within the home healthcare unit in the municipality.

Management's Convenience Themes

Assuming that the allegations are correct, it is possible to identify convenience themes for the home care management as illustrated in Fig. 6.1. The manager felt exhausted, where strain and pain can lead to deviant behavior. The motive is then threats from strain and pain. The strain perspective has become one of the leading theoretical explanations for wrongdoing (Langton & Piquero, 2007). The strain perspective argues that a range of factors influence whether individuals cope with strains through deviance (Thaxton & Agnew, 2018).

The relevant convenience theme in the organizational opportunity dimension of convenience theory seems to be chaos, where whistleblowing did not work, and where there was no freedom of speech regarding negative events in the municipality. There was a lack of control in the principal-agent relationship (Bosse & Phillips, 2016). In the willingness dimension, the accused felt that she had reported to her superiors about the problems and therefore had no guilt feelings (Benson, 1985; Chen & Moosmayer, 2020).

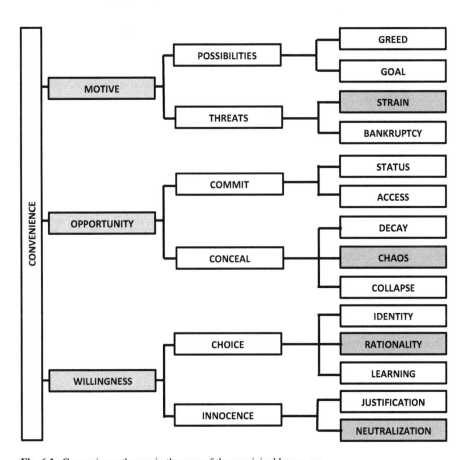

Fig. 6.1 Convenience themes in the case of the municipal home care

The Fraud Investigation Report

The report by Ernst and Young (2022) claimed that the lacking climate for expressing critical opinions and the reluctance to recognize messages from whistleblowers have caused the negative situation. The examiners suggested that municipal executives should make a real effort to correct the situation.

– The former leader of the municipal home care service felt that she received the blame and became the scapegoat in the Ernst and Young (2022) report (Sønstelie et al., 2022):

> I feel I have had to endure a lot of pressure. I have stood alone. I feel I am being wrongfully made a scapegoat, says Maj Britt Karlsen after the presentation of the Ernst & Young report. Maj Britt Karlsen says she constantly reported to care manager Trine Kløvrud about the challenges in the home care service.

After she told her story in the press quote above, the former municipal home service manager received support (Solhaug et al., 2022):

> "MB Karlsen is a very skilled leader; the problems are higher up in the system. Guaranteed," writes Finn Kristiansen in OA's comment field on Facebook. The former head of the home service responds that she has been made a scapegoat in the recent Ernst & Young report. She has 40 years behind her as an employee in Vestre Toten municipality.
>
> – I've been loyal. But now I am made a scapegoat on the wrong basis, I have the right to defend myself. I want employees and residents to hear my version as well, said the 66-year-old.

A scapegoat is a person who is blamed for the wrongdoings, mistakes, or faults of others (Gangloff et al., 2016). Scapegoating refers to the organization transferring the responsibility for an act or a situation to one or a few symbolic figures (Mulinari et al., 2021; Schoultz & Flyghed, 2021). This time, it was examiners at

Table 6.1 *Attempts to regain the social license by municipal executives*

Social legitimacy	Violation	Correction
Pragmatic legitimacy	Lack of oversight and control in home nursing	Improved openness and transparency internally and externally
Moral legitimacy	Vulnerable recipients of home care services	Whistleblowing routines and channels made more effective and efficient
Cognitive legitimacy	Perception of conflicts and dishonesty	Actions for harmonious working climate that is open to controversial views
Trust vulnerability	**Violation**	**Correction**
Risk tolerance	Turbulent working environment with service consequences	Control of working environment with improved service
Adjustment level	Helpless recipients and their close family and supporters	Empowerment of stakeholders by whistleblowing
Relative power	Management failure in overview and guardianship	Removal of blamed employee as scapegoat

Ernst and Young (2022) who were accused of scapegoating the manager in their investigation.

Regaining the Social License

The main violations of the social license to operate were concerned with inadequate handling of alerts and a culture of fear as an obstacle to an open climate for expression of opinions. Regaining the trust of employees, care recipients, and other stakeholders requires involvement of local union leaders (Ernst & Young, 2022).

The attempts to regain the social license by municipal management can be studied in terms of factors that are needed to earn the license as suggested by Saenz (2019) and Sale (2021) as illustrated in Table 6.1.

References

Baer, M. D., Frank, E. L., Matta, F. K., Luciano, M. M., & Wellman, N. (2021). Untrusted, overtrusted, or just right? The fairness of (in)congruence between trust wanted and trust received. *Academy of Management Journal, 64*(1), 180–206.

Benson, M. L. (1985). Denying the guilty mind: Accounting for involvement in a white-collar crime. *Criminology, 23*(4), 583–607.

Borgerud, I. M., Christensen, E., Finstad, L., Kassman, A., & Nylund, M. H. (2021, May 26). *Politikorrupsjon – Lederskap, risikoerkjennelse og læring (police corruption – Leadership, risk assessment and learning)*, report by the evaluation committee, Oslo, Norway.

Bosse, D. A., & Phillips, R. A. (2016). Agency theory and bounded self-interest. *Academy of Management Review, 41*(2), 276–297.

Chan, J., Logan, S., & Moses, L. B. (2020). Rules in information sharing for security. *Criminology & Criminal Justice*, published online 1–19. https://doi.org/10.1177/1748895820960199.

Chen, Y., & Moosmayer, D. C. (2020). When guilt is not enough: Interdependent self-construal as moderator of the relationship between guilt and ethical consumption in a Confucian context. *Journal of Business Ethics, 161*, 551–572.

Ernst & Young. (2022, February 14). *Rapport Vestre Toten kommune til Kontrollutvalget (report Vestre Toten municipality to the control committee)*, audit firm Ernst & Young, Oslo.

Gangloff, K. A., Connelly, B. L., & Shook, C. L. (2016). Of scapegoats and signals: Investor reactions to CEO succession in the aftermath of wrongdoing. *Journal of Management, 42*, 1614–1634.

Håkensbakken, S. (2022). Vestre Toten må forstå hvorfor det har blitt som det har blitt (Vestre Toten must understand why it has become as it has become), daily local newspaper. *Oppland Arbeiderblad*, www.oa.no, published February 15.

KPMG. (2021). *Ulven-transaksjonen – Granskingsrapport til styret i Obos (the Ulven transaction – Investigation report to the board at Obos)* (p. 34). Law Firm KPMG.

Langton, L., & Piquero, N. L. (2007). Can general strain theory explain white-collar crime? A preliminary investigation of the relationship between strain and select white-collar offenses. *Journal of Criminal Justice, 35*, 1–15.

Mpho, B. (2017). Whistleblowing: What do contemporary ethical theories say? *Studies in Business and Economics, 12*(1), 19–28.

Mulinari, S., Davis, C., & Ozieranski, P. (2021). Failure of responsive regulation? Pharmaceutical marketing, corporate impression management and off-label promotion of enzalutamide in Europe. *Journal of White Collar and Corporate Crime, 2*(2), 69–80.

Saenz, C. (2019). Building legitimacy and trust between a mining company and a community to earn social license to operate: A Peruvian case study. *Corporate Social Responsibility and Environmental Management, 26*(2), 296–306.

Sale, H. A. (2021). The corporate purpose of social license. *Sothern California Law Review, 94*(4), 785–842.

Schoultz, I., & Flyghed, J. (2021). Performing unbelonging in court – Observations from a transnational corporate bribery trial – A dramaturgical approach. *Crime, Law and Social Change*, published online https://doi.org/10.1007/s10611-021-09990-x

Solhaug, E. A., Sønstelie, E., & Fosslien, H. R. (2022). Stor støtte til hjemmetjenestens tidligere leder: "Jobbet døgnet rundt" (great support to the home service's former leader: "Worked around the clock"), daily local newspaper. *Oppland Arbeiderblad*, www.oa.no, published February 15.

Sønstelie, E., Solhaug, E. A., & Fosslien, H. R. (2022). Hjemmetjeneste-sjefen mener topplederne sviktet henne: -De har gjort meg urettmessig til syndebukk, local daily newspaper. *Oppland Arbeiderblad*, www.oa.no, published February 15.

Thaxton, S., & Agnew, R. (2018). When criminal coping is likely: An examination of conditioning effects in general strain theory. *Journal of Quantitative Criminology, 34*, 887–920.

Chapter 7
Whistleblowing Deviation

The mayor in a Norwegian municipality was charged with fraud by Norwegian police. It was a whistleblower who first notified the legal counsel in the municipality. The social license for a municipality rests on legitimacy of the administration as well as trust in both politicians and bureaucrats. The top politician is the mayor. The accused was the mayor in the municipality of Nittedal located northeast of Oslo, the capital of Norway. The municipality has 20,000 inhabitants. The accused in the mayor position represented the labor party, and she became the first mayor to be prosecuted for corruption in the country. She was prosecuted by the Norwegian national authority for investigation and prosecution of economic and environmental crime (Økokrim). The maximum sentence in Norway for corruption is 10 years in prison. However, the average for all convicted white-collar offenders in corruption cases is 2 years in prison. The public prosecutor was Esben Kyhring, while the defense lawyer was Geir Lippestad (Mikalsen et al., 2020).

The case started in September 2019 when an anonymous person blew the whistle on the mayor. The whistleblower claimed that the mayor was involved in a development project to be approved by the municipal council (Poensgen et al., 2020). Fraud examiner Erling Grimstad was hired by the municipality to conduct an internal investigation of the allegations against the mayor (Grimstad, 2021). The fraud examiner's first reaction was to notify Økokrim, which triggered a police investigation in parallel to the private investigation. After a while, Økokrim charged Thorkildsen with corruption.

Offender Convenience Themes

Assuming that the accusations and charges were correct, convenience themes can be identified as illustrated in Fig. 7.1. It was individual possibilities in the motive dimension of convenience theory. It might be a matter of climbing the hierarchy of

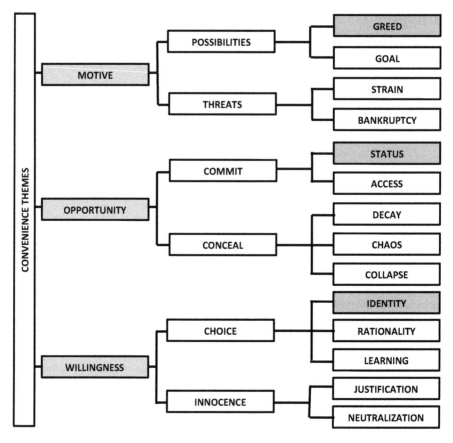

Fig. 7.1 Convenience themes for the municipal mayor

needs for economic success (Maslow, 1943) in the position of an important citizen
in the municipality. The status of a mayor is difficult to attack, which made the
opportunity structure convenient. Status is an individual's social rank within a formal or informal hierarchy or the person's relative standing along a valued social
dimension. Status is the extent to which an individual is respected and admired by
others, and status is the outcome of a subjective assessment process (McClean et al.,
2018). High-status individuals enjoy greater respect and deference from, as well as
power and influence over, those who are positioned lower in the social hierarchy
(Kakkar et al., 2020: 532):

> Status is a property that rests in the eyes of others and is conferred to individuals who are
> deemed to have a higher rank or social standing in a pecking order based on a mutually
> valued set of social attributes. Higher social status or rank grants its holder a host of tangible
> benefits in both professional and personal domains. For instance, high-status actors are
> sought by groups for advice, are paid higher, receive unsolicited help, and are credited
> disproportionately in joint tasks. In innumerable ways, our social ecosystem consistently
> rewards those with high status.

In the willingness dimension for deviant behavior, the convenience theme in the case of the mayor seems to be choice based on identity as indicated in Fig. 7.1. Identity of an individual is the person's self-concept in terms of the knowledge structure that contains all information relevant to self. Piening et al. (2020: 327) defined three self-concept levels:

> First, people define themselves in terms of their personal attributes (e.g., personality, abilities, and interests). At this individual level, one's sense of uniqueness and self-esteem is based on favorable comparisons with other people in a given social context. Second, the relational level involves self-definition based on connections and role relationships with others, with one's self-worth being influenced by the quality of these relationships. Third, the collective level refers to defining oneself in terms of the social groups one belongs to.

The identity makes deviant behavior acceptable for the elite (Petrocelli et al., 2003), often combined with narcissistic identification with own business enterprise (Galvin et al., 2015) such as the municipality. Narcissists tend to expect preferential treatment (Zvi & Elaad, 2018).

Fraud Investigation Outcome

Grimstad (2021: 2) summarized his findings in the following bullet points:

- The initial processing of the notification case gave rise to suspicion of matters that we thought the police should be informed about.
- As a result, we informed Økokrim of circumstances that could provide a basis for investigating whether a criminal act had been committed.
- The notification to Økokrim resulted in Økokrim starting an investigation.
- The defendant is charged by Økokrim for gross corruption when this report from the case processing of the notification case is submitted.
- The case handling of the development project shows that the accused individual has had relations to two specific businesspersons in the municipality. The individual did not raise the question of whether her relations could have a bearing on her impartiality in decisions or outcomes in which she participated as mayor of Nittedal.
- The accused individual has been directly involved in the processing of cases in the municipality where the two businesspersons have had financial interests, including the regulation and development of a new residential area in Bjørnholtlia at Hakadal.
- Based on her relations with the two businesspersons, it cannot be ruled out that the relationships may have had an impact on decisions that the municipality has made on the regulation and development of Bjørnholtlia.
- We recommend that the municipality makes a separate assessment of any consequences that findings in this whistleblowing case may have had for decisions made by the municipality regarding the regulation of the relevant residential area in Bjørnholtlia.

The main issue for the fraud examiners was whether the accused person in the mayor position suffered from lack of impartiality when participating in decision-making regarding the new residential area in Bjørnholtlia at Hakadal. Grimstad (2021: 28) presented the following conclusion:

> Based on the inquiries we have carried out; we believe that it is likely that the accused was not impartial to facilitate and participate in the decision-making regarding the zoning plan for Bjørnholtlia. Based on the information we have described above, we believe that the accused was not open about matters of importance for the assessment of her partiality in discussion with the then councilor, municipal attorney, or unit leader for plan, building, and geodata. She also did not request any assessment of her own partiality in connection with her participation in decisions related to the current zoning plan for Bjørnholtlia.

The trial against the suspended mayor took place in Oslo District Court where she was acquitted of the corruption charges. Økokrim decided to appeal the verdict to a court of appeals where the trial was scheduled for 2022 (Spaberg et al., 2021).

Municipal Convenience Themes

The fraud allegations against the mayor caused various reactions among citizens in the municipality. They questioned how politicians and bureaucrats had handled the whistleblowing incident (Svendsen, 2021). Fraud examiners from PwC (2022: 5) were then hired by the municipal council to address citizen questions and concerns to regain the social license to operate:

> What does the municipal counsel or the municipal councilor do when someone blows the whistle on alleged wrongdoing by the mayor in the form of receiving bribes from business-people? Are such allegations to be investigated, and who should then conduct the investigation? Who are to be alerted? For how long can the administration handle the issues without involving the political leadership? Are suspicions of wrongdoing relevant for police reporting, and who should decide to do it? Who are entitled to address all the questions that occur in these circumstances? Who decides what in such matters in a municipality? What is the political leadership expected to do when they learn about the allegations?

To answer such questions, the examiners interviewed a number of key people in the municipality. Assuming that the allegations against the municipality regarding whistleblowing mishandling were correct, the following accusations can be reflected in convenience themes:

- The legal counsel, who received the notification, should have informed the human resource function in the municipality.
- The legal counsel, who received the notification, should have initiated a review so that a reflected case description could have been presented to the municipal council.
- The duty of confidentiality was not obvious, where the police were not entitled to impose to make information confidential for the information source.
- The municipal executive should have informed the deputy mayor about the fraud allegations against the suspended mayor.
- The deputy mayor should have prepared the case for discussion in the municipal council.

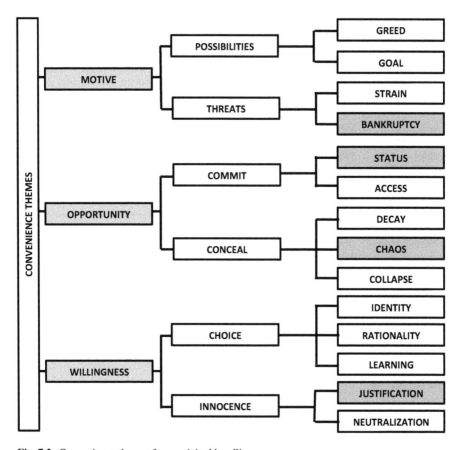

Fig. 7.2 Convenience themes for municipal handling

- The budget for external review of the matter was not approved.
- The mayor and then the deputy mayor are not automatically the legal representatives of the municipality.
- The charged mayor suffered from unfair secrecy.

The motive for these alleged wrongdoings seems to be threats along the organizational axis as indicated in Fig. 7.2. The status of the offenders as well as lack of guidelines enabled committing and concealing the deviance. The offenders might justify their actions by inexperience and confidentiality.

Regaining the Social License

Allegations of corruption at the very top of a municipality created reactions among citizens. A revised routine to handle messages from whistleblowers was expected to help regain the social license to operate public administration in the municipality.

Table 7.1 Attempts to regain the social license by municipal executives

Social legitimacy	Violation	Correction
Pragmatic legitimacy	Fraud allegations causing municipal disruption	Appointing new mayor to secure stability and continuity in the municipality
Moral legitimacy	Abuse of mayor position not acceptable	Internal investigation as well as police prosecution to demonstrate seriousness
Cognitive legitimacy	Disruption in municipal management	Municipal control and clarification of management and administration roles
Trust vulnerability	**Violation**	**Correction**
Risk tolerance	Too much trust of persons in top positions	More executives involved in decision-making
Adjustment level	Random procedure related to whistleblowing	Reliable treatment of both whistleblower and accused
Relative power	Discrepancy between politicians and bureaucrats	Alignment of politicians and bureaucrats

The attempts to regain the social license by municipal management can be studied in terms of factors that are needed to earn the license as suggested by Saenz (2019) and Sale (2021) as illustrated in Table 7.1.

References

Galvin, B. M., Lange, D., & Ashforth, B. E. (2015). Narcissistic organizational identification: Seeing oneself as central to the organization's identity. *Academy of Management Review, 40*(2), 163–181.

Grimstad, E. (2021). *Rapport etter saksbehandling av varslingssak i Nittedal kommune (report after case processing of notification case in Nittedal municipality)* (p. 29). Law Firm Grimstad.

Kakkar, H., Sivanathan, N., & Globel, M. S. (2020). Fall from grace: The role of dominance and prestige in punishment of high-status actors. *Academy of Management Journal, 63*(2), 530–553.

Maslow, A. H. (1943). A theory of human motivation. *Psychological Review, 50*(4), 370–396.

McClean, E. J., Martin, S. R., Emich, K. J., & Woodruff, T. (2018). The social consequences of voice: An examination of voice type and gender on status and subsequent leader emergence. *Academy of Management Journal, 61*(5), 1869–1891.

Mikalsen, K. S., Gustavsen, Ø., Acharki, F., & Vissgren, J. (2020). Ordføreren i Nittedal er tiltalt for grov korrupsjon (the mayor of Nittedal is accused of gross corruption), Norwegian public broadcasting corporation. *NRK*, www.nrk.no, published December 16.

Petrocelli, M., Piquero, A. R., & Smith, M. R. (2003). Conflict theory and racial profiling: An empirical analysis of police traffic stop data. *Journal of Criminal Justice, 31*(1), 1–11.

Piening, E. P., Salge, T. O., Antons, D., & Kreiner, G. E. (2020). Standing together or falling apart? Understanding employees' responses to organizational identity threats. *Academy of Management Review, 45*(2), 325–351.

Poensgen, K., Mikalsen, K. S., & and Tolfsen, C. (2020). Ordføreren i Nittedal er siktet for grov korrupsjon (the mayor of Nittedal is charged with gross corruption), Norwegian public broadcasting corporation. *NRK*, www.nrk.no, published June 23.

PwC. (2022). *Nittedal kommune: Håndtering av varsel mot ordfører (Nittedal Municipality: Handling of Notification Against Mayor), fraud investigation report*. PricewaterhouseCoopers.

Saenz, C. (2019). Building legitimacy and trust between a mining company and a community to earn social license to operate: A Peruvian case study. *Corporate Social Responsibility and Environmental Management, 26*(2), 296–306.

Sale, H. A. (2021). The corporate purpose of social license. *Sothern California Law Review, 94*(4), 785–842.

Spaberg, C., Zachariassen, S., & Gunnarshaug, S. (2021). Økokrim anker frifinnelsen av ordfører: -Jeg er sønderknust (Økokrim appeals the acquittal of the mayor: -I am totally broken), local Norwegian daily newspaper. *Romerikes Blad*, www.rb.no, published November 1.

Svendsen, E. (2021). Advokatfirma skal evaluere varslingsrutinene i Nittedal (law firm to evaluate the whistleblowing routines in Nittedal), Norwegian municipal journal. *Kommunal Rapport*, www.kommunal-rapport.no, published November 5.

Zvi, L., & Elaad, E. (2018). Correlates of narcissism, self-reported lies, and self-assessed abilities to tell and detect lies, tell truths, and believe others. *Journal of Investigative Psychology and Offender Profiling, 15*, 271–286.

Chapter 8
Fishing Rights Corruption

Nations along coast lines grant fishing rights to seafood companies. To obtain a legal license to fishing rights, the fish industry has to apply and pay fees to local governments. In some corrupt countries, government officials may have to be bribed by companies to successfully be granted a legal license. Investigative journalists sometimes detect and report such cases of government corruption. An example is investigative journalists at the broadcasting corporation Al Jazeera who have revealed corruption in many countries. While corruption can cause harm to the legal license to operate if detected and prosecuted in court, disclosure of corrupt activities will always cause some harm to the social license to operate as well. An example is Samherji, which is a large company in the fish industry with its headquarters in Iceland. While Iceland is a small country, Samherji has expanded its seafood business globally by various means.

The country's fishing group Samherji was accused of paying bribes to trawl an African country's waters. The newspaper *Financial Times* reported in November 2019 that two ministers in Namibia had resigned and that Samherji's chief executive had temporarily stepped down over allegations that the company paid bribes for fishing quotas in the southern African nation's maritime waters (Cotterill, 2019; Samherji, 2019b). The whistleblower at Samherji was Johannes Stefansson who told WikiLeaks and then Al Jazeera.

The whistleblowing caused legal actions against bribed officials in Namibia, while it caused no legal actions against bribing executives in Iceland. Samherji kept its legal license to operate. However, lack of legal actions did not prevent violation of the social license to operate for Samherji. One of the critics causing harm to Samherji's social license was the public broadcasting in Iceland. Another source of authority was the broadcasting corporation Al Jazeera.

Johannes Stefansson came to Namibia in Africa in 2011, where he was assigned the task by the Icelandic seafood company Samherji of looking for business opportunities. To complete the mission, he involved himself in questionable payments to politicians and businesspeople in Namibia and Angola. After a while, he developed

P. Gottschalk, *Financial Crime Issues*,
https://doi.org/10.1007/978-3-031-11213-3_8

a bad conscience and felt guilty of wrongdoing. He decided to give notice of the situation. The police arrested the former Minister of Fisheries in Namibia, Bernhard Esau, and indicted him for corruption and money laundering in November 2019. Stefansson provided information to WikiLeaks and then Al Jazeera, where investigative journalist James Kleinfeld interviewed local sources in Namibia. Kleinfeld (2019) then wrote a report on the "Anatomy of a bribe: A deep dive into an underworld of corruption."

Iceland public broadcasting, similar to BBC in the United Kingdom, interviewed the whistleblower and cooperated with Al Jazeera. Al Jazeera's investigative unit secretly filmed officials in Namibia demanding cash in exchange for political favors. It was a story of how foreign companies plunder Africa's natural resources. Using confidential documents provided to Al Jazeera by WikiLeaks, "Anatomy of a bribe" exposed the government ministers and public officials willing to sell off Namibia's assets in return for millions of dollars in bribes. Al Jazeera journalists spent 3 months undercover posing as foreign investors looking to exploit the lucrative Namibian fishing industry. The country's Minister of Fisheries demonstrated a willingness to use a front company to accept a $200,000 "donation." Exclusive testimony from a whistleblower, who worked for Iceland's biggest fishing company, revealed that his employer seemingly instructed him to bribe ministers and even the president in return for fishing rights worth hundreds of millions of dollars.

The prosecuting authority in Namibia claimed in December 2019 that the accused officials in the country had received 103 million Namibian dollars – equivalent to 6 million US dollars – in kickbacks to ensure the Icelandic company access to fishing quotas. According to court documents, a large number of false invoices had been made to hide the payments (Kibar, 2020a).

Samherji on Iceland hired fraud examiners at law firm Wikborg Rein in Norway to investigate all these allegations. The report of investigation was completed in the summer of 2020, but the report was never made public by the company.

Al Jazeera News Investigation

The broadcasting corporation Al Jazeera investigated allegations and published the report entitled "Anatomy of a bribe: A deep dive into an underworld of corruption," "An Al Jazeera investigation into the corrupt power brokers and global business elites defrauding the Namibian people," and "The storm is brewing – We are preparing ourselves for war" (Kleinfeld, 2019):

> Since Al Jazeera first presented the accused parties with evidence of their alleged wrongdoing, the response has been swift and overwhelming: Minister of fisheries Bernhard Esau and the minister of justice have both resigned from their cabinet positions; James Hatuikulipi has resigned as the chairman of FISHCOR, and has also resigned from his job as the managing director of Investec Asset Management. In the run-up to elections in Namibia, the #Fishrot affair has caused outrage in the country, leading to protests in the capital, Windhoek, with hundreds of people marching to the Anti-Corruption Commission demanding decisive

action against corruption in the country. On the day of the elections on November 27, most of the Namibians implicated in the investigation were arrested on charges of corruption, money laundering and fraud. All the Namibians featured in the Al Jazeera investigation deny all wrongdoing. Sacky Kadhila told The Namibian newspaper that he knew from the start that our undercover reporters were "fake businessmen." "I played along…in order to confirm my suspicions," he wrote. He added that he had reported the matter to the president's lawyer, Sisa Namandje, who in turn claimed he had alerted police.

In Iceland, the scandal has led to the suspension of Samherji's longtime CEO Thorsteinn Mar Baldvinsson, pending an internal investigation. On November 12, Samherji released a statement, saying: "Samherji will co-operate with the relevant authorities that may investigate the fisheries industry in Namibia. If such an investigation will take place, Samherji has nothing to hide." The revelations, reported by Iceland's national broadcasting service RUV (Icelandic National Broadcasting Service – Rikisútvarpiq) and the weekly magazine Stundin, have profoundly shocked this small island nation of 350,000 people. One of the few European countries with no history of colonialism or warmongering, Iceland has long prided itself on its purported "innocence." Halldora Mogensen, an Icelandic MP with the Pirate Party, put it bluntly: "The myth of Iceland's innocence is dead."

Al Jazeera is an independent news organization funded in part by the Qatari government. In 2006, Al Jazeera Satellite Network was changed to a public utility and private corporation by a public memorandum and articles of association in accordance with the provisions of Qatar Law and was renamed Al Jazeera Media Network. The investigative journalist who wrote the above report continued his investigations in Namibia where he detected corruption allegations because of a 5G deal with Huawei. Bribes were offered to politicians to ensure Chinese tech giant Huawei would win an exclusive 5G telecommunication network in Namibia (Kleinfeld, 2020).

The former Minister of Fisheries, Bernhard Esau, and the former Minister of Justice, James Hatuikulipi, were in 2021 in jail awaiting the trial on charges of corruption and money laundering. Then a new investigation by Al Jazeera detailed how the president in Namibia, Hage Geingob, allegedly instructed associates to embezzle millions of dollars (Kleinfeld, 2021).

Kveikur News Investigation

Johannes Stefansson as whistleblower did not only talk to WikiLeaks and Al Jazeera. He also appeared on Icelandic public television. He said that he had approved the payment of bribes on behalf of Samherji and each time with a green light from the company. He claimed that Samherji does whatever it takes to get its hands on the natural resources of other nations. Following the broadcast, Samherji announced that chief executive Baldvinsson had stepped down pending on the internal company probe into its Namibian activities (Cotterill, 2019).

The major newspaper in Namibia, *The Namibian*, followed the corruption scandal closely and reported a number of perspectives on the case. For example, a lawyer suddenly left Namibia after having been interviewed by the Anti-Corruption Commission in connection with the Fishrot fishing quotas corruption scandal (Menges, 2020).

Kveikur is a unit within public broadcasting on Iceland named RUV. Kveikur, the investigative series of RUV, the state broadcaster, has a weekly magazine *Stundin*. Investigative journalists at Kveikur conduct inquiries that have impacted Iceland. As a result of their work, public officials have been officially censured, the Icelandic parliament has conducted numerous debates, criminal investigations have been instigated, and many stories have led to significant public outcry. Investigative journalists Seljan et al. (2019) published the story "What Samherji wanted hidden":

> This is based on information leaked to WikiLeaks which Kveikur has investigated for the past months in collaboration with Al Jazeera Investigation Unit and Stundin. The data leaked to WikiLeaks includes thousands of documents and email communication by Samherji's employees. One of them, Johannes Stefansson, also decided to step forward and tell all. Johannes was project manager for Samherji in Namibia until 2016.
>
> "This is criminal activity. It's organized crime. They are benefiting from the country's resources, taking all the money out of the country to invest it elsewhere, in Europe or the US," he says, admitting to having violated the laws himself. "I violated the law on behalf of Samherji while I was there. I was the man to get the quotas and the connections, on my superiors' orders."
>
> For the past decade Samherji has paid ISK (Icelandic kroner) hundreds of millions to high ranking politicians and officials in Namibia with the objective of acquiring the country's coveted fishing quota. For almost a decade, Samherji's Namibian activities have involved three factory fishing trawlers fishing for horse mackerel off the coast. The trawlers have been leased from subsidiaries in Cyprus to two of Samherji's fishing companies in Namibia, Katla, later renamed Mermaria, and Arcticnam, co-owned by Samherji and groups of Namibian quota holders. Samherji has managed to obtain this coveted quota, thus guaranteeing income worth tens of billions ISK. Katla, also known as Mermaria, has been the foremost fishing company and enjoys unusual special terms from the state fishing company, FISHCOR, and utilized Namibia and Angola's international agreements.

Investigative journalists at Kveikur included Helgi Seljan Johannsson, Ingolfur Bjarni Sigfusson, Adalsteinn Kjartansson, and Stefan Adalsteinn Drengsson. Three of them published a book in Icelandic entitled *Nothing to Hide: On Samherji's Trail in Africa* in the spring 2020. In the fall 2020, Kveikur attempted to get hold of the investigation report by Wikborg Rein submitted to Samherji in the summer. The journalists found that Samherji had not done what they said they would do, which was to give a copy of the report to the public prosecutor investigating the case in Iceland. The same applied to Namibian investigators.

In 2022, Kveikur at RUV reported that Namibia requested Interpol's aid in extraditing former Samherji executives (Ciric, 2022):

> Namibia's State Prosecutor has asked Interpol for assistance in the extradition of Aðalsteinn Helgason, Egill Helgi Árnason, and Ingvar Júlíusson in connection with the investigation of the so-called Samherji scandal, RUV reports. The three men were all executives in companies owned by Icelandic seafood company Samherji in Namibia. They are all asking to be permitted to testify in the case from abroad, but the prosecutor intends to file charges against the men, for which they must appear before a judge in Namibia. Samherji was the centre of a media investigation made public in 2019, which alleged that the fishing company had bribed Namibian officials to obtain lucrative quotas, while also taking advantage of international loopholes to avoid taxes. Aðalsteinn and Egill Helgi were Samherji's managing directors in Namibia. The charges against Egill Helgi are in connection with his work for Esja Holding and Mermaria Seafood Namibia. Ingvar was a CFO for Samherji and the charges against him are in connection with his work for Saga Seafood, Esja Investment and Heinaste Investments. Last year, the State Prosecutor requested that the three men be extra-

dited from Iceland, but the request was rejected, as the Icelandic government does not extradite Icelandic citizens. The State Prosecutor says Namibian authorities have more than enough evidence in hand to justify Interpol's involvement and that the three men have not provided any evidence to the contrary. She says the trio is attempting to destroy all evidence of their involvement in the case.

The Al Jazeera news investigation as well as the Kveikur news investigation was reviewed by Bjarnadóttir (2020). She identified four issues of concern reported in the media: corruption within, exploitation of Namibian resources, reputation of Iceland internationally, and mistrust and disputes in government. Reputation of Iceland internationally reflected the potential violation of the social license not only for Samherji but for other businesses in the country as well.

Samherji Fishing Press Release

Samherji (2020a) published the following press release on July 29, 2020, using the company website (https://www.samherji.is/en/moya/news/samherjis-namibia-investigation-finalized):

The Samherji board of directors has received Wikborg Rein's investigation report in relation to the allegations against the company's operations in Namibia. In November 2019, allegations were directed at Samherji and the company's operations in Namibia. The board mandated Norwegian and international law firm Wikborg Rein to assist Samherji in its investigation into the relevant facts. Wikborg Rein is ranked among the leading Nordic law firms within this particular area of law. The firm's lawyers have over decades done vast amounts of similar work for Nordic authorities and international companies.

– Already from the outset we knew that some allegations were outrageous and without basis in reality. One such example related to the German-owned crewing company Cape Cod. The company was dominantly used to pay wages to crews in several countries but portrayed in media as having been a vehicle for a variety of illegal purposes in relation to Namibia. We were further deeply offended by the portrayal of Samherji having exploited a developing nation and walked away with large profits. The total taxes paid in Namibia over the years by entities Samherji was invested in, including income tax, employee tax, export levies, import levies, social security and a number of other payments made to the Namibian state, were about 4 billion Icelandic kroner. That is remarkable in itself considering that Samherji's operations in Namibia were ultimately unprofitable and loss-making, says Mr. Eirikur S. Johannsson, chairman of the Samherji board.

– Other allegations concerned facts about a small part of our global operation in a foreign culture, far from Iceland where we saw a need to have external assistance mapping the relevant facts for us. The alleged facts were simply unknown to us and needed to be scrutinized. So having been faced with serious and fragmented allegations it was very helpful for the Samherji board to receive Wikborg Rein's comprehensive and balanced review of the relevant facts over the years of operation in Namibia, says Mr. Johannsson.

Wikborg Rein has uploaded and analyzed more than a million documents. A large number of relevant personnel have been interviewed. Time has been spent on the ground in several countries, including Namibia. Forensic accounting firm Forensic Risk Alliance (FRA) was also engaged and analyzed payments and other transactions of interest related to the Namibian business. After eight months of work, Wikborg Rein has submitted a comprehensive report substantiating the factual conclusions.

– Having our organization and operations scrutinized is nothing new to Samherji, says Mr. Johannsson.
– In the so-called Central Bank case Samherji was scrutinized for seven years, after which Samherji emerged fully vindicated and victorious. This time we commenced our own investigation and scrutiny in order to get to the bottom of the relevant facts. We have spent vast internal and external resources on this process. Even though the allegations painted a distorted image of our operations, it was important to the company to display to our stakeholders that we take such allegations very seriously, says Mr. Johannsson.

Long before Wikborg Rein's conclusions emerged, Samherji put in place a number of measures to safeguard against further exposure to wrongdoing committed by individuals. All operations in Namibia were stopped already in 2019. On 17 January 2020 Samherji announced that it was in process of launching a modern state-of-the art compliance program which is being implemented throughout our global organization this year: https://www.samherji.is/en/moya/news/samherji-to-implement-corporate-governance-and-compliance-system.

That work is already well underway. Samherji's ambition is to be a pioneer in compliance, governance and internal control within the global fisheries industries.

Samherji will also proactively keep reaching out to relevant authorities that show dedication to mutual cooperation, offering assistance and cooperation during ongoing investigations into the Namibia-related allegations. An agreement is now made for Wikborg Rein to meet with the Icelandic District Prosecutor in the fall. Several meetings have further been held with Namibian authorities in an effort to explore the basis for similar cooperation there.

Once Wikborg Rein have met with relevant authorities, there will be a number of considerations to be taken into account in terms of what findings can be made public and how. We need to assess whether publishing information will jeopardize ongoing investigation in any country. We further need to assess whether publishing certain information will infringe upon laws and regulations concerning protection of individuals mentioned in any findings. Other aspects also need to be taken into consideration.

– We have a need to comment in more detail on the contents of the findings and to rebut allegations that we reacted strongly to when they were made against us last year, says Mr. Johannsson.
– We have respected the integrity of the investigation and left many allegations publicly unanswered despite an urge to comment on them. We equally respect the integrity of still ongoing public investigations. But we will in the coming weeks take a stronger and more vocal stand publicly also in relation to concrete details. Samherji firmly denies that its management ever intended for any subsidiary to engage in wrongful activity, including bribery or money laundering, in order to achieve benefits and will rigorously rebut any further allegation to this effect.

Björgolfur Johannsson was appointed temporarily as chief executive at Samherji, while Wikborg Rein investigated accusations of corruption and money laundering. He expressed already in December 2019 that he did not believe in the allegations that bribes were paid (Schultz & Trumpy, 2019b).

DNB Bank Corrupt Transactions

The alleged corruption payments from Samherji traveled via the Norwegian bank DNB to Esau in Namibia (Finanstilsynet, 2020). DNB is Norway's largest lender that faced allegations concerning the Icelandic company having transferred money via the bank to bribe Namibian officials. DNB had to investigate the claims. When

DNB made the announcement of an internal investigation, Iceland's biggest fishing company, Samherji, said in a statement that it had also hired a law firm to investigate the allegations (Schultz, 2019).

While Samherji published the long statement cited above in 2020, at first, Samherji denied any wrongdoing the year before (Samherji, 2019a):

> It has recently been brought to our attention that a former executive of a subsidiary of the company in Namibia, Johannes Stefansson, has spoken to the media and made serious allegations against Samherji's executives, both current and former. We take this very seriously and have engaged the international law firm Wikborg Rein based in Norway to assist us in thorough investigation of our operations in Africa. Until the investigation has been concluded we will not comment on specific allegations (...).
>
> "All the activities of Samherji and its affiliates were under investigation by authorities for years and no wrongdoings were ever found. All our accounting, e-mails and all other data were thoroughly examined, including that of the companies that have been operating in African waters since 2007. We will not now, like in the past, accept false and misleading allegations of a former employee who once again are prepared by the same parties and media as in the Central Bank-case a few years back," says Thorsteinn Mar Baldvinsson, CEO of Samherji.
>
> At this point in time, we believe it is important to disclose that in the beginning of 2016 we came to suspect that something was wrong without operations in Namibia. In order to get better information, we hired a former police officer from the special prosecutor's office to go to Namibia and look into the matter. His investigation led to the dismissal of the aforementioned employee in mid-2016 for unacceptable behavior and conduct. Since then, our staff has been trying to take control of our operations in Namibia. During this process the former employee has demanded large sums of money from Samherji.

This statement in a press release from Samherji (2019a) carries the date November 11. It denies any knowledge of wrongdoing and blames the whistleblower Stefansson, who received the blame for misconduct in Namibia. This kind of initial statement is common and similar to initial accounts from companies when they face allegations of misconduct and crime (Gottschalk & Benson, 2020: 949):

> Our analysis shows that denial of wrongdoing in several cases is replaced by admission of wrongdoing and scapegoating, while obfuscation of wrongdoing is replaced by denial or acceptance of responsibility and scapegoating.

A scapegoat is a person burdened with the wrongdoing of others (Eren, 2020). While CEO Baldvinsson spoke in the above statement on November 11, he had to step aside 3 days later, on November 14, when Samherji issued a new press statement (Samherji, 2019b):

> The CEO and board of directors of Samherji have agreed that the CEO Thorsteinn Mar Baldvinsson will step aside for the time being until the pending internal investigation into the company's subsidiaries' alleged wrongdoing in Namibia has revealed the key material facts of the matter.

This executive destiny for Baldvinsson is typical as illustrated in the research by Gottschalk and Benson (2020). They found that corporations tend to distance themselves from individuals so that the corporations can survive. Corporations reassign, force to resign, or fire senior leaders. At Samherji, the board hired a new CEO, Björgolfur Johannsson, when Baldvinsson had to step down in November 2019. Four months later, Baldvinsson returned to Samherji, now in a position as co-CEO with Johannsson without any real executive power. The company then stated that the fraud examination by Wikborg Rein was to continue (Samherji, 2020a):

> Wikborg Rein's reporting lines will remain to the board of directors, and Mr. Johannsson will remain dedicated to providing any assistance needed for Wikborg Rein.

According to Reuters (2019), Samherji transferred more than $70 million through a shell company in the tax haven Marshall Islands from 2011 to 2018. Samherji transferred the money through bank accounts in DNB, Norway. The bank's largest shareholder is the Norwegian state, which holds 34% stake in the bank (Reuters, 2019):

> The money consisted partly of proceeds from Samherji's questionable and possibly unlawful operations in Namibia where the company bribes officials to get secure access to fishing quotas. The company in the Marshall Islands was used to pay salaries to the crews of Samherji's factory trawlers. These trawlers fished horse mackerel in Mauritania, Morocco, and Namibia.

The Norwegian bank DNB was heavily involved in the Panama Papers scandal, where the bank had helped rich people in their wealth management program to hide large sums of money in tax havens (Brustad & Hustadnes, 2016; Langset et al., 2016; Tanum, 2016). Fraud examiners from law firm Hjort (2016) investigated the case. The bank ignored to monitor its client transactions through the bank and thus risked being a vehicle for money laundering and tax evasion.

The Samherji scandal forced the bank to conduct yet another internal investigation (Reuters, 2019):

> "Like every other bank, we are guided to take action if the clients do not give us the necessary information that we need to have so that the bank can have good control over how the client uses the bank," said DNB's spokesman, Even Westerveld. "This can sometimes mean that the bank freezes the accounts of clients or off boards him. Unfortunately, we do not officially hold count how often this happens within the bank."

On April 20, 2020, Margret Olafsdottir, chief communications officer at Samherji on Iceland, responded to a request for the Wikborg Rein report:

> Wikborg Rein has informed the Samherji board of directors that the investigation is likely to conclude during the course of this second quarter of 2020. When their work is finished, they will first meet with the Samherji board to present the results. They will next meet with relevant authorities and present their findings and conclusions to them. There will then be a number of considerations to be taken into account in terms of what can be published and how, including whether publishing information will jeopardize ongoing investigations by public authorities in any country, whether publishing certain information will infringe upon laws and regulations concerning protection of individuals mentioned in any findings, etc. All such questions will be discussed thoroughly with relevant authorities at such time.

On September 17, 2020, Margret Olafsdottir, chief communications officer at Samherji on Iceland, responded to a new request for the Wikborg Rein report:

> The vast majority of investigation reports are not published in its entirety, for good reasons. The report is very substantial and there are a large number of elements to be taken into account when assessing what can be published and how, including protection of individuals portrayed in the report. The Samherji board of directors commissioned the report to enable them to address the allegations against the Samherji groups and to identify effective measures against future exposure to individuals' actions. Such work is ongoing in a systemized

manner and will continue to do so until the board is satisfied. Although it is not common practice for private companies to make entire investigation reports public, it is more normal to release compressed information about key findings. Samherji will do so during the course of this fall, following meetings to be held between Wikborg Rein and a number of relevant stakeholders in this process, including public authorities.

Økokrim is the Norwegian national authority for investigation and prosecution of economic and environmental crime, similar to the serious fraud office in the United Kingdom or the fraud units at the FBI in the United States. They started investigating Samherji and DNB in November 2019 (Ekroll & Breian, 2019):

Økokrim is launching an investigation into DNB related to the Icelandic fisheries case. Økokrim has started an investigation at DNB after disclosure of possible corruption and money laundering in an Icelandic fishing company where DNB has been their bank. The Icelandic fishing group Samherji faced accusation of corruption and illegal cooperation with Namibian state officials. Several of them are now in prison, and others are on the run in the country. Samherji faces allegations of having used DNB to transfer money via tax havens, and to an African official who owns a company in Dubai. In total, Samherji allegedly used DNB to transfer NOK 640 million to a tax haven, according to Icelandic media. Økokrim is now investigating Norway's largest financial group.

"The purpose of the investigation is to find out what has happened and whether criminal offenses have been committed. It is natural that we cooperate with the authorities of other countries working on the case complex. We are at an early stage and will not be providing more information about the investigation now," acting Økokrim chief, Hedvig Moe, writes in a press release.

In an email on April 20, 2020, communication director at Norwegian bank DNB, Even Westerveld, stated:

No investigation has been carried out in this case, and consequently no investigation report has been made. The board has had the case thoroughly reviewed several times, and the case is also known to be under investigation by Økokrim. We do not know the status of the investigation right now.

Økokrim is the Norwegian national authority for investigation and prosecution of economic and environmental crime and the main source of specialist skills for the police and the prosecuting authorities in their combat against crime of this kind. The board at DNB was headed by Olaug Svarva, and the chief executive at the bank was Kjerstin Braathen. Norwegian business newspaper *Dagens Næringsliv* also reported that Økokrim had started an investigation into DNB's involvement in the Samherji scandal (Solgård & Trumpy, 2019):

On Wednesday afternoon, Økokrim writes in a press release that they will investigate DNB Bank in connection with the Samherji case, which has been covered by a number of national and international media in recent weeks. "Økokrim has started an investigation against DNB Bank. As reported in several media, the case concerns an Icelandic fisheries group and alleged corruption in Namibia. DNB Bank is referred to as a bank client for the fishing group," the report states.

– The aim of the investigation is to find out what has happened, and whether criminal acts have been committed. It is natural that we cooperate with the authorities in other countries that work on the same case complex. We are in an early phase and will not provide more information about the investigation now, says acting Økokrim executive Hedvig Moe in the press release.

> The case concerns the Icelandic fishing giant Samherji on Iceland, which for a number
> of years is said to have used DNB to squander money via tax havens – and to an African
> official who owns a company in Dubai. It is unknown how much of the funds can be linked
> to possible money laundering and potential bribery.

Norwegian bank DNB ended the client relationship with Samherji in 2018. This was more than 1 year after bank executives at DNB learned about the risk and the potential scandal. In 2015, DNB did make a customer update regarding Samherji registered on the Marshall Island, but bank executives failed in establishing an overview of the real owners (Schultz & Trumpy, 2019a; Solgård & Trumpy, 2019).

On the previous and following pages, it is referred to Økokrim, which is the serious fraud office in Norway investigating and prosecuting financial crime. When a new chief executive at Økokrim was appointed, the police agency could no longer investigate the role of the bank DNB in potential money laundering of funds from Island to Namibia via Norway. The reason for Økokrim's lack of integrity and impartiality in the case was the background of the newly appointed chief executive. Pål Lønseth, the new executive, was recruited to the agency from the private fraud examination team at audit and accounting firm PricewaterhouseCoopers. In his role as fraud examiner, he had been investigating financial transactions linked to the Samherji scandal. Since the principle is that all subordinates are automatically disqualified if someone higher up is disqualified to handle a matter, Økokrim had to declare that the whole agency might suffer from partiality. Therefore, the investigation of the bank DNB on suspicion of money laundering had to be transferred to one of the police districts in Norway. Each police district has a unit specializing in financial crime. However, those local units are by far as qualified at the national agency Økokrim. Therefore, it was reason to expect that DNB would avoid serious scrutiny by a police district unit and thus survive charges even if they were guilty of helping Samherji launder money for bribes.

Different from Økokrim, local police districts are not part of international law enforcement networks. Therefore, the director of public prosecutions at the higher prosecuting authorities in Norway did not know what to do with the DNB investigation several months after Pål Lønseth had disqualified Økokrim for the investigation. Lønseth was appointed head of Økokrim on Friday, June 12, 2020. Four months later, on October 15, prosecution director Jørn Sigurd Maurud had still not decided what to do with the DNB investigation that was terminated at Økokrim. Police inspector Ole Rasmus Knudsen who was in charge of white-collar crime investigations in the Oslo Police District had heard nothing about the case being transferred to them. The likely outcome for DNB was again that DNB executives would avoid prosecution in the Samherji scandal, like they avoided prosecution in the Panama Papers scandal 4 years earlier. However, an investigative journalist became interested in why Maarud did seemingly nothing to allocate the DNB investigation. Maarud then replied on November 2 that the higher prosecuting authorities were in the process of transferring the case to the Oslo Police District.

As mentioned above, Samherji transferred more than $70 million through a shell company in the tax haven Marshall Islands from 2011 to 2018 (Reuters, 2019). Samherji transferred the money allegedly through bank accounts in DNB, Norway.

Norwegian police seemed in the fall of 2020 reluctant to investigate the matter, almost 1 year after they first learned about the potential money laundering in the Norwegian bank. Attorney general Maurud published a press release on September 29, 2020:

> The chief at Økokrim has informed the public prosecutor that he considers himself incompetent in four cases that are under investigation by the unit. The attorney general bases the assessment of the question of impartiality on his judgment, and has decided that the case responsibility will be transferred from Økokrim to another regional public prosecutor's office with an associated police district. Until the cases have been moved, no further investigation is currently being carried out. There will be a clarification relatively soon concerning who will take over case responsibility, so that no significant consequences are expected for, among other things, the progress of the investigation. The other public prosecutor's offices and police districts regularly handle cases of financial crime, including extensive and complicated matters, and the attorney general therefore has confidence that the investigation and prosecution are well taken care of in the cases that are transferred. It is in the nature of the cases that Økokrim – as a unit with special responsibility for the case area – in some cases possesses competence that is not as easy to find elsewhere. To the extent that assistance from Økokrim is deemed necessary so that the quality of the investigation does not suffer, the attorney general has, pursuant to section 60 of the criminal procedure act, the opportunity to decide that certain employees at Økokrim may assist in the further investigation, under the direction of the new public prosecutor. Whether this may become relevant will depend on, for example, what kind of criminal act is being investigated, which investigative methods are relevant, and how far the investigation has come already. The attorney general will return to this issue after a closer assessment in the individual case.

However, shortly after, the Norwegian prosecution authority closed the case against Norwegian bank DNB and potential offenders within the bank (Tomter, 2021).

Convenience theory can be applied to the deviance at DNB as illustrated in Fig. 8.1. In wealth management and large international transactions for corporate clients, there are possibilities to make bank profit. There was a lack of control and oversight in the bank labeled chaos. It was a rational choice in the bank to have Samherji as a customer despite substantial risk. The rational choice assumption about offending is based on a normative foundation where advantages and disadvantages are subjectively compared (Müller, 2018). There was no sign of guilt feeling in the bank when Finanstilsynet (2020) reviewed the matter.

The financial supervisory authority of Norway – Finanstilsynet – found that the bank had no control or guardianship as indicated in Fig. 8.1 (Finanstilsynet, 2020: 16):

> The bank does not appear to have had control over the customer's role holders vis-à-vis DNB or to have carried out customer control of these. It appears from e-mail correspondence with the customer's contact person in 2017 that two of the online banking users were not legitimized. The customer stated that the two would no longer be online banking users, but it does not appear whether other users were added, or who after the changes had online banking access. According to the bank, no persons with a documented role in the company have ever had access to online banking.

The financial supervisory authority of Norway is an independent government agency that builds on laws and decisions emanating from the Norwegian parliament, the government, and the ministries. The authority's main goal is to promote financial stability and well-functioning financial markets.

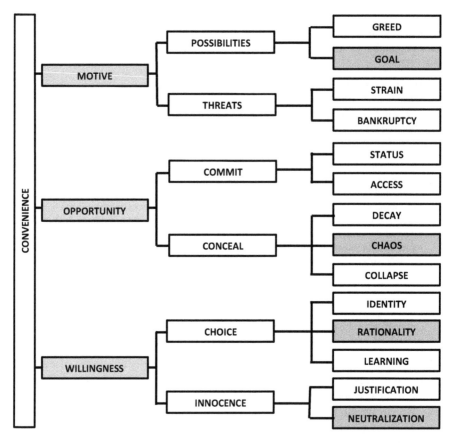

Fig. 8.1 Convenience themes in the case of DNB bank

Whistleblower Johannes Stefansson

Johannes Stefansson remained active and willing to respond to media requests for interviews. After the press release from Samherji cited above, the whistleblower was interviewed by Norwegian business newspaper *Dagens Næringsliv*. The heading of the interview was entitled "The whistleblower: He announced the biggest corruption case a Norwegian bank has been involved in, but Johannes Stefansson was never contacted by Økokrim" (Kibar, 2020a: 33):

- Nobody from Norway has contacted me or my lawyer so far, says Johannes Stefansson, the man who reported the biggest known corruption case a Norwegian bank has been involved in (…).
- It is very strange that I have not heard anything. And there is some concern related to developments in Norway and Iceland. Investigators in Namibia have said that the investigation drags out there and other places, the whistleblower says (…).

- Økokrim has probably known about the case since early 2019, says Stefansson. In a few weeks, he will be ready to return to Namibia for the first time since he blew the whistle – together with a bodyguard with a background from some special forces (…).
- Johannes Stefansson was for many years a very autonomous leader for our business in Namibia. We are in a comprehensive process of implementing systems in our global business so that it can never happen again, writes acting CEO Björgolfur Johannsson in an email to us. He characterizes Stefansson's statements about the company as "incorrect, in some respects grossly incorrect" (…).
- Can it affect your credibility that you yourself have been involved in corruption?
- That is okay. The documents will speak for themselves. I am just the tour guide.

When a scandal hits a company, then the blame game starts, and scapegoating occurs. Management tries to separate the company from the scandal by identifying an individual to blame (Gottschalk & Benson, 2020). A typical example is here the statement above that "Johannes Stefansson was for many years a very autonomous leader for our business in Namibia."

Stefansson worked for 14 months with investigators in Namibia before the case became public knowledge. Namibian investigators sought the assistance of Interpol to conduct investigations in Dubai, the Democratic Republic of the Congo, Zimbabwe, Angola, Cyprus, and Spain, in addition to Iceland and Norway. The arrested officials in Namibia were called The Fishrot Six.

Johannes Stefansson was originally a fisherman like his father. After being at sea for more than a decade aboard large trawlers in the Atlantic, the Indian Ocean, and eastern Russia, he gradually gained management positions in production facilities at various seafood companies. Soon he got a job in Iceland's largest fishing company with a position that involved a lot of travel. The task for him was to open up new markets for Samherji. He got his first managerial position at Samherji's Moroccan company. As a foreign company, Samherji could not come up with direct bids. However, local actors who won the tenders could resell their rights to parts of an annual quota of tons of horse mackerel. Stefansson quickly had sound agreements signed with three local quota owners.

Bribes in Namibia were seldom in cash. It happened most of the time with invoices. Stefansson had access to the Samherji bank accounts in Namibia. Some minor payments came directly from Norway.

When the scandal became public, Samherji headquarters wanted Stefansson to return immediately to Iceland. He was reluctant to do so in fear of potential reprisals and retaliations. He established contact with an IT expert in South Africa to gather as much information as possible that could document his claims about the company's allegedly corrupt business practice. He saved all the emails from his computer in South Africa. He delayed his return to Iceland with various excuses, at the same time as he shut the rest of the company out of his own dropbox. While Samherji management thought he was on his way home, he secured a total of 40 gigabytes of documentation. He stored everything on several hard drives, which he sent by courier to different parts of the world. It took him 2 days to empty his personal computer and secure the contents.

Stefansson then received numerous threats, and he could observe hacking attempts on his digital equipment. Rumors to harm Stefansson were spreading about him regarding extravagant lifestyle, women stories, alcohol addiction, and drug abuse. At one point in time, he stayed in hiding for 5 days after receiving a message that they wanted to take him out. He got help from Christian Yema, a Congolese friend he had only known for 6 months and who was an experienced bodyguard with a background from the military and special force units. Stefansson also got help from the organization Platform to Protect Whistleblowers in Africa, which has provided protection to people in some of the largest corruption cases that have been detected on the African continent – including the latest corruption disclosure related to Angola's president daughter Isabel dos Santos' business activities.

Stefansson blew the whistle on white-collar crime in the fisheries sector. Witbooi et al. (2020) argued that organized crime in the fisheries sector threatens a sustainable ocean economy:

> The threat of criminal activity in the fisheries sector has concerned the international community for a number of years. In more recent times, the presence of organized crime in fisheries has come to the fore (…) Organized criminal groups may share characteristics with conventional businesses, such as their structure and capability, and frequently operate in the white-collar realm. The ability of the network to protect its operations (the protection economy) – through violence, bribery or extortion – is a common, but not necessarily defining, feature of organized crime.

According to the Whistleblower Network News, Johannes Stefansson's health became a major concern because there had been attempts on his life (Turner, 2021):

> When he travels outside Iceland, he needs bodyguards. "If we die with this, then we die with this, we are going to fight to the end," he tells me. "I was never supposed to survive."

In 2022, eight Namibian government officials were on trial where they faced charges of corruptly receiving payments to give a competitive advantage to Icelandic fishing company Samherji. The prosecutor had invited Stefansson to testify in court. However, the prosecutor stated that "we have enough evidence to convict the accused without Mr. Stefansson's evidence" (Routh, 2022).

Wikborg Rein Fraud Investigation

Law firm Wikborg Rein headquartered in Oslo, Norway, was hired by Samherji on Iceland to investigate allegations of wrongdoing in Namibia. The law firm was also hired by the Icelandic company to help solve current issues in Namibia. The examiners thus accepted a double role that is problematic. One problem is that the examiners might make mistakes and wrongdoing while solving current issues in Namibia. If they do, then they cannot investigate those mistakes or that wrongdoing, simply because you cannot investigate your own actions. Another problem is the trustworthiness of the investigation report in terms of independence and objectivity. Critics may easily argue that the report is biased to satisfy the client, who has provided the firm with additional legal work.

Unfortunately, the practice of some law firms of taking on additional assignments for clients is not uncommon. While a private investigation by fraud examiners should be independent and objective, where investigators are accountable, it is tempting for a law firm to take on more work for the client. Some law firms are the main legal advisors to the clients on a continuous basis. Some audit firms are the main external auditor of the clients' accounts on a continuous basis. This is unfortunate, as the reader should be skeptical of investigation reports from such firms.

The following email exchange between the journalist Osman Kibar at daily Norwegian business newspaper *Dagens Næringsliv* and examiners Geir Sviggum and Elisabeth Roscher at Wikborg Rein in August 2020 illustrates the issue:

> Kibar: Icelandic media have questioned that Wikborg Rein assisted Samherji in negotiations related to the business even before you were hired for the investigation. Has this been a topic and what is Wikborg Rein's possible comment on this?
>
> Sviggum: Wikborg Rein had no ongoing assignments for Samherji when we were instructed by the board to carry out this assignment. We have also never before had any involvement with Samherji's operations in Namibia. So, this is incorrect. During the process, it has been desirable for Samherji that we should assist in matters that have had a close and immediate connection to the investigation process and the facts that have been revealed there. This applies, for example, to a controlled closure of the business in Namibia and a legal exit from the country in dialogue with the Namibian authorities. We further assisted in implementing immediate measures to prevent further exposure to the conditions that were the subject of accusations. But all this derives directly from the accusations the company was exposed to in November last year.

It comes as no surprise that the whistleblower, Stefansson, did not want to contribute to Samherji's own investigation of the allegations against the company. Stefansson was repeatedly invited to an interview with Wikborg Rein as part of Samherji's own investigation process. Whistleblowers tend to suffer retaliation (Mesmer-Magnus & Viswesvaran, 2005; Park et al., 2020; Rehg et al., 2009; Shawver & Clements, 2019), misleading presentation of their views, as well as wrongful judgment of their statements in reports of investigations. The preference of cooperating with the criminal justice system, such as public prosecutors, but not with fraud examiners paid by the scandalized company, makes sense.

Given the lack of contribution from the whistleblower Stefansson, the findings in the report of investigation by Wikborg Rein became even less trustworthy. The task of reconstructing past events and sequence of events obviously suffered from the lack of access to the whistleblower as the main source of information. Examiners from law firm Wikborg Rein were simply not perceived as trustworthy by the whistleblower Stefansson. Therefore, the report of investigation became even less complete and objective.

The email exchange between the journalist Osman Kibar at daily Norwegian business newspaper *Dagens Næringsliv* and examiners Geir Sviggum and Elisabeth Roscher at Wikborg Rein ended up in a newspaper article early September 2020 under the heading "Both cleaned up and investigated fishing giant" (Kibar, 2020b: 18):

Law firm Wikborg Rein assisted the Icelandic fishing giant Samherji in negotiations con-
nected to the business activity after the company hired the firm to investigate Samherji.
Norwegian law professors have different views on the roles of Wikborg Rein.

We wrote in the beginning of August that Wikborg Rein has handed over a comprehensive report of investigation of the Icelandic fishing giant Samherji accused of corruption to
the client Samherji. The law firm shall, among other things, have reviewed more than one
million documents. Icelandic media, led by the state channel RUV, have reported that
Wikborg Rein assisted Samherji in negotiations related to business activities in Namibia,
after the firm was hired to conduct the investigation – and whether this could affect the
independence and impartiality of the law firm.

Professor Petter Gottschalk in the department of leadership and organizational behavior
at BI Norwegian Business School says that Wikborg Rein behaves reprehensible.

- Investigators must be independent of everything that has happened, is happening, and
  can happen. If investigators in other roles perform actions that prove to be unfortunate
  and harmful, the investigators cannot examine such matters. One cannot examine oneself. Therefore, it is reprehensible that Wikborg Rein has taken on other assignments for
  Samherji in addition to the investigation, says Gottschalk.
- That Wikborg Rein has undertaken other assignments for Samherji weakens the credibility of the investigation report. The report can now easily be perceived as commissioned work, he adds.

Samherji remained silent and rejected to disclose the investigation report by
Wikborg Rein. Instead, a new press release referred to the report in a manipulative
manner to present the white-collar crime case as a matter of a rotten apple. A single,
stand-alone white-collar criminal can be described as a rotten apple, but when several are involved in crime, and corporate culture virtually stimulates offenses, then
it is more appropriate to describe the phenomenon as a basket of rotten apples or as
a rotten apple orchard, like Punch (2003: 172) defines them:

The metaphor of "rotten orchards" indicate(s) that it is sometimes not the apple, or even the
barrel that is rotten but the system (or significant parts of the system).

Margrét Ólafsdóttir at the seafood company Samherji attempted implicitly to blame
the whistleblower in her new press release entitled "Fees for quota were in line with
market prices in Namibia" (Samherji, 2020b):

After Norwegian law firm Wikborg Rein finalized its investigation, into the activities of
companies affiliated with Samherji in Namibia on July 28th and presented its findings to
Samherji's board, the company has in various ways corrected and refuted allegations that
have been made against it. Samherji has now commissioned an analysis of the pricing of the
quotas that companies affiliated with Samherji leased while operating in Namibia. The
analysis consisted of a comparison of prices in catching agreements between unrelated parties. The comparison confirms that companies affiliated with Samherji paid the market price
for quotas. Companies affiliated with Samherji were never allocated any catch quotas in
Namibia. Instead, the companies leased the right to quotas that had been allocated to locals.

We have already released information about the losses suffered in Namibia and the taxes
paid to local authorities. This statement, however, is related to an audit that Samherji commissioned due to allegations that the price paid for the lease of fishing rights under agreements with FISHCOR and Namgomar was far below the market price. While Samherji's
companies were operating in Namibia, they leased catching rights from private entities,
such as the joint ventures and the company Namgomar, which was granted quotas pursuant
to an international fishing agreement between Angola and Namibia. They also leased catching rights from FISHCOR, a Namibian-owned fishing company. Samherji firmly denies

that quotas were leased from these parties at a price that was lower than the market price. Allegations to that effect are unfounded. In fact, the price paid under the agreements with FISHCOR and Namgomar was always equal to or higher than the price paid by Samherji-affiliated companies to other quota holders in Namibia.

The allegations that have been made about the price for quotas form part of a larger narrative according to which companies affiliated with Samherji are accused of having paid bribes to secure catching agreements grossly below market prices. It has also been claimed that companies in the Samherji Group did everything in their power to pay as low tax in Namibia as possible and that these contributing factors, together with the rich profits from operations in Namibia, mean that Samherji was in fact robbing a developing country.

In order to find out what the correct market price was for catch quotas during the years that companies affiliated with Samherji had had operations in Namibia, agreements with six unrelated Namibian companies that held catch quotas were reviewed. Each of these companies was profit-driven and operated in the open market. The price in these agreements was then compared with the price paid by companies affiliated with Samherji under agreements with FISHCOR and Namgomar. A total of thirty-nine comparisons were made. In all but one case, the price paid by Samherji for catch quotas under agreements with FISHCOR and Namgomar was equal to or higher than the price paid under agreements with other companies. A price comparison was also made in similar agreements made by other commercial fishing companies, domestic and foreign, with quota holders in Namibia. This was done to ensure that the price paid by Samherji's affiliates under agreements with FISHCOR and Namgomar was not unreasonably low and also to dispel suspicions that the agreements relied on had been selected explicitly to ensure a favorable outcome. In the vast majority of the contracts examined in this second wave of comparisons, the FISHCOR and Namgomar fees were equal to, or higher than, fees in other commercial fishing companies' contracts with Namibian quota holders.

Despite the fact that individual employees did not follow procedures and working methods that Samherji strives for in all its operations, it is clear that the company is responsible for discipline and supervision and must intervene decisively when the required vigilance is not maintained. It seems clear that the leasing of catch quotas in Namibia has in some cases lacked such control and intervention. However, this does not change the main conclusion of this analysis, which is that companies affiliated with Samherji paid market prices for the quota they leased. In the near future, Samherji will continue to correct misrepresentations and at the same time report on procedures and working methods that were deficient.

I emailed Margret Olafsdottir at Samherji with reference to the quote above saying "Despite the fact that individual employees did not follow procedures and working methods that Samherji strives for in all its operations" and asked who those employees were and how they did deviate from procedures and working methods. She replied in an email on October 5, 2020:

> Thank you for your email in which you ask two questions. The first relates to individuals that are current or former employees of Samherji subsidiaries. Whether certain acts or omissions are to have consequences for individuals is a matter between the particular employee and the legal entity in which he or she was employed at the time. It is also a matter between him or her and relevant public authorities. Although no current or former employee has been charged, indicted or incarcerated in this matter, several individuals have voluntarily met with relevant authorities and shared information of relevance. We consider it to be inappropriate to name any individual in question pending ongoing investigations, as would it be unethical for any media to publish names. In our 29 July press release we emphasized that we "need to assess whether publishing certain information will infringe upon laws and regulations concerning protection of individuals mentioned in any findings." This attitude has been and remains highly consistent.

> Your second question is how certain employees deviated from procedures and working methods. This is a question of particular findings in the concluded investigation. This question was addressed in the last paragraph of my email to you on 17 September:
>
> Although it is not common practice for private companies to make entire investigation reports public, it is more normal to release compressed information about key findings. Samherji will do so during the course of this fall, following meetings to be held between Wikborg Rein and a number of relevant stakeholders in this process, including public authorities.

I replied to her that I found something strange in her email:

> This is really strange. Employees did what they were told from Samherji headquarters. When their corporate wrongdoing on behalf of Samherji is exposed, Samherji headquarters does not support them.

On October 7, 2020, Margret Olafsdottir, chief communications officer at Samherji on Iceland, responded to me:

> You of course do not have any knowledge with regard to the support provided by Samherji or its subsidiaries to current or former employees. We do not know what you refer to in terms of "Employees (allegedly doing) what they were told from Samherji headquarters." We are of course prepared to address such allegations in appropriate fora should this become necessary and prudent.
>
> Samherji is in daily dialogue with a large number of relevant stakeholders regarding accurate facts of this matter as scrutinized and analysed. We do not consider you to be such relevant stakeholder. Still, we have shown you the courtesy of replying to your emails as far as we are able to comment publicly at this point. Inappropriate rudeness is however not a good basis for further dialogue.

I wrote back to her that I assumed that it would be acceptable to her that I included her latest email above as a quote in this book. She did not respond. Instead, she hired a public relations advisor to inquire when the book would be published. The advisor Bjørn Richard Johansen at First House called me on October 12. The firm First House has been criticized in the media for more than a decade for their unethical communication advice (e.g., Johnsen, 2014).

Attorney Eva Joly expressed concern about the situation that the Wikborg Rein fraud investigation report was not made publicly available. She argued that it was important for the public to learn about the role of Norwegian bank DNB in potential money laundering as well as to learn about the role of Icelandic seafood company Samherji in corruption (NTB, 2020).

White-Collar Crime Convenience

Both the briber and the bribed in a corruption relationship have their financial motives, organizational opportunities, and willingness for deviant behaviors. They enter into a relationship with mutual illegal benefits (Huang & Knight, 2017). In Fig. 8.2, themes for the briber are with texture, while themes for the bribed are in dark gray. The briber has a motive of obtaining fishing rights in the Namibian ocean

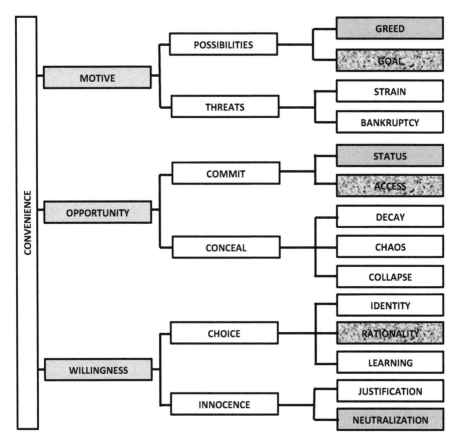

Fig. 8.2 Convenience themes in the case of Samherji

zone, which is corporate crime (Bittle & Hébert, 2020), while the bribed can make an extraordinary profit, which is possible because of the individual's decision rights as the Minister of Fishery. This is occupational crime (Goldstraw-White, 2012; Shepherd & Button, 2019).

Johannes Stefansson had access to resources (Berghoff & Spiekermann, 2018) in terms of corruption payments from Samherji via the Norwegian bank DNB to Esau and others in Namibia, as suggested by the axis opportunity-commit-access in the figure. It was a rational choice for the briber (Kamerdze et al., 2014) to get involved in corruption to improve corporate profitability in the Icelandic fishing empire of Samherji.

The bribed can neutralize potential feelings of guilt by arguing that he would have triggered the same agreements anyway (Benson, 1985). The briber, Samherji, can neutralize guilt feelings by claiming that they do so much good in Namibia by creating jobs in fisheries and paying taxes to the local government. Samherji can claim that it was necessary to carry out the offense since Namibia is a corrupt country. The offender then claims that the offense belongs in a larger context, where the crime is an illegal element among many legal elements to ensure an important result. The offense was a required and necessary means to achieve an important goal. A bribe represents nothing in dollar value compared to the potential income from a large contract abroad and compared to the local benefit of jobs and business abroad.

Regaining the Social License

On June 22, 2021, Samherji published a statement and apology on its website. In an apology, the actor admits violating a rule, accepts the validity of the rule, and expresses embarrassment and anger at self. However, the apology in the following quote was limited to not having oversight and guardianship in Namibia against opportunistic employees such as Johannes Stefansson. The actual corruption is not admitted but rather attributed to the whistleblower (Samherji, 2021):

> Samherji firmly rejects the allegations of bribery but accepts the criticism that in the circumstances, it was necessary to pay more attention to how payments were made, who they were made to and on what basis, who had the authority to give instructions about them and where they should be received. It is also clear that the underlying agreements behind the payments should have been precise and formal (…).
>
> "It is my and Samherji's firm position that no criminal offences were committed in Namibia by companies on our behalf or their employees, apart from the conduct that the former managing director has directly confessed to and acknowledged. Nonetheless, as Samherji's top executive, I am responsible for allowing the business practices in Namibia to take place. It has upset our staff, friends, families, business partners, customers and others in our community. I am very sorry that this happened, and I sincerely apologize to all those involved, both personally and on behalf of the company. Now it's important to ensure that nothing like this happens again. We will certainly strive for that," says Thorsteinn Már Baldvinsson, CEO of Samherji.

The statement by Samherji (2021) claimed to present the main findings by examiner Elisabeth Roscher at law firm Wikborg Rein in Norway. The corporate statement made indirect references to the investigation report as there are no quotes in the statement. The contents of the investigation report might thus have been subject to manipulation by Samherji before publication of the so-called main findings. Maybe Samherji avoided text in the report of investigation that directly criticized Samherji and potentially made the firm legally liable. Maybe Samherji chose text in the investigation report for publication that blamed others for incidents in the wrongdoing. Maybe Samherji (2021) in their statement selected findings that they easily and conveniently could comment.

The statement by Samherji was probably not enough for regaining the social license to operate. Media reports had emphasized not only reputation damage to the company but also to Iceland (Bjarnadóttir, 2020: 34):

> Prime minister, Katrin Jakobsdóttir, said to Mbl "that if allegations against Samherji are substantiated, it is a matter of great concern for the Icelandic economy and shame for Samherji. The issue can affect the nation as a whole." In the same article, it is stated that

Iceland was placed on the grey list of the FATF, an international working group on measures against money laundering and terrorist financing, almost a month ago. Katrin says then that being on the list is disappointing and that she has concerns about our reputation but states that Samherji's case "is not descriptive of Icelandic society as a whole."

It would indeed be a challenge for Samherji to regain its social license to operate. The national reputation problem added to the challenge. Stakeholders abroad might remember the banking collapse in Iceland, where greedy Icelanders were in the lead roles. The Panama Papers revealed that wealthy Icelanders had the world record in the number of offshore accounts relative to the number of citizens (Bjarnadóttir, 2020). Therefore, it remained an open question whether Samherji in the future would regain their social license to operate in foreign waters.

References

Benson, M. L. (1985). Denying the guilty mind: Accounting for involvement in a white-collar crime. *Criminology, 23*(4), 583–607.

Berghoff, H., & Spiekermann, U. (2018). Shady business: On the history of white-collar crime. *Business History, 60*(3), 289–304.

Bittle, S., & Hébert, J. (2020). Controlling corporate crimes in times of de-regulation and re-regulation, chapter 30. In M. L. Rorie (Ed.), *The handbook of white-collar crime* (pp. 484–501). Wiley & Sons.

Bjarnadóttir, S. M. (2020, September 15). *Iceland's involvement in bribes and corruption in Namibia's fishing industry – Discourse analysis of the media.* Master thesis in culture communication and globalization, Denmark: Aalborg University.

Brustad, L., & Hustadnes, H. (2016). Bjerke har forsømt lederansvaret uansett (-Bjerke has neglected the management responsibility regardless), daily Norwegian newspaper. *Dagbladet,* www.dagbladet.no, published April 11.

Ciric, J. (2022). Namibia requests Interpol's aid in extraditing former Samherji executives. *Iceland Review,* www.icelandreview.com, published February 21.

Cotterill, J. (2019). Two Namibian ministers resign in Icelandic fishing scandal. *Financial Times,* www.ft.com, published November 14.

Ekroll, H. C., Breian, Å., & NTB (2019). Økokrim starter etterforskning av DNB i forbindelse med islandsk fiskerisak (Økokrim is launching an investigation into DNB related to the Icelandic fisheries case), daily Norwegian newspaper. *Aftenposten,* www.aftenposten, published November 29.

Eren, C. P. (2020). Cops, firefighters, and scapegoats: Anti-money laundering (AML) professionals in an era of regulatory bulimia. *Journal of White Collar and Corporate Crime,* 1–12. Published online https://doi.org/10.1177/2631309X20922153

Finanstilsynet. (2020). Tilsynsrapport fra undersøkelser av DNBs etterlevelse av hvitvaskingsloven (review report from investigation of DNB's compliance with the money laundering act). *The Financial Supervisory Authority of Norway,* www.finanstilsynet.no. December 4.

Goldstraw-White, J. (2012). *White-collar crime: Accounts of offending behavior.* Palgrave Macmillan.

Gottschalk, P., & Benson, M. L. (2020). The evolution of corporate accounts of scandals from exposure to investigation. *British Journal of Criminology, 60,* 949–969.

Hjort. (2016). *Rapport til styret i DNB (report to the board at DNB), bank mentioned in the Panama papers, report of investigation* (p. 18). Law Firm Hjort.

Huang, L., & Knight, A. P. (2017). Resources and relationships in entrepreneurship: An exchange theory of the development and effects of the entrepreneur-investor relationship. *Academy of Management Review, 42*(1), 80–102.

Johnsen, N. (2014). Frank Aarebrot om first house: -vi vet ikke hvem de representerer (frank Aarebrot about first house: -we do not know who they represent), daily Norwegian newspaper. *VG*, www.vg.no, published May 21.

Kamerdze, S., Loughran, T., Paternoster, R., & Sohoni, T. (2014). The role of affect in intended rule breaking: Extending the rational choice perspective. *Journal of Research in Crime and Delinquency, 51*(5), 620–654.

Kibar, O. (2020a). Varsleren (the whistleblower), daily Norwegian business newspaper. *Dagens Næringsliv*, Saturday, August 8, 32–37.

Kibar, O. (2020b). Både ryddet opp for og gransket fiskerikjempe (Both cleaned up and investigated fishing giant), daily Norwegian business newspaper. *Dagens Næringsliv*, Tuesday, September 1, 18–19.

Kleinfeld, J. (2019). Anatomy of a bribe: A deep dive into an underworld of corruption, news organization. *Al Jazeera*, www.aljazeera.com, published December 1.

Kleinfeld, J. (2020). Corruption allegations in Namibian 5G deal with Huawei, news organization. *Al Jazeera*, www.aljazeera.com, published July 15.

Kleinfeld, J. (2021). Namibian president caught in new fishing corruption allegations, news organization. *Al Jazeera*, www.aljazeera.com, published April 2.

Langset, M., Ertesvåg, F. and Ensrud, S. (2016). BI-professor: -Det vil bli rettssaker (BI professor: -there will be court cases), daily Norwegian newspaper. *VG*, Wednesday, April 6, p. 7.

Menges, W. (2020). Fishrot lawyer fights to stay on as executor. *The Namibian*, www.namibian.com, published August 6.

Mesmer-Magnus, J. R., & Viswesvaran, C. (2005). Whistleblowing in an organization: An examination of correlates of whistleblowing intentions, actions, and retaliation. *Journal of Business Ethics, 62*(3), 266–297.

Müller, S. M. (2018). Corporate behavior and ecological disaster: Dow chemical and the Great Lakes mercury crisis, 1970-1972. *Business History, 60*(3), 399–422.

NTB. (2020). Kritisk til at rapport om fiskeriselskap ikke gjøres offentlig (critical to the fact that the report on fishing company is not made public), daily Norwegian financial newspaper. *Finansavisen*, www.finansavisen.no, published August 5.

Park, H., Bjørkelo, B., & Blenkinsopp, J. (2020). External whistleblowers' experiences of workplace bullying by superiors and colleagues. *Journal of Business Ethics, 161*, 591–601.

Punch, M. (2003). Rotten orchards. «pestilence», police misconduct and system failure. *Policing and Society, 13*(2), 171–196.

Rehg, M. T., Miceli, M. P., Near, J. P., & Scotter, J. R. V. (2009). Antecedents and outcomes of retaliation against whistleblowers: Gender differences and power relationships. *Organization Science, 19*(2), 221–240.

Reuters. (2019). Norway's DNB investigates allegedly improper Samherji payments to Namibia. *Under Current News*, www.undercurrentnews.com, published November 15.

Routh, R. (2022). Kanyangela accused of 'holding back'. *New Era*, www.neweralive.na, published February 22.

Samherji. (2019a). *Statement from Samherji: Press release*, www.samherji.is, published November 11 by margret@samherji.is.

Samherji. (2019b). *Samherji CEO steps aside while investigations are ongoing*, www.samherji.is, published November 14 by margret@samherji.is.

Samherji. (2020a). *Samherji's Namibia investigation finalized,* Samherji ice fresh seafood, website https://www.samherji.is/en/moya/news/samherjis-namibia-investigation-finalized, Akureyri, Iceland, published by margret@samherji.is.

Samherji. (2020b). *Fees for quotas were in line with market prices in Namibia*, Samherji seafood, www.samherji.is, published September 25 by Margrét Ólafsdóttir, margret@samherji.is.

Samherji. (2021). Statement and apology from Samherji, Samherji seafood, www.samherji.is, published June 22.

Schultz, J. (2019). Wikborg Rein-gransker om Samherji: -Planen er å være ute av Namibia innen få måneder (Wikborg Rein investigator about Samherji: -the plan is to be out of Namibia within a few months, daily Norwegian business newspaper. *Dagens Næringsliv*, www.dn.no, published December 1.

Schultz, J., & Trumpy, J. (2019a). NRK: DNB brukte mer enn et år på å stenge Samherji-kontoer (NRK: DNB spent more than a year to close Samherji accounts), Norwegian daily business newspaper. *Dagens Næringsliv*, www.dn.no, published August 26.

Schultz, J., & Trumpy, J. (2019b). Björgolfur Johannsson ble Samherji-sjef etter hvitvaskingsavsløring: -Jeg tror ikke det har vært noen bestikkelser, Norwegian daily business newspaper. *Dagens Næringsliv*, www.dn.no, published December 13.

Seljan, H., Kjartansson, A., & Drengsson, S. A. (2019). What Samherji wanted hidden, Kveikur at *RUV*, public broadcasting on Iceland, www.ruv.is/kveikur/fishrot/fishrot

Shawver, T., & Clements, L. H. (2019). The impact of value preferences on whistleblowing intentions of accounting professionals. *Journal of Forensic and Investigative Accounting, 11*(2), 232–247.

Shepherd, D., & Button, M. (2019). Organizational inhibitions to addressing occupational fraud: A theory of differential rationalization. *Deviant Behavior, 40*(8), 971–991.

Solgård, J., & Trumpy, J. (2019). Økokrim har startet etterforsking av DNB (Økokrim has started investigating DNB), Norwegian daily business newspaper. *Dagens Næringsliv*, www.dn.no, published November 28.

Tanum, A. C. (2016). DNB *Luxembourg – Redegjørelse fra styret (DNB Luxembourg – Statement from the board)*, brev til Nærings- og fiskeridepartementet ved statsråd Monica Mæland (letter to the department of industry and fishery attention minister Monica Mæland), April 11, Oslo, Norway.

Tomter, L. (2021). Varsleren på island: -DNB burde vært stilt til ansvar for hvitvasking (the whistleblower in Iceland: -DNB should have been held responsible for money laundering), Norwegian broadcasting corporation. *NRK*, www.nrk.no, published February 12.

Turner, J. (2021). Johannes Stefansson. *Whistleblower Network News*, www.whistleblowersblog. org, published March 1.

Witbooi, E., Ali, K. D., Santosa, M. A., Hurley, G., Husein, Y., Maharaj, S., Okafor-Yarwood, I., Quiroz, I. A., & Salas, O. (2020). Organized crime in the fisheries sector threatens a sustainable ocean economy. *Nature*, published online https://doi.org/10.1038/s41586-020-2913-5

Chapter 9
Banking Mismanagement

At Wirecard in Germany, speculations in the media about financial mismanagement were so strong and loud that the company attempted to obtain a clean bill of health from fraud examiners at KPMG (2020). While the management was not successful in their attempt, the fraud examiners avoided conclusions about misconduct or crime. The fraud examiners did neither confirm nor reject accounting manipulation and other kinds of financial wrongdoing. Therefore, Wirecard management quickly stated that "no evidence was found for the publicly raised allegations of balance sheet manipulation" (Storbeck, 2020a). The social license to operate could easily be violated as Angela Merkel, the chancellor of Germany, had personally helped Wirecard in her position as the most influential politician in Europe at that time. She lobbied for Wirecard even after irregularities at the company had come to light (Chazan & Storbeck, 2020b). The first draft of the KPMG report was not accepted by Wirecard management. KPMG then revised the report of investigation before it eventually was published (Storbeck, 2020a). Thereby, Wirecard could maintain the social license to operate for a short time longer.

German House of Wirecards

Among the accusations that violated the social license to operate were allegations that Wirecard management recorded higher revenues through fictitious customer relationships, suspicious loan relationships through what is called merchant cash advance, over-reporting of profits in the Singapore branch and in the United Arab Emirates, and a suspicious transaction by a company in India (McCrum, 2019). The accusations were concerned with deficiencies in the accounts and mysterious collaborations with third-party companies in countries such as Singapore, the United Arab Emirates, and India (McCrum, 2020; Storbeck, 2020a). The suspected fraud focused on bankruptcy fraud where trusted executives removed funds to secret destinations.

The reason why Wirecard wanted to launch an independent investigation was to secure its social license to operate amidst accusations in the media. Especially in the newspaper *Financial Times*, a number of articles were published suggesting that Wirecard used fictitious customers and trading partners to be able to report more income and wealth than was real (Chazan, 2021; Chazan & Storbeck, 2020a, b; Storbeck, 2020a, b, 2021a, b; Storbeck & Morris, 2021; McCrum, 2015, 2019, 2020).

Wirecard as a technology-based financial services firm in Germany began its operations in 2002 as a German payment processor. The company entered the prestigious DAX Index, which lists Germany's top 30 most valuable enterprises (Reuters, 2020). Markus Braun was the charismatic chief executive officer at Wirecard (Bloomberg, 2021; Harenbrock & Mergenthaler, 2021).

The suspicion started already in 2015 when the *Financial Times* published a series of articles under a title saying "The House of Wirecards" (McCrum, 2015), which indicated misconduct and collapse inspired by the American political thriller "House of Cards":

> Wirecard is a little known German tech stock worth €5bn, and a puzzle. It offers payment services, owns a Munich bank, and transacts millions of online credit card payments behind the scenes at familiar websites. It grows at breakneck pace but buys obscure payment companies around the world which keep the growth going. The company says it was founded in 1999, but it went bust after the dotcom crash. The real beginning was 2002, when chief executive Markus Braun took over and injected cash. Three years later Wirecard joined the stock market through the reverse takeover of a defunct call-center business. Allegations of balance sheet inconsistencies were made in 2008. The accuser subsequently landed in jail, and the stock has since been a rocket, rising eightfold. Enthusiastic investors have given Wirecard half a billion euros to spend, and the company used much of it to buy customers, so-called portfolios of relationships, piling almost all the cash its business has produced since 2009 into these customer relationships.

In the *Financial Times* article, McCrum (2015) accused Wirecard, among other things, of a shortfall of €250 million in the balance sheet, which corresponded to 3 years of company profits. Wirecard denied these allegations, blaming short-selling propaganda. Analysts also agreed with Wirecard that the charges were not true. Furthermore, in 2016, anonymous short sellers of the Wirecard shares made statements in which they accused Wirecard of being involved in money laundering and illegal online gambling. This created greater attention and suspicion among people at the financial supervisory authority in Germany and among private investors. Over the next few years, journalists and short sellers who had spoken badly of Wirecard received so-called fishing emails. There was suspicion that Wirecard was behind these emails in the hope of gaining control of the computers of the critics that potentially could violate the social license to operate. In 2019, there was even greater suspicion against Wirecard when the office in Singapore was investigated due to suspicion of fraud. In addition, Wirecard partnered with a third-party company addressed in the Philippines. When investigators from KPMG (2020) went down to this address, they found that the address belonged to a retired fisherman who was unaware that a multinational company was using the same address. On the basis of such findings, there was indeed reason for suspicion of financial wrongdoing at Wirecard and great doubt about the company's legitimacy both legally and socially.

Offender Convenience Themes

Assuming that the allegations and accusations were correct, the Wirecard fraud of deceiving potential customers, banks, and investors served the purpose of making them believe that the financial business of Wirecard was more profitable than it actually was. This in turn could potentially lead to financial gains for Wirecard such as greater flow of customer funds, more investors, and improved loan terms for the business.

The motive for the alleged fraud can be assessed on the basis of what seems most logical. When Wirecard entered into the German stock exchange DAX, this put a lot of pressure on the company from shareholders, who expected a high annual return. The company had seemingly several successful years, and the shareholders received a high annual return. To maintain a good annual return, Wirecard lead by CEO Braun saw the opportunity to emerge as a larger and stronger company than they really were, to attract new investors. This opportunity arose due to their distinctive organizational structure through the third-party companies they partnered with in Asia and the United Arab Emirates. This was a convenient solution for Wirecard to appear as a large and lucrative company.

The negative gap between performance and public statements increased rapidly. Externally, the company continued as long as possible to appear financially sound and sustainable, while large losses started to occur in 2015. Company management searched for a solution to financial threats. The management of the company, led by CEO Markus Braun, was accused of having falsified the company's accounts to remain attractive to investors and other stakeholders. Braun himself had a large sum invested in stocks at Wirecard, and company decline and collapse would thus have personal consequences for him.

In the Wirecard case, the suspicion is thus that financial crime was committed by manipulating customer relationships as well creating non-existing partnerships for the purpose of window-dressing to keep everyone happy. Irregularities in the accounting of subsidiaries in Singapore and fake activities in the Philippines were just some of the elements of the fraud scheme to remain in business. The executives' gain increased when the shares of Wirecard rose in value, as not only Braun but also others in top management had most of their fortune in Wirecard stocks.

At first, the motive was possibilities of creating a market value for Wirecard so high that it exceeded the market value of Deutsche Bank and thereby enabled a possible takeover of Deutsche Bank by Wirecard (Håland, 2020). It was corporate crime to develop possibilities as illustrated in Fig. 9.1.

An important part of the opportunity structure for Wirecard was the lack of regulation and oversight by federal authorities in Germany, combined with enthusiastic support from leading politicians for the innovative banking concept. When the

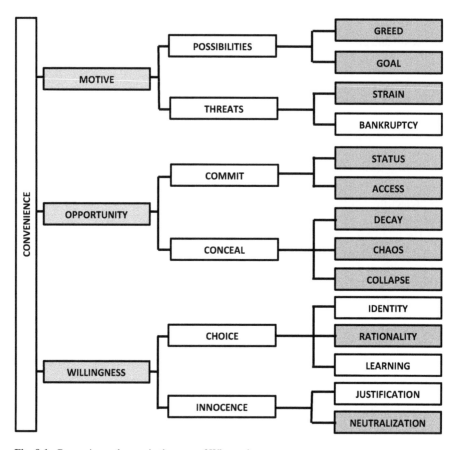

Fig. 9.1 Convenience themes in the case of Wirecard

Wirecard scandal was a fact, the German parliament launched an inquiry (Chazan & Storbeck, 2020b).

There were signs of chaos, such as lack of control in principal-agent relationships (Wall-Parker, 2020), where the board did not know what top management was doing and top management did not know what local branch managers were doing. Sensemaking of actions was difficult for outsiders (Weick et al., 2005). While there was an instance of whistleblowing related to misconduct in Singapore, costs did exceed benefits for whistleblowers (Tankebe, 2019). In addition to lack of control in principal-agent relationships, problems in sensemaking of actions for outsiders, and costs exceeding benefits for whistleblowers, an ethical climate conflict also contributed to chaos (Potipiroon & Wongpreedee, 2020).

In the willingness dimension of convenience theory, there are themes related to the convenience of deviant behavior. Convenience themes address the choice of crime and the feeling of innocence as illustrated in Fig. 9.1. The rational choice of accounting manipulation had benefits exceeding costs if Wirecard was successful in taking over Deutsche Bank. The rational choice perspective suggests that crime is a rational choice if benefits exceed costs (Müller, 2018). Wirecard executives were sliding on the slippery slope over on the wrong side of the law (Gamache & McNamara, 2019). Some Wirecard executives lacked self-control (Craig & Piquero, 2016).

Project Panther Deutsche Bank

Storbeck (2020a) wrote about the Wirecard scandal in the UK newspaper *Financial Times* under the heading "Wirecard: The frantic final months of a fraudulent operation":

> A plan to buy Deutsche Bank is now seen as part of a desperate effort to disguise fraud at the German payments group. The codename was "Project Panther." Markus Braun, the chief executive of German payments group Wirecard had hired McKinsey & Co to help prepare his most audacious idea yet, a plan to take over Deutsche Bank. In a 40-page presentation last November, the consultants insisted the new entity, to be dubbed "Wirebank," would be "thinking and acting like a fintech, at the scale of a global bank." By 2025, it could generate €6bn in additional profit, McKinsey claimed.
>
> While Germany's largest bank sat on €1.4tn in assets, it was a mere €14bn on the stock market, roughly the same as Wirecard. The McKinsey report promised that the combined stock market valuation would double to close to €50n. A deal to acquire Deutsche Bank would have been the crowning achievement for a company which within a few years had become one of the most valuable in the country, winning the label of "Germany's PayPal." An upstart financial technology company would be running Germany's most illustrious bank. A tie-up with Deutsche Bank had another potential attraction: A deal offered the prospect of a miraculous exit from the massive fraud Wirecard had been operating. Around €1.9bn in cash was missing from its accounts and large parts of its Asian operations were actually an elaborate sham. By blending Wirecard's business into Deutsche's vast balance sheet, it might be possible to somehow hide the missing cash and explain it away later in post-merger impairment charges. There was one catch. To even start preparing such a deal in earnest, the company needed to get a clean bill of health from KPMG, which was conducting a special audit of Wirecard's books.

Wirecard had hired audit firm KPMG (2020) to conduct a fraud examination into alleged increase in revenue through fictitious customer relationships and other forms of accounting manipulation. Wirecard's motive to hire KPMG was to get a clean bill of health from fraud examiners according to Storbeck (2020a):

> With the KPMG investigation in full flow, the Wirecard executives behind the fraud saw Project Panther and a deal with Deutsche, which was first reported by Bloomberg, as one possible way to fend off discover, says an adviser to the payments group who was involved in the discussions. But they also worked on a separate plan: a vast cover-up operation in Asia.

KPMG did not provide a clean bill of health, since fraud examiners in their report criticize Wirecard's internal controls and compliance functions. However, fraud examiners did neither confirm nor reject accounting manipulation and other kinds of financial wrongdoing. Therefore, Wirecard management quickly stated that "no evidence was found for the publicly raised allegations of balance sheet manipulation" (Storbeck, 2020a). Nevertheless, the company collapsed half a year later.

Chief executive Markus Braun at Wirecard resigned on June 19 and was arrested on June 22, 2020. Jan Marsalek, Wirecard's second-in-command who oversaw operations in Asia, escaped arrest and was on the run in August 2020. A key Wirecard business partner died. Thomas Eichelmann was the finance director at Wirecard. Susanne Steidl was the chief product officer. Consultants from McKinsey & Co had helped Wirecard prepare a plan of Project Panther to take over Deutsche Bank. To do so, the value of Wirecard needed to exceed the value of Deutsche Bank. The scheme was detected by investigative journalists at *Financial Times* (Storbeck, 2020a).

Markus Braun denied allegations of fraud and embezzlement. He denied having inflated sales and profits. Nevertheless, he had been eager to carry out Project Panther and make a deal with Deutsche Bank to fend off discovery of potential wrongdoing.

Fraud Investigation Outcome

KPMG (2020) conducted the investigation on the premises of Wirecard AG, as well as at KPMG's branch offices between October 31, 2019, and April 24, 2020. In addition, KPMG inspected documents on the premises of the auditor and conducted interviews with Wirecard business partners on their premises in Dubai and the Philippines and, in one case, via video conferencing. KPMG determined the scope and nature of the relevant investigation activities independently and at their discretion in accordance with the examination mandate.

KPMG (2020: 12) examined the amount and existence of revenues from the TPA business relationships between Cardsystems Middle East, Wirecard UK & Ireland, as well as Wirecard Technologies and the respective relevant TPA partners:

> KPMG can, as a result of the forensic investigation conducted in relation to the investigation period 2016 to 2018, neither make a statement that the revenues exist and are correct in terms of their amount, nor make a statement that the revenues do not exist and are incorrect in terms of their amount. To this extent, there is an obstacle to the investigation.

In our perspective of evaluating the KPMG investigation and the collapse of Wirecard a few months later, the examiners failed in establishing facts concerning the existence or nonexistence of revenues. A different approach in terms of knowledge strategy and information strategy might have been successful. However, the investigation did not result in a clean bill of health that could reaffirm the social license to operate.

Within a few days of investigation, KPMG realized that Wirecard's core payments processing operations in Europe were not making any money – a fact that Wirecard had never disclosed to investors (Storbeck, 2020a):

> All of the profit was generated by the operations overseen by Mr. Marsalek, Wirecard's Asia business, where the processing of transactions was outsourced to third-party business partners.

Jan Marsalek claimed that 1.9 billion euros in cash were transferred from Singapore to the Philippines and into a bank account in the name of Manila-based lawyer Mark Tolentino. KPMG discovered that 2 months after the money supposedly was paid into Tolentino's account, Wirecard still did not have a contractual relationship with the new trustee, nor had they conducted background checks on him (Storbeck, 2020b).

In their final report, KPMG examiners detailed shortcomings in Wirecard's internal controls and compliance functions and outlined severe doubts about the company's accounting practices (Storbeck, 2020a, b), but they did not draw any definitive conclusions. KPMG neither verified the existence of the outsourced business nor the cash in escrow accounts, and they described "the dogged obstruction by Wirecard and its business partners" (Storbeck, 2021a, b).

The examiners' report presented results of the investigation activities into third party acquiring in regard to (1) existence and revenues from third-party acquirers (TPA) business, (2) customer relationships in the TPA business, and (3) descriptions of the TPA business in Wirecard's annual statements:

1. Questionable amount and existence of revenues, in particular with reference to allegedly questionable customer relationships. KPMG (2020: 13) examiners could not make a statement regarding existence and correctness of numbers: "This is due to deficiencies in the internal organization and, in particular, to the unwillingness of the Third-Party Acquirers to participate in this special investigation in a comprehensive and transparent manner."
2. Questionable customer relationships. KPMG (2020: 28) examiners could not verify the existence and correctness of customer names: "According to the information available, the names given in the press were 'account name' designations or aliases under which the revenues of customers referred to a TPA partner were recorded at the time. As we could not be provided with the actual names of the 43 alleged customers (aliases) quoted in the press, KPMG was unable to verify the existence of these customer relationships for the investigation period 2016 to 2018."
3. Questionable descriptions of third-party business in annual statements. KPMG (2020: 30) provides no clear answer: "The presentation of debtor risk and existing customer risk in the report casts doubt on whether the scope of these risks in relation to the TPA business is sufficiently apparent to addressees of the financial statements. With regard to the debtor risk, the presentation made in the management report could give the impression that the risk from chargebacks is exclusively related to the receivables from the acquiring area. However, according to the information obtained, the chargeback risk in Wirecard's TPA business actually affects a considerable portion of the escrow accounts reported as cash and cash equivalents."

The examiners' report presented results of the investigation activities into digital lending business in regard to (1) amount and composition of the merchant cash advance business, (2) legal permissibility of business activities in Turkey and Brazil,

(3) business background of certain lending activities, (4) acts at subsidiaries in Singapore, and (5) payment to middleman in India:

1. Questionable amount and composition of the merchant cash advance business in the context of the company's disclosures. KPMG (2020: 37) provided no clear answer: "According to an internal memorandum submitted to KPMG, the published information on the volume of merchant cash advance should be used to explain business models. It is said not to be a defined product, but a value-added service, which is in part an integral component of Wirecard's services. This volume is therefore a management estimate based on various assumptions and calculations." Examiners neither questioned the management estimate nor inquired into assumptions and calculations.
2. Questionable legal permissibility of Wirecard's business activities in Turkey and Brazil in connection with the merchant cash advance product. KPMG (2020: 39) conducted no independent investigation in Turkey but trusted instead a law firm paid for by Wirecard: "In the course of the investigation of the permissibility of the merchant cash advance business in Turkey, KPMG reviewed results summarized in the memorandum of a law firm commissioned by Wirecard. With regard to the appropriateness of the structure of the merchant cash advance business with international customers ('international merchants'), including Wirecard Bank, KPMG concluded that the transactions with international customers in Turkey were legally permissible." Similar conclusion was drawn for Brazil based on "the information we received" (KPMG, 2020: 40). The passivity of examiners in obtaining information is striking.
3. Questionable business background of possible unsecured loans granted to a specific company. Again, KPMG (2020: 42) was unable to reconstruct past events: "In 2018, Wirecard Asia Holding Pte. Ltd., Singapore, granted company 4 several unsecured loans with a total volume of EUR 115 million with a one-year term for the purpose of 'merchant cash advance business.' Since KPMG did not receive any information on the customers of company 4 in the course of the investigation – in particular, not on the customers forwarded by Wirecard to company 4 – KPMG could not determine which companies or persons participated economically and to what extent in the loans granted to company 4 for 'merchant advance purposes'." The passivity of examiners in obtaining information is again striking.
4. Whistleblower alleging that there are indications of fraudulent acts at Wirecard subsidiaries in Singapore. KPMG (2020: 45) based again their assessment on secondary sources: "In response to the whistleblower's accusations in spring 2018, Wirecard AG engaged Law Firm 1 to conduct a compliance audit and, at a later date, engaged Law Firm 2 to conduct an internal investigation. The background was that the compliance audit of Law Firm 1 has weaknesses. For example, the data basis, in particular consisting of accounting data and e-mail traffic, was not completely saved. The incompleteness of the data basis could not be fully remedied in the course of the investigation by Law Firm 2. EY Audit has supplemented individual results of the compliance audit and the internal investi-

gation of the Law Firms 1 and 2 respectively, with its own auditing activities – including the use of EY FIS. As a result, the investigation activities of Law Firm 2 and the auditing activities of EY Audit under the extended audit procedures were not carried out on a complete data and information basis. Therefore, it cannot be ruled out that the investigation activities of Law Firms 1 and 2 and the auditing activities of EY Audit within the framework of the extended audit procedures would have come to a different conclusion if a complete database had been available. EY Audit has carried out auditing activities on the basis of the available data in relation to the accusations made." While fraud examiners here express that deviance is possible, they made no attempt to interview the whistle-blowers or others who could tell where to find evidence.

5. Questionable payment of excessive purchase price to middleman in India. Fraud examiners at KPMG (2020: 50) admitted another failure despite attempted background research: "The auditors were unable to identify the beneficial owner of Fund 1. The background research by KPMG also failed to identify the beneficial owner of Fund 1. Consequently, the accusation that Fund 1 is an intermediary cannot be conclusively clarified. Since knowledge of the beneficial owner is of essential importance for the question of who benefited from the purchase price, further investigations are not useful at this time as long as the identity has not been clarified. According to the information provided to KPMG, Wirecard AG does not know the beneficial owner of Fund 1."

KPMG (2020: 59) then presented the following text under the heading "Conclusion":

> KPMG issues this report to the best of its knowledge and belief on the basis of the documents submitted to KPMG, information provided and its own investigation activities, and with reference to the Code of Professional Conduct.

This is certainly no conclusion regarding findings. However, as there were no findings and no fraud investigation outcome, the chosen conclusion text illustrates the complete failure of examiners Sven-Olaf Leitz and Alexander Geschonneck at KPMG.

Regaining the Social License

There was no way of regaining the social license in this case of Wirecard in Germany as the financial institution collapsed shortly after the fraud investigation was completed. The financial institution went bankrupt (Kagge, 2021). Wirecard shareholders had to pay the price for the fraud scandal (Harenbrock & Mergenthaler, 2021):

> German fintech star Wirecard is left in shambles after €1.9 billion were found missing from its books last year. While CEO Braun is in custody and the firm's CFO Marsalek is on the run, shareholders are left in the lurch.

The Wirecard scandal was a series of accounting frauds that resulted in the insolvency of the German payment processor and financial services provider (Storbeck, 2020b). Erikstad (2020) suggested that Wirecard may have been drained of funds before bankruptcy. Wirecard failed in 2019 in its attempt to take over Deutsche Bank, which had not made any profits since 2014 (Håland, 2020). Wirecard's chief executive, Markus Braun, was ambitious both on behalf of the company and on behalf of himself (Solgård, 2020). Wirecard auditor Ernst & Young was in trouble for failing to uncover the fraud (Bugge, 2020).

Markus Braun refused to answer questions after his arrest (Chazan & Storbeck, 2020a):

> Mr. Braun refused to answer any questions from MPs, citing his right under German law to remain silent. He declined to answer even basic inquiries, such as what the subject of his PhD thesis was or if he had a daughter.

In March 2022, German prosecutors charged Wirecard's former chief executive and two other high-ranking managers for the colossal commercial fraud that led to the collapse of the payment company. They were charged for market manipulation, embezzlement, and gang fraud on a commercial scale.

References

Bloomberg. (2021). Jailed ex-Wirecard CEO sues chubb to pick up his legal bills. *Bloomberg.* www.bloomberg.com, published May 10.

Bugge, W. (2020). Wirecard-revisor i trøbbel for å ikke ha avdekket milliardsvindelen [Wirecard auditor in trouble for failing to uncover billionaire fraud]. Daily Norwegian business newspaper *Dagens Næringsliv.* www.dn.no, published June 26.

Chazan, G. (2021). Wirecard given no 'privileged treatment' says German finance deputy. *Financial Times.* www.ft.com, published April 21.

Chazan, G., & Storbeck, O. (2020a). Wirecard: The scandal spreads to German politics. *Financial Times.* www.ft.com, published September 29.

Chazan, G., & Storbeck, O. (2020b). Wirecard's Markus Brown says regulators not to blame in scandal. *Financial Times.* www.ft.com, published November 20.

Craig, J. M., & Piquero, N. L. (2016). The effects of low self-control and desire-for-control on white-collar offending: A replication. *Deviant Behavior, 37*(11), 1308–1324.

Erikstad, T. (2020). Wirecard kan ha blitt tappet for midler før konkurs [Wirecard may have been drained of funds before bankruptcy]. Daily Norwegian business newspaper *Dagens Næringsliv.* www.dn.no, published August 11.

Gamache, D. L., & McNamara, G. (2019). Responding to bad press: How CEO temporal focus influences the sensitivity to negative media coverage of acquisitions. *Academy of Management Journal, 62*(3), 918–943.

Håland, S. (2020). De elendige: Hva feiler det tyske banker? [The miserable: What is wrong with German banks?]. Daily Norwegian business newspaper *Dagens Næringsliv.* www.dn.no, published July 27.

Harenbrock, K., & Mergenthaler, T. (2021). Wirecard shareholders pay the price for fraud scandal. *Deutsche Welle.* www.dw.com, published March 19.

Kagge, G. (2021, April 22). Merkel må forklare seg om hjelp til selskap anklaget for milliardsvindel [Merkel must explain herself about help to companies accused of billion fraud]. Daily Norwegian newspaper *Aftenposten*, p. 24.

KPMG. (2020, April 27). *Report concerning the independent special investigation at Wirecard AG*. Audit firm KPMG, Munich, Germany, 74 pages.

McCrum, D. (2015). The house of Wirecard. *Financial Times*. www.ft.com, published April 27.

McCrum, D. (2019). Wirecard's suspect accounting practices revealed. *Financial Times*. www.ft.com, published October 15.

McCrum, D. (2020). Wirecard: The timeline. *Financial Times*. www.ft.com, published June 25.

Müller, S. M. (2018). Corporate behavior and ecological disaster: Dow chemical and the Great Lakes mercury crisis, 1970–1972. *Business History, 60*(3), 399–422.

Potipiroon, W., & Wongpreedee, A. (2020). Ethical climate and whistleblowing intentions: Testing the mediating roles of public service motivation and psychological safety among local government employees. *Public Personnel Management*. Published online https://doi.org/10.1177/0091026020944547.

Reuters. (2020). Germany's DAX index gets shake-up in wake of Wirecard scandal. *Reuters*. www.reuters.com, published November 24.

Solgård, J. (2020). «Bestemors favorittbank» ga milliardlån til tidligere Wirecard-sjef ["Grandma's favorite bank" gave billions in loans to former Wirecard boss]. Daily Norwegian business newspaper *Dagens Næringsliv*. www.dn.no, published July 9.

Storbeck, O. (2020a). Wirecard: The frantic final months of a fraudulent operation. *Financial Times*. www.ft.com, published August 25.

Storbeck, O. (2020b). Whistleblower warned EY of Wirecard fraud four years before collapse. *Financial Times*. www.ft.com, published September 30.

Storbeck, O. (2021a). Prosecutors delayed arrest warrant for Wirecard's Jan Marsalek. *Financial Times*. www.ft.com, published January 29.

Storbeck, O. (2021b). German parliament expands probe into EY's audits of Wirecard. *Financial Times*. www.ft.com, published April 22.

Storbeck, O., & Morris, S. (2021). BaFin files insider trading complaint against Deutsche Bank board member. *Financial Times*. www.ft.com, published April 19.

Tankebe, J. (2019). Cooperation with the police against corruption: Exploring the roles of legitimacy, deterrence and collective action theories. *British Journal of Criminology, 59*, 1390–1410.

Wall-Parker, A. (2020). Chapter 3: Measuring white collar crime. In M. L. Rorie (Ed.), *The handbook of white-collar crime* (pp. 32–44). Wiley.

Weick, K. E., Sutcliffe, K. M., & Obstfeld, D. (2005). Organizing and the process of sensemaking. *Organization Science, 16*(4), 409–421.

Chapter 10
Social License Issues

This chapter reviews a number of social license issues derived from fraud investigation reports in a number of countries. The fraud investigation reports are concerned with issues in Austria, Canada, Congo, Denmark, Germany, Iceland, Japan, Moldova, the Netherlands, New Zealand, Norway, South Sudan, Sweden, the United States, and Vietnam. The total of 26 investigation reports from 16 nations represents a convenience sample that is not representative of fraud investigation reports generally around the globe. Rather, the presented sample of reports is the total number of fraud investigations since 2015 that were possible to detect and retrieve for relevant analysis and comparison. Generally, fraud investigation reports tend to be kept secret both by investigators and clients for various reasons discussed by Gottschalk and Tcherni-Buzzeo (2017).

The sample of investigation reports has in common that there were social license issues. For example, the investigation issues at the International Biathlon Union in Austria could threaten the financing of the organization and its activities if sponsors, media, spectators, and other sources of income would react to the allegations of corruption. Similarly, public and private funding of humanitarian aid could suffer if it was evidenced in Congo that foreign aid workers received kickbacks from local suppliers of goods and services.

The presented sample includes previously discussed case studies of the corporate member revolt at Obos in Norway, the military regime cooperation in Myanmar by Bestseller in Denmark, the fishing rights corruption in Namibia by Samherji in Iceland, and the banking mismanagement by Wirecard in Germany.

Violating the social license to operate can have a variety of consequences from the least serious to the most serious consequence. For example, in Vietnam, abusing embassy positions in rentals might be solved by the rotten apple approach by dismissing the suspect from employment at the embassy. On the other hand, in Denmark, for example, helping Russian oligarchs launder proceeds in the bank might result in the Danish financial supervisory authority's direct involvement in controls and guardianship.

P. Gottschalk, *Financial Crime Issues*,
https://doi.org/10.1007/978-3-031-11213-3_10

Fraud Investigation Reports

The sample of investigation reports is listed in Table 10.1. The first column lists the countries where the client organizations for the reviews are located. The second column lists the client organizations for the investigations. The third column lists the investigators who conducted the reviews. The final column lists the years that the investigation reports were published. For example, the commission conducted an investigation at the International Biathlon Union in Austria in 2021.

The accusations and allegations that triggered fraud investigations are listed in Table 10.2. For example, in Austria, the president of the International Biathlon Union was accused of receiving bribes from the Russian Biathlon Union. The bribes were in terms of hunting trips and other favors in return for downplaying and ignoring rumors of doping among Russian athletes in the sports.

Table 10.1 Characteristics of fraud investigation reports

Country	Organization	Investigator	Year
Austria	International Biathlon Union	Commission	2021a
Canada	Town of Pelham	KPMG	2017
Congo	Mercy Corps Humanitarian	Smith	2020
Denmark	Bestseller Clothing	Christoffersen Mikkelsen	2021
Denmark	Danske Bank Banking	Bruun Hjejle	2018
Denmark	Social Security Agency	PwC	2019
Denmark	Banedanmark Railroad	Kammeradvokaten	2020a
Denmark	Ejendomsstyrelse Properties	Kammeradvokaten	2020b
Denmark	Danske Bank Banking	Plesner	2020
Germany	Wirecard Banking	KPMG	2020
Iceland	Samherji Fishing	Al Jazeera	2019
Japan	Toshiba Equipment	Deloitte	2015
Moldova	Three Local Banks	Kroll	2017
Netherlands	Oceanteam Offshore	Sands	2019
New Zealand	Fuji Xerox Equipment	Deloitte	2017
Nigeria	Nigeria National Petroleum	PwC	2015
Norway	Obos Social Housing	KPMG	2021
Norway	Norfund Foreign Aid	PwC	2020a
Norway	Equinor Energy	PwC	2020b
South Sudan	Lundin Energy	Commission	2021b
Sweden	Swedbank Banking	Clifford Chance	2020
Sweden	Nasdaq Clearing	Finansinspektionen	2021
United States	University of California, Berkeley	State Auditor	2020
United States	Wells Fargo Community Bank	Committee	2017
United States	Apollo Global Management	Dechert	2021
Vietnam	Embassy of Norway	Duane Morris	2016

Table 10.2 Allegations reviewed in fraud investigation reports

Country	Organization	Allegation
Austria	International Biathlon Union	Receiving bribes from Russia
Canada	Town of Pelham	Bribing town officials for construction site
Congo	Mercy Corps Humanitarian	Receiving kickbacks from local vendors
Denmark	Bestseller Clothing	Supporting military junta in Myanmar
Denmark	Danske Bank Banking	Laundering money in Estonia
Denmark	Social Security Agency	Embezzling client social benefits
Denmark	Banedanmark Railroad	Receiving bribes from vendor
Denmark	Ejendomsstyrelse Properties	Receiving bribes from vendor
Denmark	Danske Bank Banking	Claiming termination of client funds
Germany	Wirecard Banking	Accounting manipulation
Iceland	Samherji Fishing	Bribing officials in Namibia
Japan	Toshiba Equipment	Manipulating management accounting
Moldova	Three Local Banks	Transferring funds abroad
Netherlands	Oceanteam Offshore	Covering private executive expenses
New Zealand	Fuji Xerox Equipment	Contracting new before termination
Nigeria	Nigeria National Petroleum	Embezzling oil revenues
Norway	Obos Social Housing	Ignoring membership demands
Norway	Norfund Foreign Aid	Losing state fund transfer
Norway	Equinor Energy	Lacking oversight and guardianship
South Sudan	Lundin Energy	Supporting human rights violations
Sweden	Swedbank Banking	Laundering money in Estonia
Sweden	Nasdaq Clearing	Manipulating stock exchange
United States	University of California, Berkeley	Receiving bribes for college admission
United States	Wells Fargo Community Bank	Abusing consumer savings
United States	Apollo Global Management	Conspiring with Jeffrey Epstein
Vietnam	Embassy of Norway	Abusing embassy position in rentals

Sources of License Authority

Violations of the license to operate might engage sources of license authority as listed in Table 10.3. For example, there was the threat of financial supporters reducing or withdrawing funding from the International Biathlon Union in Austria if it was determined that the organization could be characterized by corruption.

Table 10.3 illustrates the variety of sources that are relevant as license authorities. They are stakeholders who can have an impact at violations of the social license.

Table 10.3 Sources of license authority related to fraud investigation reports

Country	Organization	Source of license authority
Austria	International Biathlon Union	Financial supporters (e.g., sponsors)
Canada	Town of Pelham	Town citizens about municipal spendings
Congo	Mercy Corps Humanitarian	Funders of development aid
Denmark	Bestseller Clothing	Customers of the garment industry
Denmark	Danske Bank Banking	Danish financial supervisory authority
Denmark	Social Security Agency	Ministry of Social Affairs
Denmark	Banedanmark Railroad	Citizens as taxpayers
Denmark	Ejendomsstyrelse Properties	Citizens as taxpayers
Denmark	Danske Bank Banking	Customers with bank accounts
Germany	Wirecard Banking	Politicians supporting innovation
Iceland	Samherji Fishing	Politicians for national reputation
Japan	Toshiba Equipment	Shareholders in the company
Moldova	Three Local Banks	Investigative journalists in the media
Netherlands	Oceanteam Offshore	Shareholders in the company
New Zealand	Fuji Xerox Equipment	Customers of equipment contracts
Nigeria	Nigeria National Petroleum	National Bank of Nigeria
Norway	Obos Social Housing	Members of the housing cooperative
Norway	Norfund Foreign Aid	Funders of development aid
Norway	Equinor Energy	Government as shareholder
South Sudan	Lundin Energy	Investigative journalists and researchers
Sweden	Swedbank Banking	Swedish financial supervisory authority
Sweden	Nasdaq clearing	Swedish financial supervisory authority
United States	University of California, Berkeley	State of California
United States	Wells Fargo Community Bank	Customers with bank accounts
United States	Apollo Global Management	Media, criminal justice system
Vietnam	Embassy of Norway	Ministry of Foreign Affairs

Substance of Social License

The substance of social license is listed in Table 10.4. For example, the substance in Austria would be funding for the International Biathlon Union, while the substance in Denmark for Danske Bank would be the freedom of self-governance as a financial institution.

Table 10.4 Substance of social license related to fraud investigation reports

Country	Organization	Substance of social license
Austria	International Biathlon Union	Financial resources for the organization
Canada	Town of Pelham	Citizen trust in political bodies
Congo	Mercy Corps Humanitarian	Financial resources to foreign aid
Denmark	Bestseller Clothing	Customers buying their garments
Denmark	Danske Bank Banking	Permission as a financial institution
Denmark	Social Security Agency	Political acceptance of spending
Denmark	Banedanmark Railroad	Public procurement acceptance
Denmark	Ejendomsstyrelse Properties	Public procurement acceptance
Denmark	Danske Bank Banking	Permission as a financial institution
Germany	Wirecard Banking	Permission as a financial institution
Iceland	Samherji Fishing	Permitted provider on fishing quotas
Japan	Toshiba Equipment	Funding from investors as shareholders
Moldova	Three Local Banks	Permission by national bank
Netherlands	Oceanteam Offshore	Funding from investors as shareholders
New Zealand	Fuji Xerox Equipment	Customers buying their lease agreements
Nigeria	Nigeria National Petroleum	Government approval of operations
Norway	Obos Social Housing	Members' acceptance of decision-making
Norway	Norfund Foreign Aid	Financial resources to foreign aid
Norway	Equinor Energy	Shareholder acceptance of operations
South Sudan	Lundin Energy	Permission for oil exploration
Sweden	Swedbank Banking	Permission as a financial institution
Sweden	Nasdaq Clearing	Permission as a financial institution
United States	University of California, Berkeley	Permission as a public university
United States	Wells Fargo Community Bank	Permission as a financial institution
United States	Apollo Global Management	Permission for securities management
Vietnam	Embassy of Norway	Employment of local citizens

References

Al Jazeera. (2019). Anatomy of a bribe: A deep dive into an underworld of corruption, by J. Kleinfeld, www.aljazeera.com, published December 1.

Bruun Hjejle. (2018). *Report on the non-resident portfolio at Danske Bank's Estonian branch* (pp. 87). Law Firm Bruun Hjejle.

Christoffersen, J., & Mikkelsen, M. S. (2021, May 10). *Redegjørelse: Bestseller A/S' samfundsansvar i Myanmar (Statement: Bestseller Ltd.'s Social Responsibility in Myanmar)* (pp. 122). Law Firm Offersen Christoffersen.

Clifford Chance. (2020). *Report of investigation on Swedbank* (pp. 218). Law Firm Clifford Chance.

Commission. (2021a, January 28). *Final report of the IBU external review commission*, Redacted Version, Austria, pp. 220.

Commission. (2021b, September 23). *Human rights violations and related economic crimes in the Republic of South Sudan* (pp. 59). Human Rights Council.

Committee. (2017). *Independent directors of the Board of Wells Fargo & company: Sales practices investigation report* (pp. 113). Community Bank, Report of investigation, Law Firm Shearman Sterling.

Dechert. (2021). *Investigation of Epstein/Black relationship and any relationship between Epstein and Apollo Global Management* (pp. 21). Law Firm Dechert, Report of Investigation.

Deloitte. (2015). *Investigation report, summary version, independent investigation Committee for Toshiba Corporation.* Report of Investigation, Audit Firm Deloitte Tohmatsu.

Deloitte. (2017). *FujiFilm holdings corporation: Independent investigation Committee's investigation report and future measures in New Zealand* (pp. 89). Report of Investigation, Audit Firm Deloitte Tohmatsu.

Duane Morris. (2016). *Project house – Report, conclusions and notes from interviews with selected landlords, real estate agents and locally engaged employees of the Royal Norwegian Embassy in Hanoi* (pp. 172). Report of Investigation, Hanoi, Vietnam.

Finansinspektionen. (2021, January 27). *Warning and administrative fine – Finansinspektionen's decision (to be announced 27 January 2021 at 8:00)* (pp. 46). Swedish Financial Supervisory Authority.

Gottschalk, P., & Tcherni-Buzzeo, M. (2017). Reasons for gaps in crime reporting: The case of white-collar criminals investigated by private fraud examiners in Norway. *Deviant Behavior, 38*(3), 267–281.

Kammeradvokaten. (2020a, October 5). *Undersøgelse af forholdet mellem visse ansatte hos Banedanmark og private virksomheter (Review of the Relationship Between Certain Employees at Banedanmark and Private e Enterprises)* (pp. 191). Law Firm Poul Schmith.

Kammeradvokaten. (2020b, October 6). *Advokatundersøgelse af det økonomiske kontrolmiljø i forsvarsministeriets ejendomsstyrelse (Attorney review of the economical control function in the defense Department's Property Management)* (pp. 270). Law Firm Poul Schmith.

KPMG. (2017). *The Corporation of the Town of Pelham: Forensic review of certain concerns regarding the East Fonthill development project* (pp. 100). Report of Investigation, Audit Firm KPMG.

KPMG. (2020, April 27). *Report concerning the independent special investigation at Wirecard AG* (pp. 74). Audit Firm KPMG.

KPMG. (2021). *Ulven-transaksjonen – Granskingsrapport til styret i Obos (The Ulven transaction – Investigation report to the board at Obos), law firm KPMG* (34 pages). Oslo.

Kroll. (2017). *Project Tenor II, summary report, report prepared for The National Bank of Moldova, report of investigation* (pp. 58), Audit Firm Kroll. (2016: Project Tenor – Scoping Phase, 84 pages. 2018: Project Tenor II, Confidential Working Papers Part I to the Detailed Report, Detailed tracing analysis, 60 pages. 2018: Project Tenor II – Confidential working papers – Part II, Evidence Packs – Funds traced to: Ilan Shor, Alexandr Macloivici and Olga Bondarciuc. 2018: Project Tenor II – Detailed Report, Report Prepared for The National Bank of Moldova, 154 pages).

Plesner. (2020). *Response to DFSA-letter: Anmodning om redegørelse om Danske Bank A/S' gældsinddrivelsessystem (Response to DFSA letter: Request for account concerning Danske Bank Inc.'s debt collection system)* (pp. 120). Investigation Report by Danske Bank, Law Firm Plesner.

PwC. (2015). *Auditor-general for the federation: Investigative forensic audit into the allegations of unremitted funds into the federation accounts by the NNPC* (pp. 199). Nigerian National Petroleum Corporation, Report of Investigation, Audit Firm PricewaterhouseCoopers.

PwC. (2019). *Ekstern undersøgelse af tilskudsadministrationen 1977–2018: Udarbejdet for Socialstyrelsen (External investigation of benefits administration 1977–2018: Provided to the social security administration)* (pp. 80). Report of Investigation, Audit Firm PricewaterhouseCoopers.

PwC. (2020a, June 30). *Independent assessment of the LOLC incident: Report developed for Norfund, report of investigation* (pp. 34). PricewaterhouseCoopers.

PwC. (2020b, October 9). Equinor in the USA: Review of Equinor's US onshore activities and learnings for the future. In *Prepared for Equinor ASA's Board of Directors.* Audit Firm PricewaterhouseCoopers, Oslo, Norway.

Sands. (2019). *Factual report Oceanteam: Investigation of related party transactions* (pp. 256). Report of Investigation, Law Firm Sands.

Smith. (2020). *Operational review of exposure to corrupt practices in humanitarian aid implementation mechanisms in the DRC*. Adam Smith International, Final Report by Nicole Henze, Francois Grunewald, and Sharanjeet Parmar, Department for International Development.

State Auditor. (2020). *University of California*, California State Auditor, 621 Capitol Mall, Sacramento, California, Report of Investigation, pp. 82.

Chapter 11
Bottom-Up Status Control

Traditionally, control in organizations is concerned with top-down approaches, where executives attempt to direct their employees' attention, behaviors, and performance to align with the organization's goals and objectives. More recently, the control perspective has extended to include customization and transmutation of control mechanisms, where transmutation captures the idea that organizational units implement control regimes that are different from the mandated control mechanism from management (Chown, 2021: 711):

> Researchers are now beginning to bring these literatures together, marrying the top-down managerial perspective with the lived experiences of employees throughout the organization.

This chapter takes a new approach by turning the problem of control upside down as it focuses on control of executives who find white-collar crime convenient. The bottom-up approach to executive compliance focuses on organizational measures to make white-collar crime less convenient for potential offenders (Haines et al., 2022). Compliance refers to obeying the formal rules and regulations in force at a given time and place (Durand et al., 2019).

Control is concerned with a negative discrepancy between the desired and current state of affairs. Control mechanisms attempt to reduce the discrepancy through adaptive action in the form of behavioral reactions (Direnzo & Greenhaus, 2011). Control mechanisms attempt to influence and manage the process, content, and outcome of work (Kownatzki et al., 2013). Control involves processes of negotiation in which various strategies are developed to produce particular outcomes. Control is therefore a dynamic process that regulates behavior through a set of modes, rules, or strategies (Gill, 2019).

There are various types of control mechanisms with various targets (Chown, 2021: 752):

> For example, prominent frameworks delineate controls based on whether they are formal or informal, coercive, normative, peer-based, or concertive. Controls are also divided based on

whether they target employees' behaviors by implementing processes or rules that ensure individuals perform tasks in a particular manner, target their outputs by assessing employees based on measurable items such as profits or production, or target the inputs to the production process by controlling the human capital and material inputs utilized by the organization.

Corporate white-collar crime control is mainly focused on attempts to prevent, detect, and reduce negative discrepancy between desired and current state of executive affairs. Control attempts to influence the process of work in normative ways. Control targets executive behavior to ensure that executive individuals perform tasks in a legitimate manner. As argued by Kownatzki et al. (2013), behavior control relies on subjective, organizationally relevant criteria to assess executive activity and measures performance in the context of long-term progress toward the development of a particular way of doing things. Behavior control not only provides checks and balances for executive performance but also provides a common vocabulary that facilitates dialogue among stakeholders and fosters the creation of ambitious behavioral norms. When behavior rather than outcome is the focus, controls may provide a buffer for external short-term pressures.

Within an organization, struggles are about conceptions of control (Yue et al., 2013). Control mechanisms have to satisfy a number of requirements to be successful, such as fairness perceived by controlled individuals (Long et al., 2011). Social control is based on attachment, commitment, involvement, and belief, where a control mechanism is informal punishment in the appearance of shaming (Amry & Meliala, 2021).

Research has documented the failure of the traditional top-down approach to executive compliance, in particular control of chief executive officers (Bosse & Phillips, 2016; Galvin et al., 2015; Khanna et al., 2015; Pillay & Kluvers, 2014; Williams, 2008; Zahra et al., 2005; Zhu & Chen, 2015).

Some CEOs will employ illegal or objectionable means in striving to reach goals. This type of behavior is not necessarily different from the behavior of others in positions of power and authority (e.g., politicians, officers of universities, church officials, heads of major philanthropies, etc.), but the degrees of freedom enjoyed by many CEOs make the CEO position nevertheless very special in terms of convenience. For example, a CEO may conveniently cheat and defraud owners (Khanna et al., 2015; Williams, 2008; Zahra et al., 2005) because there is lack of oversight and guardianship in the agency relationship (Bosse & Phillips, 2016; Pillay & Kluvers, 2014).

While there is considerable variance in narcissistic tendencies across CEOs, many CEOs have narcissistic personality traits such as self-focus, self-admiration, a sense of entitlement, and a sense of superiority (Zhu & Chen, 2015: 35):

Narcissistic CEOs tend to favor bold actions, such as large acquisitions, that attract attention. They are less responsive than other CEOs to objective indicators of their performance and more responsive to social praise. For instance, while narcissistic CEOs tend to aggressively adopt technological discontinuities, they are especially likely to do so when such behavior is expected to garner attention and admiration from external audiences.

Galvin et al. (2015: 163) found that some CEOs suffer from narcissistic identification with the organization:

> It is not uncommon to learn of individuals in positions of power and responsibility, especially CEOs, who exploit and undermine their organizations for personal gain. A circumstance not well explained in the literature, however, is that some of those individuals may highly identify with their organizations, meaning that they see little difference between their identity and the organization's identity – between their interests and the organization's interest. This presents a paradox, because organizational identification typically is not noted for its adverse consequences on the organization.

The CEO is the only person at that top hierarchical level in the organization. Below the CEO, there are a number of executives at the same hierarchical level. Above the CEO, there are a number of board members at the same hierarchical level. However, the CEO is alone at his or her level. The CEO is supposed to face control by the board, but the board only meets occasionally to discuss business cases. Executives below the CEO are typically appointed by the CEO and typically loyal to the CEO (Bendiktsson, 2010; Bigley & Wiersma, 2002; Chatterjee & Pollock, 2017; Chen & Nadkarni, 2017; Davidson et al., 2019; Gamache & McNamara, 2019; Gangloff et al., 2016; Khanna et al., 2015; König et al., 2020; McClelland et al., 2010; Schnatterly et al., 2018; Shen, 2003; Zhu & Chen, 2015).

The board of directors is typically incapable of controlling chief executive activities (Ghannam et al., 2019). Examples of former CEOs as white-collar crime convicts include Thomas Middelhoff at Alcantor in Germany, Boris Benulic at Kraft & Kultur in Sweden, Hisao Tanaka at Toshiba Corporation in Japan, Are Blomhoff at Betanien Foundation in Norway, and Trond Kristoffersen at Finance Credit in Norway – in addition to all the well-known names from the United States.

Control of executives is necessary to ensure the legitimate success and survival of organizations. As argued by Gill (2019), there are two important conceptual dimensions that draw together insights from studies of control and resistance in the workplace. The dimension of compatibility considers executives' subjective experiences of the fit between their personhood and modes of control, where alignment can inspire fulfillment and misalignment can prompt suffering and deviant behavior. The dimension of coherence considers executives' perception of the consistency between modes, which can be fragmented or unified to reinforce organizationally prescribed compliance and ethics, where "ethics is not equivalent to laws" (Dion, 2019: 836).

At its core, top-down control refers to the manner in which "an organization's managers can use different types of control mechanisms – such as financial incentives, performance management, or culture – to monitor, measure, and evaluate workers' behaviors and influence them toward achieving the organization's goals in efficient and effective ways" (Chown, 2021: 713). Similarly at its core, bottom-up control refers to the manner in which organizational members can use different types of control mechanisms – such as whistleblowing, transparency, resource access, or culture – to monitor, measure, and evaluate executives' avoidance of deviant behaviors and influence them toward achieving the organization's goals in efficient and effective ways. While the hierarchical structure remains with executives at the top of the organization in charge of the business, bottom-up control is a matter of stakeholder involvement in compliance. While top-down control is often a formal and rigid system, bottom-up control can be an informal and flexible system based on social influence (Haines et al., 2022: 185):

> Criminalization, foundational analytical territory for criminology, forms part of a "bottom up" strategy where it becomes "social property," untethered from law and formal criminal justice. Criminalization as social property comprises a central element of "social control influence" over corporate harm. This is justice in the vernacular with media, social movements and citizen watchdogs exerting pressure, demanding change and bringing business to account.

When noticing wrongdoing at the top of the organization, improvisation might be a key capability for organizational members and citizen watchdogs. Capability refers to the ability to perform (Paruchuri et al., 2021), while improvisation refers to the spontaneous process by which planning and execution happen at the same time (Mannucci et al., 2021). Rather than following formal reporting lines to people who are not trustworthy, improvisation is a matter of spontaneous action in response to unanticipated occurrences, in which individuals find a way to manage the unexpected problem.

Disclosure of Executive Language

Status is the first opportunity theme in convenience theory. Status can allow executive language that nobody understands. For example, one might suggest that elite members are considered too big to fail and too powerful to jail (Pontell et al., 2014), and there is power inequality between the elite and others (Patel & Cooper, 2014). Therefore, subordinates tend to accept executive language that they do not really understand (Ferraro et al., 2005), and they get distracted from observing deviant behavior by offender humor (Yam et al., 2018). A consequence of strange language and offender humor might be an acceptance of blame game by misleading attribution to others (Eberly et al., 2011).

Executives and others in the elite may use language that followers do not necessarily understand. Followers nevertheless tend to trust executive messages. Language shapes what people notice and ignore (Ferraro et al., 2005), and language is a window into organizational culture (Holt & Cornelissen, 2014; Srivastava & Goldberg, 2017; Weick, 1995). Offender language can cause obedience among followers (Mawritz et al., 2017).

Individuals with high social status in privileged positions thus sometimes use language that people simply do not understand. Executives and others in the elite may use language that followers not necessarily understand – however nevertheless they trust executive messages (Ferraro et al., 2005). Cryptology is concerned with techniques for secure communication in the presence of third parties called adversaries. Cryptology is about constructing and analyzing protocols that prevent third parties or the public from understanding messages. Similarly, in an organizational context, executive communication applies a management language that few others understand.

According to Ferraro et al. (2005), language affects what people see or not see; how they see it; and the social categories and descriptors that they use to interpret their reality. Language shapes what people notice and ignore and what they believe is and is not important. Reality is socially constructed, and language plays an important role in such constructions. Srivastava and Goldberg (2017) argue that language is a window into culture. Subcultures develop in the organization, where the language is different from other parts of the organization. The language through which people in the elite communicate with colleagues on the job illustrates how people fit into an organization's culture or subculture. Language use can predict an individual's influence and adaption on the job and can reveal distinct linguistic patterns for executives involved in misconduct and crime.

Removal of Powerful People

Hostile and abusive supervision by powerful executives is detrimental to the well-being of the corporation. Mawritz et al. (2017) argue that abusive supervision, defined as subordinates' perceptions of the extent to which supervisors engage in the sustained display of hostile verbal and non-verbal behaviors, can create substantial costs to organizations and their employees. One recommendation for curbing such behavior is the non-acceptance of a primitive impulsive system found among some executives (Liang et al., 2016). Sometimes, failing self-control among executives is caused by poor-performing subordinates (Liang et al., 2016; Mawritz et al., 2017). Then a recommendation might imply that poor performance is corrected or compensated in joint efforts by empowered employees.

Executives need to have an internal locus of control, where locus of control refers to individuals' perceptions about whether the consequences of their behaviors are within (internal) or beyond (external) their own personal control. They have a need to influence their own outcomes, rather than their circumstances (Valentine et al., 2019).

Hostile and abusive supervision by powerful executives can reduce the status of those executives since status is a property that rests in the eyes of others (Kakkar et al., 2020: 532):

> Status is a property that rests in the eyes of others and is conferred to individuals who are deemed to have a higher rank or social standing in a pecking order based on a mutually valued set of social attributes. Higher social status or rank grants its holder a host of tangible benefits in both professional and personal domains. For instance, high-status actors are sought by groups for advice, are paid higher, receive unsolicited help, and are credited disproportionately in joint tasks. In innumerable ways, our social ecosystem consistently rewards those with high status.

Harvin and Killey (2021: 509) studied whether a firm's CEO who has an extraordinary personal reputation or superstar status can have an adverse impact on the independence of an auditor who is engaged in the audit of the firm's financial statement:

> As indicated in the experiment that was conducted in the study, the superstar status of a CEO of a firm being audited appears to have the potential to have a negative impact of the strategic risk assessment of an auditor's overall risk assessment of an audit during the planning stage of an audit. It would be very troublesome if an auditor unwittingly or consciously lowered the strategic risk assessment as a result of the CEO's superstar status. The strategic risk assessment of an audit determines the level of substantive audit tests that are performed as well as the amount of audit time that is devoted to the completion of the audit.

Declining status in a hostile environment can cause executive falling of powerful people from the privileged elite (Kakkar et al., 2020). Then white-collar offenders no longer are too powerful to fail or too powerful to jail (Pontell et al., 2014). Friends in key positions and elite networks may abandon them since they are no asset anymore to the relationships, but rather potential liabilities (Dewan & Jensen, 2020).

Dewan and Jensen (2020) studied high social status individuals in times of scandals that can change the role of status from being an asset to being a liability. They defined scandal as the disruptive publicity of misconduct, that is, a situation after detection and disclosure to the public. While the importance of status in convenience theory is related to prevention of blame before disclosure, Dewan and Jensen's (2020: 1657) research was concerned with status after disclosure:

> Because scandal diminishes the effectiveness of factors that make status an asset, status offers less protection during a scandal. At the same time that scandal decreases the protective benefits of status; the factors that make status a liability remain or are augmented.

Status can thus be a liability in the context of blaming, shaming, and labeling of misconduct and crime. High status creates high expectations that are seriously violated in a scandal. The disappointment causes an expectation of consequence for the person responsible for the disappointment.

Removal of powerful people might include prosecution for corporate wrongdoing (Henning, 2017: 503):

> The Department of Justice has made it a priority in corporate criminal investigations to require that companies single out those within the organization responsible for any wrongdoing.

Attempts to emphasize individual culpability can cause an upsurge of prosecutions of corporate executives who oversee companies that engage in misconduct. When executives push hard for profits and the personal gain that comes from corporate success, Henning (2017) argued that there should be no blurred line into fraud and corruption.

Detection of Misleading Attribution

Executives may reinforce a culture of financial crime by ignoring criminal actions and otherwise facilitate unethical behavior. At the same time, they try to distance and disassociate themselves from criminal actions (Pontell et al., 2021: 9):

> High status corporate criminals often go to great lengths to distance themselves from the crimes committed by their subordinates and to hide any incriminating evidence of their role in the decisions that authorized those criminal acts.

Misleading attribution of blame to subordinates by executives is both a matter of detection and reaction (Eberly et al., 2011). Generally, attribution is concerned with how individuals make judgments about responsibility (Piening et al., 2020: 335):

> Attributions of responsibility involve a series of yes-no judgments in which individuals first determine whether a negative event has been caused by internal or external factors. If the event is attributed to internal causes, the process continues to determine whether the cause was controllable or not, whereas in case of external causality, the organization cannot be held responsible, so the process stops.

Linked to the blame game is shaming, where suspected elite members express social disapproval of innocent individuals in the organization, thereby attempting to gain social control on perceptions of criminality. Shaming implies stigmatization and disapproval (Amry & Meliala, 2021). Social control is based on attachment, commitment, involvement, and belief, where a control mechanism is informal punishment in the appearance of shaming.

The attribution perspective implies that white-collar offenders attempt to attribute causes of crime to everyone else but themselves in the organization. Attribution theory is about identifying causality predicated on internal and external circumstances (Eberly et al., 2011). External attributions place the cause of a negative event on external factors, absolving the account giver and the privileged individual from personal responsibility. Innocent subordinates receive blame for crime committed by elite members (Lee & Robinson, 2000). According to Sonnier et al. (2015: 10), affective reactions influence blame attribution directly and indirectly by altering structural linkage assessments:

> For example, a negative affective reaction can influence the assessment of causation by reducing the evidential standards required to attribute blame or by increasing the standards of care by which an act is judged.

When the Siemens corruption scandal emerged in the public, top management attempted to blame lower-level managers (Berghoff, 2018: 423):

> At first the company defended itself with set phrases like "mishaps of individuals" and isolated offenses committed by a "gang" of criminals, or "This is not Siemens."

Status-related factors such as influential positions, upper-class family ties, and community roles often preclude perceptions of blameworthiness (Slyke & Bales, 2013). According to the attribution perspective, parties involved in a personal conflict or crime suspicion will naturally wonder "Why is this happening?" in the hope that if they understand the negative event, they might be able to predict its cause. The cause can be either individual behavior (personal attribution) or organizational behavior (system attribution). The attribution perspective suggests that, all else being equal, the odds are in favor of making a personal attribution (Keaveney, 2008). If a white-collar offender fails to attribute crime to another individual, then there is the alternative of blaming the system.

However, bottom-up detection of misleading attribution can cause self-conscious emotions of guilt and shame among potential and actual white-collar offenders, making deviance less convenient (Zhong & Robinson, 2021: 1439):

> These are painful emotions that individuals experience when they perceive their actions have violated a standard, prompting a negative evaluation of their behavior in the case of guilt or a negative evaluation of their global self in the case of shame. Prior studies have revealed that many forms of wrongdoing can beget guilt and/or shame, including transgressions, cheating, psychological aggression, ostracism, lying and deception, and unethical behavior.

Katz (1979) found that financial crime higher up in the organization will be ignored to a larger extent than lower down in the organization, or blame is allocated elsewhere (Keaveney, 2008; Lee & Robinson, 2000; Sonnier et al., 2015). For example, the blame for the ignition switch failure at General Motors was moved away from the chief executive officer and far down the hierarchy to some middle managers in the organization (Jenner Block, 2014).

Attribution theory explains individuals' attribute responsibility for both own and others' behavior. The central premise is that attributions of responsibility depend on whether individuals view the causes of behavior as a result of internal or external factors. If individuals determine that a behavior results from internal factors in terms of actor personality characteristics and actor disposition, then they typically will attribute the behavior to the actor. Alternatively, individuals can attribute the behavior to other people or the situation such as social structure or organizational context. The strength of attribution in terms of responsibility can depend on a number of factors such as causality, knowledge, intentions, and seriousness (Gailey & Lee, 2005). Blameworthiness is the extent to which it is clear that an individual engaged in a questionable act (Dewan & Jensen, 2020).

Disregard of Offender Humor

White-collar offenders attempt to use humor to distract attention from their crime. Offender humor distraction as suggested by Yam et al. (2018) implies that potential white-collar offenders can influence the organizational opportunity structure by aggressive humor. Aggressive humor is a negatively directed style of humor that an individual carries out at the expense and detriment of one's relationships with others.

It can be teasing with a humorous undertone, or it can be victimization of the receiver. It can be the opposite of self-irony, where the offender makes jokes about others and makes them look ridiculous. The more aggressive an offender's style, the more a sense of humor will signal acceptability of norm violations for the offender. Aggressive humor is a form of hostile behavior.

Aggressive leader humor expands the organizational opportunity for white-collar crime, and it influences the willingness of victims of such humor (Yam et al., 2018: 349):

> The more aggressive a leader's style, the more a sense of humor will signal acceptability of norm violations, which will be positively associated with deviance.

Aggressive humor refers to a specific style of humor aimed at teasing or ridiculing. It may include sarcasm humorously to convey disapproving information to followers. Aggressive humor may signal to followers that the accepted social norm of being respectful toward others is not important. It signals that violating norms of human decency is acceptable.

The leader humor perspective suggests that leader sense of humor is positively associated with followers' perceived acceptability of norm violations. When leaders display humor and, as a result, violate norms, followers will likely perceive that it is socially acceptable to violate norms in the organization for two reasons (Yam et al., 2018: 352):

> First, leaders' formal position makes them strong sources of normative expectations. Leaders, as role models, are more likely to be observed by followers who are scanning the environment for information on how to behave in the work context. In other words, leaders who make light of norm violations in order to produce humor are likely to imply to followers that mild norm violations in the organizations are generally acceptable. Second, when a leader acts in a humorous manner, others will likely react with laughter and amusement, an implicit signal of approval. Followers will be likely to interpret this social information as signaling the acceptability of norm violations. When a norm violation is enacted – and interpreted by others – in a playful, humorous way, it also signals to followers that violations need not be taken seriously or scrutinized.

Therefore, a bottom-up approach to executive deviance is to avoid acceptance of executive language that they do not really understand (Ferraro et al., 2005) and avoid distraction from observing deviant behavior by offender humor (Yam et al., 2018). A consequence of ignorance of strange language and offender humor might be detection of the blame game by misleading attribution to others (Eberly et al., 2011). Furthermore, leaders with an aggressive humor might practice morally ambiguous leadership (Dion, 2020), where their ambiguity can become vulnerable to bottom-up criticism.

Correction of Power Inequality

Marxist criminology views the competitive nature of the capitalist system as a major cause of financial crime (Siegel, 2011). It focuses on what creates stability and continuity in society, and it adopts a predefined political philosophy. Marxist criminology focuses on why things change by identifying the disruptive forces in capitalist societies and describing how power, wealth, prestige, and perceptions of the world divide every society. The economic struggle is the central venue for the Marxists. Marx divided society into two unequal classes and demonstrated the inequality in the historical transition from patrician and slave to capitalist and wage worker. It is the rulers versus the ruled. Marx also underlined that all societies have a certain hierarchy wherein the higher class has more privileges than the lower one. In a capitalist society, where economic resources equate to power, it is in the interest of the ascendant class to maintain economic stratification in order to dictate the legal order (Petrocelli et al., 2003).

Conflict theory provides an explanation of crime, since it is concerned with social inequality, class and racial differences, and the power used by the ruling class through its criminal justice apparatus. Conflict theorists see inequality based on differences in wealth, status, ideas, and religious beliefs. Not only do capitalist societies generate vast inequalities of wealth but also those who own the wealth, who control large corporations and financial and commercial institutions, influence those who have political power to get the laws they want (Lanier & Henry, 2009b).

Conflict theory is a perspective in criminology that emphasizes the social, political, or material inequality of a social group and that draws attention to power differentials, such as class conflict. Crime stems from conflict between different segments of society fueled by a system of domination based on inequality, alienation, and justice. Crime is harm that comes from differences in power (Lanier & Henry, 2009a).

While there is power inequality between executives and employees (Patel & Cooper, 2014), corporate white-collar control mechanisms have to be perceived as fair to be successful. Fairness issues play a key role in determining how willing executives are to work toward the performance standards the organization seeks to enforce (Long et al., 2011).

High social status in privileged positions creates power inequality compared to those without any status in their positions. The perspective of power inequality suggests that, for example, family members in family firms wield significant influence in their firms. Family members often have legitimate access to firm resources that nonfamily executives in the firm cannot question (Patel & Cooper, 2014). Kempa (2010) found that white-collar offenders have unlimited authority to get it the way they want.

Power inequality is reduced when white-collar crime by executives and others in the elite are punished. One of the peculiar aspects of white-collar crime is that the privileged and powerful punish their own: Why does the ruling class punish their own?

Reason 1: Reduce Conflict   Since white-collar crime is crime by the wealthy and powerful, it seems to contradict social conflict theory. There are no reasons why the wealthy and powerful would like to see laws that turn their own actions into regular criminal offences. When Sutherland (1939) first coined the term "white-collar crime," there were indeed reactions in the audience of upper-class people. They asked why one should define actions by privileged individuals of the influential classes as crime at the level of street crime by ordinary criminals. According to

Brightman (2009), Sutherland's theory of white-collar crime first presented in 1939 was controversial, particularly since many of the academics in the audience perceived themselves to be members of the upper echelon in American society. The audience was the American Sociological Association where Sutherland gave his address and first presented his theory of white-collar crime. What Podgor (2007) found to be the most interesting aspect of Sutherland's work is that a scholar needed to proclaim that crime of the upper socioeconomic class is in fact crime that should be prosecuted. It is apparent that prior to the coining of the term "white-collar crime," wealth and power allowed many persons to escape criminal liability.

Veblen's (1899) sociological study of the "leisured classes" and their rapacious conspicuous consumption had an influence on Sutherland's (1939) research. Josephson (1962) who coined the term "robber barons" in the 1930s was also an influential scholar at that time. Therefore, Sutherland's work on white-collar crime seems to fit with conflict theory, where he might have seen a need to reduce the level of conflict in society by defining obvious unjustified misconduct by privileged individuals as regular crime. This is in line with Arrigo and Bernard (1997), who apply conflict theory to explain initiatives for more prosecution of white-collar criminals. Seron and Munger (1996: 187) quoted that "The plain fact is that in a new stage of capitalism, class divides as ruthlessly as it did in the age of the Robber Barons."

Reason 2: Government Influence   Another reason for starting to define capitalists and other persons of respectability and high social status as regular criminals when they abuse their powers for personal or organizational profit is the need of governments to gain some kind of control over the business sector and the market economy. Business and professional elites had achieved political influence beyond what most democratic governments found acceptable. Even worse, some enterprises were so powerful that they became almost untouchable for government interventions. They were too powerful to fail and too powerful to jail (Pontell et al., 2014).

Criminological attention on the activities of business enterprises and other organizations, their creativity and power, remains in a conflict with political influence of business executives, capitalists, and members of the professional elites. Haines (2014: 20) discusses corporate fraud as an example, where she argues that:

> Criminalization of corporate fraud deflects attention to one of these actors, the business and its directors, without clear recognition of the role played by government itself.

Haines (2014) argues that governments critically, in close consultation with the professions, enact legal and regulatory reforms that engender confidence in both the accuracy of accounts and materiality of money while also further institutionalizing their underlying ambiguities. Hence, even as governments are excited to sanction corporate criminals with more vigor, they are at the same time implicated in the creation of corporate criminals. Corporate fraud implies that there has been a criminal misrepresentation of a financial or business state of affairs by one or more individuals for financial gain, where banks, shareholders, and tax authorities are among the victims. Yet, misrepresentation is a matter of opinion rather than accuracy. For example, estimating values of products in stock is no exact science. If nobody wants to buy products in stock, they have no value. While governments work at arm's length through external auditors, law enforcement is reluctant to prosecute unless misrepresentation of the value of a business is completely out of range.

Reason 3: "Our" Laws A third reason for the prosecution of the wealthy and powerful individuals and corporations is that their own laws did not intend to target members of their own class. The lawmakers had others in society in mind. Caught by surprise that members of their own class violate their own laws leads the ruling class to turn laws against their own allies. When those allies demonstrate nonconforming and deviant behavior, others in the ruling class take on the task of prosecuting deviating members of the elite. "As we are reminded today, those who make the laws don't have the right to break the laws," Richard Frankel, the specialist agent in charge of the Criminal Division of the New York office of the Federal Bureau of Investigation, said at a news conference.

FBI held its news conference as Sheldon Silver, the speaker of the State Assembly in New York, faced prosecution for corruption. State prosecutors charged Silver with having exploited his position as one of the most powerful politicians in the state of New York to obtain millions of dollars in bribes and kickbacks. Prosecutors accused Silver's law practice of being a fiction where the sources of large payments of bribes were hiding (Rashbaum & Kaplan, 2015: A24). Silver was arrested on Manhattan on a five-count indictment in January 2015. US attorney Preet Bharara alleged that the Manhattan democrat used New York's ethics laws to hide his scheme – allowing him to become wealthy off his position in power (Spector, 2015).

Silver resigned a few weeks later as speaker (McKinley, 2015). At the same time, Malcolm A. Smith, a former majority leader of the New York State Senate, was convicted of federal corruption charges including bribery, wire fraud, and extortion (Vega, 2015).

Reason 4: Deviant Behavior A fourth reason might be disappointment within the ruling class. The ruling class in society faces decisions over which values to enforce. When individuals in their own upper-level class violate some of these values, then the majority defines it as a crime. Those who violate values of fair competition among capitalists and market access, for example, are potential criminals, even if they belong to the same class as those condemning them.

President George W. Bush's connections to Enron and CEO Kenneth Lay were well documented in major American newspapers. However, when Enron emerged as a deviant organization with a bad apple CEO, Lay and other top executives were prosecuted. Lay died of a heart attack before his conviction (Bendiktsson, 2010).

Reason 5: Crime Victims A fifth and final reason might be the victim of crime. If the victim of white-collar crime were another person in the upper class, then the ruling class would like to protect that person. Victimization of upper-class members by other upper-class members can be considered a crime. Upper-class members need protection against deviant individuals in their own class. It is an inter-group conflict in the dominant class (Wheelock et al., 2011). Maybe Madoff can serve as an example. Rich Jews placed their money in Madoff's investment fund with the promise and expectation that the rate of return would be extraordinarily good. Instead, they lost their money. Wealthy people were victims of Madoff's Ponzi scheme. The government had to sanction such behavior by Madoff, and he received a record prison sentence of 150 years (Ragothaman, 2014).

References

Amry, M. A., & Meliala, A. (2021). Lifestyle-related shaming: The significance of reintegrative shaming on drug relapse offenders in Indonesia. *Journal of Social and Political Sciences, 4*(1), 145–153.

Arrigo, B. A., & Bernard, T. J. (1997). Postmodern criminology in relation to radical and conflict criminology. *Critical Criminology, 8*(2), 39–60.

Bendiktsson, M. O. (2010). The deviant organization and the bad apple CEO: Ideology and accountability in media coverage of corporate scandals. *Social Forces, 88*(5), 2189–2216.

Berghoff, H. (2018). "Organised irresponsibility?" The Siemens corruption scandal of the 1990s and 2000s. *Business History, 60*(3), 423–445.

Bigley, G. A., & Wiersma, M. F. (2002). New CEOs and corporate strategic refocusing: How experience as heir apparent influences the use of power. *Administrative Science Quarterly, 47*, 707–727.

Bosse, D. A., & Phillips, R. A. (2016). Agency theory and bounded self-interest. *Academy of Management Review, 41*(2), 276–297.

Brightman, H. J. (2009). *Today's white-collar crime: Legal, investigative, and theoretical perspectives*. Routledge/Taylor & Francis Group.

Chatterjee, A., & Pollock, T. G. (2017). Master of puppets: How narcissistic CEOs construct their professional worlds. *Academy of Management Review, 42*(4), 703–725.

Chen, J., & Nadkarni, S. (2017). It's about time! CEOs' temporal dispositions, temporal leadership, and corporate entrepreneurship. *Administrative Science Quarterly, 62*(1), 31–66.

Chown, J. (2021). The unfolding of control mechanisms inside organizations: Pathways of customization and transmutation. *Administrative Science Quarterly, 66*(3), 711–752.

Davidson, R. H., Dey, A., & Smith, A. J. (2019). CEO materialism and corporate social responsibility. *The Accounting Review, 94*(1), 101–126.

Dewan, Y., & Jensen, M. (2020). Catching the big fish: The role of scandals in making status a liability. *Academy of Management Journal, 63*(5), 1652–1678.

Dion, M. (2019). A Gadamerian perspective on financial crimes. *Journal of Financial Crime, 26*(3), 836–860.

Dion, M. (2020). Bribery, extortion and "morally ambiguous" leadership in organizations. *Journal of Financial Crime, 27*(4), 1027–1046.

Direnzo, M. S., & Greenhaus, J. H. (2011). Job search and voluntary turnover in a boundaryless world: A control theory perspective. *Academy of Management Review, 36*(3), 567–589.

Durand, R., Hawn, O., & Ioannou, I. (2019). Willing and able: A general model of organizational responses to normative pressures. *Academy of Management Review, 44*(2), 299 320.

Eberly, M. B., Holley, E. C., Johnson, M. D., & Mitchell, T. R. (2011). Beyond internal and external: A dyadic theory of relational attributions. *Academy of Management Review, 36*(4), 731–753.

Ferraro, F., Pfeffer, J., & Sutton, R. I. (2005). Economics language and assumptions: How theories can become self-fulfilling. *Academy of Management Review, 30*(1), 8–24.

Gailey, J. A., & Lee, M. T. (2005). An integrated model of attribution of responsibility for wrong-doing in organizations. *Social Psychology Quarterly, 68*, 338–358.

Galvin, B. M., Lange, D., & Ashforth, B. E. (2015). Narcissistic organizational identification: Seeing oneself as central to the organization's identity. *Academy of Management Review, 40*(2), 163–181.

Gamache, D. L., & McNamara, G. (2019). Responding to bad press: How CEO temporal focus influences the sensitivity to negative media coverage of acquisitions. *Academy of Management Journal, 62*(3), 918–943.

Gangloff, K. A., Connelly, B. L., & Shook, C. L. (2016). Of scapegoats and signals: Investor reactions to CEO succession in the aftermath of wrongdoing. *Journal of Management, 42*, 1614–1634.

Ghannam, S., Bugeja, M., Matolcsy, Z. P., & Spiropoulos, H. (2019). Are qualified and experienced outside directors willing to join fraudulent firms and if so, why? *The Accounting Review, 94*(2), 205–227.

Gill, M. J. (2019). The significance of suffering in organizations: Understanding variation in workers' responses to multiple modes of control. *Academy of Management Review, 44*(2), 377–404.

Haines, F. (2014). Corporate fraud as misplaced confidence? Exploring ambiguity in the accuracy of accounts and the materiality of money. *Theoretical Criminology, 18*(1), 20–37.

Haines, F., Bice, S., Einfeld, C., & Sullivan, H. (2022). Countering corporate power through social control: What does a social licence offer? *The British Journal of Criminology, 62*, 184–199.

Harvin, O., & Killey, M. (2021). Do "superstar" CEOs impair auditor's judgement and reduce fraud detection opportunities? *Journal of Forensic and Investigative Accounting, 13*(3), 500–514.

Henning, P. J. (2017). Why it is getting harder to prosecute executives for corporate misconduct. *Vermont Law Review, 41*(3), 503–522.

Holt, R., & Cornelissen, J. (2014). Sensemaking revisited. *Management Learning, 45*(5), 525–539.

Jenner Block. (2014). *Report to board of directors of General Motors company regarding ignition switch recalls* (325 pages). Law Firm Jenner Block.

Josephson, M. (1962). *The robber barons: The classic account of the influential capitalists who transformed America's future.* Orlando.

Kakkar, H., Sivanathan, N., & Globel, M. S. (2020). Fall from grace: The role of dominance and prestige in punishment of high-status actors. *Academy of Management Journal, 63*(2), 530–553.

Katz, J. (1979). Concerted ignorance: The social construction of cover-up. *Urban Life, 8*(3), 295–316.

Keaveney, S. M. (2008). The blame game: An attribution theory approach to marketer-engineer conflict in high-technology companies. *Industrial Marketing Management, 37*, 653–663.

Kempa, M. (2010). Combating white-collar crime in Canada: Serving victim needs and market integrity. *Journal of Financial Crime, 17*(2), 251–264.

Khanna, V., Kim, E. H., & Lu, Y. (2015). CEO connectedness and corporate fraud. *The Journal of Finance, 70*, 1203–1252.

König, A., Graf-Vlachy, L., Bundy, J., & Little, L. M. (2020). A blessing and a curse: How CEOs' trait empathy affects their management of organizational crises. *Academy of Management Review, 45*(1), 130–153.

Kownatzki, M., Walter, J., Floyd, S. W., & Lechner, C. (2013). Corporate control and the speed of strategic business unit decision making. *Academy of Management Journal, 56*(5), 1295–1324.

Lanier, M. M., & Henry, S. (2009a). Chapter 3: Conflict and radical theories. In *Essential criminology* (3rd ed.). Westview, Member of the Perseus Books Group.

Lanier, M. M., & Henry, S. (2009b). Chapter 10: Capitalism as a criminogenic society – Conflict, Marxist, and radical theories of crime. In *Essential criminology* (3rd ed.). Westview, Member of the Perseus Books Group.

Lee, F., & Robinson, R. J. (2000). An attributional analysis of social accounts: Implications of playing the blame game. *Journal of Applied Social Psychology, 30*(9), 1853–1879.

Liang, L. H., Lian, H., Brown, D. J., Ferris, D. J., Hanig, S., & Keeping, L. M. (2016). Why are abusive supervisors abusive? A dual-system self-control model. *Academy of Management Journal, 59*(4), 1385–1406.

Long, C. P., Bendersky, C., & Morrill, C. (2011). Fairness monitoring: Linking managerial controls and fairness judgments in organizations. *Academy of Management Review, 54*(5), 1045–1068.

Mannucci, P. V., Orazi, D. C., & Valck, K. (2021). Developing improvisation skills: The influence of individual orientations. *Administrative Science Quarterly, 66*(3), 612–658.

Mawritz, M. B., Greenbaum, R. L., Butts, M. M., & Graham, K. A. (2017). I just can't control myself: A self-regulation perspective on the abuse of deviant employees. *Academy of Management Journal, 60*(4), 1482–1503.

McClelland, P. L., Liang, X., & Barker, V. L. (2010). CEO commitment to the status quo: Replication and extension using content analysis. *Journal of Management, 36*(5), 1251–1277.

McKinley, J. (2015, February 6). Settlement in suit against ex-lawmaker. *The New York Times*, p. A20.

Paruchuri, S., Han, J. H., & Prakash, P. (2021). Salient expectations? Incongruence across capability and integrity signals and investor reactions to organizational misconduct. *Academy of Management Journal, 64*(2), 562–586.

Patel, P. C., & Cooper, D. (2014). Structural power equality between family and nonfamily TMT members and the performance of family firms. *Academy of Management Journal, 57*(6), 1624–1649.

Petrocelli, M., Piquero, A. R., & Smith, M. R. (2003). Conflict theory and racial profiling: An empirical analysis of police traffic stop data. *Journal of Criminal Justice, 31*(1), 1–11.

Piening, E. P., Salge, T. O., Antons, D., & Kreiner, G. E. (2020). Standing together or falling apart? Understanding employees' responses to organizational identity threats. *Academy of Management Review, 45*(2), 325–351.

Pillay, S., & Kluvers, R. (2014). An institutional theory perspective on corruption: The case of a developing democracy. *Financial Accountability & Management, 30*(1), 95–119.

Podgor, E. S. (2007). The challenge of white collar sentencing. *Journal of Criminal Law and Criminology, 97*(3), 1–10.

Pontell, H. N., Black, W. K., & Geis, G. (2014). Too big to fail, too powerful to jail? On the absence of criminal prosecutions after the 2008 financial meltdown. *Crime, Law and Social Change, 61*(1), 1–13.

Pontell, H. N., Tillman, R., & Ghazi-Tehrani, A. K. (2021). In-your-face watergate: Neutralizing government lawbreaking and the war against white-collar crime. *Crime, Law and Social Change*. Published online https://doi.org/10.1007/s10611-021-09954-1, 19 pages.

Ragothaman, S. C. (2014). The Madoff debacle: What are the lessons? *Issues in Accounting Education, 29*(1), 271–285.

Rashbaum, W. K., & Kaplan, T. (2015, January 23). U.S. says assembly speaker took millions in payoffs, abusing office. *The New York Times*, pp. A1 and A24.

Schnatterly, K., Gangloff, K. A., & Tuschke, A. (2018). CEO wrongdoing: A review of pressure, opportunity, and rationalization. *Journal of Management, 44*(6), 2405–2432.

Seron, C., & Munger, F. (1996). Law and inequality: Race, gender…and, of course, class. *Annual Review of Sociology, 22*, 187–212.

Shen, W. (2003). The dynamics of the CEO-board relationship: An evolutionary perspective. *Academy of Management Review, 28*(3), 466–476.

Siegel, L. J. (2011). *Criminology* (11th ed.). Wadsworth Publishing.

Slyke, S. R. V., & Bales, W. D. (2013). Gender dynamics in the sentencing of white-collar offenders. *Criminal Justice Studies, 26*(2), 168–196.

Sonnier, B. M., Lassar, W. M., & Lassar, S. S. (2015). The influence of source credibility and attribution of blame on juror evaluation of liability of industry specialist auditors. *Journal of Forensic & Investigative Accounting, 7*(1), 1–37.

Spector, J. (2015, January 23). Lawmaker accused in graft scheme. *USA Today*, p. 4A.

Srivastava, S. B., & Goldberg, A. (2017). Language as a window into culture. *California Management Review, 60*(1), 56–69.

Sutherland, E. H. (1939). White-collar criminality. *American Sociological Review, 5*(1), 1–12.

Valentine, S. R., Hanson, S. K., & Fleischman, G. M. (2019). The presence of ethics codes and employees' internal locus of control, social aversion/malevolence, and ethical judgment of incivility: A study of smaller organizations. *Journal of Business Ethics, 160*, 657–674.

Veblen, T. (1899). *The theory of the leisure class: An economic study of institutions.* Macmillan.

Vega, T. (2015, February 6). Ex-state senate chief is guilty of bribery. *The New York Times*, p. A20.

Weick, K. E. (1995). What theory is not, theorizing is. *Administrative Science Quarterly, 40*, 385–390.

Wheelock, D., Semukhina, O., & Demidov, N. N. (2011). Perceived group threat and punitive attitudes in Russia and the United States. *British Journal of Criminology, 51*, 937–959.

Williams, J. W. (2008). The lessons of Enron: Media accounts, corporate crimes, and financial markets. *Theoretical Criminology, 12*(4), 471–499.

Yam, K. C., Christian, M. S., Wei, W., Liao, Z., & Nai, J. (2018). The mixed blessing of leader sense of humor: Examining costs and benefits. *Academy of Management Journal, 61*(1), 348–369.

Yue, L. Q., Luo, J., & Ingram, P. (2013). The failure of private regulation: Elite control and market crises in the Manhattan banking industry. *Administrative Science Quarterly, 58*(1), 37–68.

Zahra, S. A., Priem, R. L., & Rasheed, A. A. (2005). The antecedents and consequences of top management fraud. *Journal of Management, 31*, 803–828.

Zhong, R., & Robinson, S. L. (2021). What happens to bad actors in organizations? A review of actor-centric outcomes of negative behavior. *Journal of Management, 47*(6), 1430–1467.

Zhu, D. H., & Chen, G. (2015). CEO narcissism and the impact of prior board experience on corporate strategy. *Administrative Science Quarterly, 60*(1), 31–65.

Chapter 12
Bottom-Up Access Control

Corporate executive access to resources is the second opportunity theme in convenience theory. The perspective here is to discuss how a bottom-up approach to executive compliance can reduce the extent of white-collar crime convenience from executive access to resources. Access convenience themes listed in Fig. 2.2 are discussed in this chapter.

A white-collar offender has typically legitimate and convenient access to resources to commit crime (Füss & Hecker, 2008; Huisman & Erp, 2013; Lange, 2008; Pinto et al., 2008; Reyns, 2013). A resource is an enabler applied and used to satisfy human and organizational needs. A resource has utility and limited availability. According to Petrocelli et al. (2003), access to resources equates access to power. Other organizational members are losers in the competition for resources (Wheelock et al., 2011). In the conflict perspective suggested by Petrocelli et al. (2003), the upper class in society exercises its power and controls the resources. Valuable resources are typically scarce, unique, not imitable, not transferrable, combinable, exploitable, and not substitutable (Davis & DeWitt, 2021).

Restrictions on Access to Systems

White-collar crime can be distinguished from ordinary crime ("street crime") based on the status of offenders, their access to legitimate professions, the common presence of an organizational form, and the extent of the costs and harmfulness of such crime (Cullen et al., 2020). While street criminals hide themselves after an offense, white-collar criminals hide the offense while staying in the same positions (Michel, 2016). This is because they have legitimate access to premises and systems to commit financial crime (Benson & Simpson, 2018).

While executive access to premises and systems has to be monitored, customization and transmutation are needed to ensure that control mechanisms achieve the intended control outcomes based on executives' own assessment of their management challenges (Chown, 2021). Transmutation captures the idea that organizational units including management implement control regimes that are different from the mandated and general control mechanism of the organization. While there is no more need for trust regarding executive work versus others' work in an organization, control mechanisms implemented in management need to ensure intended control outcomes.

Berghoff and Spiekermann (2018: 291) argued that all economic transactions depend on a certain degree of trust, without which transaction costs would simply be too high for economic activity:

> White-collar criminals abuse the good faith of various stakeholders, from customers to the general public, from shareholders to the authorities. Therefore, white-collar crime often coincides with the breach of trust.

Offenders take advantage of their positions of power with almost unlimited authority in the opportunity structure (Kempa, 2010), because they have legitimate and often privileged access to physical and virtual locations in which crime is committed, are totally in charge of resource allocations and transactions, and are successful in concealment based on key resources used to hide their crime. Offenders have an economic motivation and opportunity (Huisman & Erp, 2013), linked to an organizational platform and availability and in a setting of people who do not know, do not care, or do not reveal the individual(s) with behavioral traits who commit crime. Opportunity includes people who are loyal to the criminal either as a follower or as a silent partner, for example, when the follower perceives ambitious goals as invariable.

In the rare case of detection of possible crime, the potential offender has access not only to better defense as a strategic resource but also often access to an alternative avenue of private investigation. When suspicion of misconduct and crime emerges, then the organization may hire a fraud examiner to conduct a private investigation into the matter. The enterprise takes control of suspicions by implementing an internal investigation. An external law firm or auditing firm is engaged to reconstruct past events and sequence of events. Typically, the resulting investigation report points to misconduct while at the same time concluding that there have been no criminal offenses. The police will monitor the internal investigation and await its conclusion. When the conclusion states that there may be misconduct, but no crime, then the police and prosecution tend to settle down with it (King, 2020).

However, the threat of dismissal following corporate scandals limits corporate involvement in executive destiny. Even when the executive is not necessarily to blame, the executive is a potential scapegoat that the organization deprives of access to resources. Dismissal occurs instantly, where the former privileged individual has no access anymore to defense attorneys, documents, or colleagues. The corporation has to survive at the expense of an executive (Ghannam et al., 2019).

Legitimate access to crime resources can be illustrated by the case of a chairman of the board who published his autobiography (Olav, 2014, 2015). The chairman used a tax haven where he had an account when he ran business through another company there (Bjørklund, 2018; Oslo tingrett, 2015). A tax haven is a country or place with very low or no rates of taxation for foreign investors, where foreigners enjoy complete secrecy about their investments. Money laundering of proceeds from criminal activity is an attractive opportunity in tax havens. On the legitimate side, the use of tax havens enables transfer-pricing strategies to lower overall tax burdens for multinational corporations. Subsidiaries located in tax havens serve multinationals to avoid taxes by shifting income from high-tax countries to low-tax countries. Firms also use tax havens in strategies that involve inter-company debt or leasing arrangements to shift income across jurisdictions. Tax authorities in various countries attempt to challenge this kind of tax evasion (Dyreng et al., 2019; Guenther et al., 2019). Chairman Olav was sentenced to 5 years in prison.

Disclosure of Entrepreneurialism

High social status in privileged positions is sometimes associated with entrepreneurship, where an entrepreneurial individual can create opportunities for deviant behavior (Ramoglou & Tsang, 2016). The entrepreneurship perspective emphasizes that entrepreneurs discover and create innovative and entrepreneurial opportunities (Smith, 2009; Tonoyan et al., 2010; Welter et al., 2017). Criminal entrepreneurs actualize illegal opportunities in the shadow economy (McElwee & Smith, 2015). Scheaf and Wood (2021: 2) found that entrepreneurial fraud has stimulated a wide array of research related to white-collar crime, where they provided the following definition of entrepreneurial fraud:

> Enterprising individuals (alone or in groups) deceiving stakeholders by sharing statements about their identity, individual capabilities, elements of new market offerings, and/or new venture activities that they know to be false in order to obtain something of value.

While the common understanding of entrepreneurship is focused on the positive and productive aspects, entrepreneurial fraud focuses on the dark aspects. It is all about deception used to obtain valuable resources from stakeholders (Scheaf & Wood, 2021).

Ramoglou and Tsang (2016: 738) argued that opportunities are not the result of innovation, discovery, or creation: "They are objectively existing propensities to be creatively actualized." Criminal entrepreneurs thus actualize illegal opportunities in the shadow economy (McElwee & Smith, 2015). Criminal entrepreneurship represents the dark side of entrepreneurialism. To understand entrepreneurial behavior by white-collar criminals, important behavioral areas include "modus essendi," "modus operandi," and "modus vivendi." Modus essendi is a philosophical term relating to modes of being. Modus operandi is method of operating, which is an accepted criminological concept for classifying generic human actions from their visible and consequential manifestations. Modus vivendi represents the shared symbiotic relationship between different entrepreneurial directions (Smith, 2009). Entrepreneurs are often important economic agents, driving forward employment, opportunities, and economic development. Entrepreneurship is associated with innovation, adaptation, change and dynamism, hard work, willpower, and overcoming challenges and struggles. According to Welter et al. (2017), entrepreneurship is a broadly available social technology for creating organizations that may pursue a myriad of goals. Tonoyan et al. (2010) found that viewing illegal business activities as a widespread business practice provides the rationale for entrepreneurs to justify their own corrupt activities.

Review of Specialized Access

White-collar offenders have legitimate access to premises (Benson & Simpson, 2018; Williams et al., 2019), and they have specialized access in routine activities (Cohen & Felson, 1979). The routine activity perspective suggests three conditions for crime to occur: a motivated offender, an opportunity in terms of a suitable target, and the absence of a capable or moral guardian. The existence or absence of a likely guardian represents an inhibitor or facilitator for crime. The premise of the routine activity perspective is that crime is to a minor extent affected by social causes such as poverty, inequality, and unemployment. Motivated offenders are individuals who are not only capable of committing criminal activity but are willing to do so. Suitable targets are financial sources that offenders consider particularly attractive. Lack of guardians is not only lack of protective rules and regulations, audits and controls, but also lack of mental models in the minds of potential offenders that reduce self-control against attraction from criminal acts. Reyns (2013) expanded the routine activity perspective into online routines where insider business cybercrime occurs without direct manual contact.

Corruption is a typical crime category among white-collar offenses. Lange (2008) defines organizational corruption as the pursuit of individual interests by one or more organizational actors through the intentional misdirection of organizational resources or perversion of organizational routines. Pinto et al. (2008) make a distinction between corrupt organizations and organizations of corrupt individuals. A corrupt organization is usually a top-down phenomenon in which a group of organizational members – typically, the dominant coalition, organizational elites, or top management team – undertakes corrupt actions. An organization of corrupt individuals is an emergent, bottom-up phenomenon in which informal processes facilitate personally corrupt behaviors that cross a critical threshold such that the organization deserves the characteristic of being corrupt.

Limits to Strategic Resources

A white-collar offender has usually access to resources that are valuable (application of the resource provides desired outcome), unique (very few have access to the resource), not imitable (resource cannot be copied), not transferrable (resource cannot be released from context), combinable with other resources (results in better outcome), exploitable (possible to apply in criminal activities), and not substitutable (cannot be replaced by a different resource). According to Petrocelli et al. (2003), access to resources equates access to power. Others are losers in the competition for resources (Wheelock et al., 2011). In the conflict perspective suggested by Petrocelli et al. (2003), the upper class in society exercises its power and controls the resources.

Opportunity is dependent on social capital available to the criminal. The structure and quality of social ties in hierarchical and transactional relationships shape opportunity structures. Social capital is the sum of actual or potential resources accruing to the criminal by virtue of his or her position in a hierarchy and in a network. Social capital accumulated by the individual in terms of actual and potential resources, which are accessible because of profession and position, creates a larger space for individual behavior and actions that others can hardly observe. Many initiatives by trusted persons in the elite are unknown and unfamiliar to others in the organization. Therefore, white-collar criminals do not expect consequences for themselves.

Allocation of control rights to strategic resources might vary with governance structures (Rashid et al., 2022). In addition, residual rights of control occur because of incomplete organizing of exchanges. Alvarez and Parker (2009) argued that incomplete contract theory suggests that the relevant party to an exchange should receive these residual rights in order to maximize its overall value for the organization. That is the party that expects to create the most value from the exchange.

The resource-based perspective postulates that differences in individuals' opportunities find explanation in the extent of resource access and the ability to combine and exploit those resources. Executives and other members of the elite are potential offenders that are able to commit financial crime to the extent that they have convenient access to resources suitable for illegal actions. Access to resources in the organizational dimension makes it more relevant and attractive to explore possibilities and avoid threats using financial crime. The willingness to exploit a resource for fraud and corruption increases when a potential offender has a perception of relative convenience. Criminal acts disappear from easy detection in a multitude of legal transactions in different contexts and different locations performed by different people. The organizational affiliation makes crime look like ordinary business. Offenders conceal economic crime among apparently legal activity. Offenders leverage resources that make it convenient to conceal crime among regular business transactions. In particular, businesses that practice secrecy rather than transparency enable convenient concealment of financial crime (Transparency, 2018). Chasing profits leaves people more creative in finding ways to make more legal as well as illegal profits for themselves and the organization, and people become more creative in concealing crime in various ways (Füss & Hecker, 2008). Offenders attempt to carry out crime in such a way that the risk of detection is minimal and even microscopic (Pratt & Cullen, 2005).

Strategic resources are normally used by executives in legitimate actions to achieve business objectives. Executives typically develop strategic plans, then mobilize strategic resources, and finally apply the resources in a process of strategic plan implantation. This is the typical top-down approach by the board and management in most organizations when conducting legitimate business activities.

In a bottom-up approach to prevent deviance by executives, strategic planning is not relevant. Rather, the opposite of planning is most effective. The opposite of planning followed by implementation at a later point in time is improvisation. Improvisation is defined as the spontaneous process by which planning and execution happen at the same time. It is the convergence of planning and execution such as the more proximate the design and solving in time, the more that activity is improvisational. Improvisation is a reactive, spontaneous action in response to unanticipated occurrences, in which law-abiding individuals find a way to manage the unexpected problem and thus sometimes create something novel in response to the unknown (Mannucci et al., 2021: 614):

> Drawing on these shared definitional elements, we developed a working definition of improvisation that we used as our compass as we navigated between theory and the field: improvisation is a spontaneous action in response to unanticipated occurrences that is characterized by the convergence of planning and execution.

Situated improvising is localized attempts to cope practically with novel complexities and accomplish specific tasks. It is distributed rather than focused and experimental rather than planned. The locus of change is practice, and a practitioner is the entrepreneur at work. Practitioners act as entrepreneurial change agents only to the extent their situated improvising break with the dominant logic in their field, but not in the sense that they deliberately intend to discard existing legal and institutional arrangements. It is the urgency of the work at hand that calls for improvising own handling of unknown complexity. Improvising thus generates institutional change that accidentally happens. It is propelled by the urgency of the challenge that directs the improvisation so that the improvisation itself is not random (Smets et al., 2012).

Mannucci et al. (2021) suggested stages of improvisation for knowledge workers such as attorneys in law firms discussed by Smets et al. (2012). Stages of growth models for maturity levels help to assess and evaluate a variety of phenomena (e.g., Masood, 2020; Röglinger et al., 2012; Solli-Sæther & Gottschalk, 2015). Stage models predict the development or evolution of improvisation maturity from basic performance to superior results (Iannacci et al., 2019: 310):

> They also suggest that this development is progressive (i.e., each successive stage is better than the previous one), stepwise (i.e., each step is a necessary prerequisite for the following step in the sequence), and prescriptive (i.e., each step must occur in a prescribed order in accordance with a pre-existing plan or vision), thus emphasizing the chain of successful events rather than the mechanisms by which subsequent stages come about.

Mannucci et al. (2021: 630) described their three-stage model from imitative improvisation via reactive improvisation to generative improvisation:

> In the initial stage of improvisation development, players' sensemaking process is limited by their basic understanding of structures. As they do not fully grasp how to initiate improvisational action in response to unexpected events, they develop imitative improvisation skills by observing and taking inspiration from others' improvisational actions (…) Over time, players complement imitative improvisation with the more reactive improvisation skills that extant literature typically describes. Reactive improvisation focuses on "what is happening" and "how to react." When improvising reactively, players engage in a sensemaking process to interpret unfolding events and develop an appropriate and original response (…) Some players further broaden their improvisation skillset by becoming the originators of unexpected events.

At the third level of generative improvisation, knowledge workers like elite law firm lawyers initiate improvisational actions without the need for an external trigger. They focus less on "what is happening" and "how to react" by directing their attention to "what could happen" and "how can I change what happens." The lawyer has a desire to co-create rather than just modify what will happen. Personal initiative is a core feature at generative improvisation (Mannucci et al., 2021).

References

Alvarez, S. A., & Parker, S. C. (2009). Emerging firms and the allocation of control rights: A bayesian approach. *Academy of Management Review, 34*(2), 209–227.

Benson, M. L., & Simpson, S. S. (2018). *White-collar crime: An opportunity perspective* (3rd ed.). Routledge.

Berghoff, H., & Spiekermann, U. (2018). Shady business: On the history of white-collar crime. *Business History, 60*(3), 289–304.

Bjørklund, I. (2018). *Må betale over 137 mill I erstatning* [Must pay over 137 million in compensation]. Daily Norwegian business newspaper *Dagens Næringsliv*. www.dn.no, published January 19.

Chown, J. (2021). The unfolding of control mechanisms inside organizations: Pathways of customization and transmutation. *Administrative Science Quarterly, 66*(3), 711–752.

Cohen, L. E., & Felson, M. (1979). Social change and crime rate trends: A routine activity approach. *American Sociological Review, 44*, 588–608.

Cullen, F. T., Chouhy, C., & Jonson, C. L. (2020). Chapter 14: Public opinion about white-collar crime. In M. L. Rorie (Ed.), *The handbook of white-collar crime* (pp. 211–228). Wiley.

Davis, G. F., & DeWitt, T. (2021). Organization theory and the resource-based view of the firm: The great divide. *Journal of Management, 47*(7), 1684–1697.

Dyreng, S. D., Hanlon, M., & Maydew, E. L. (2019). When does tax avoidance result in tax uncertainty? *The Accounting Review, 94*(2), 179–203.

Füss, R., & Hecker, A. (2008). Profiling white-collar crime. Evidence from German-speaking countries. *Corporate Ownership & Control, 5*(4), 149–161.

Ghannam, S., Bugeja, M., Matolcsy, Z. P., & Spiropoulos, H. (2019). Are qualified and experienced outside directors willing to join fraudulent firms and if so, why? *The Accounting Review, 94*(2), 205–227.

Guenther, D. A., Wilson, R. J., & Wu, K. (2019). Tax uncertainty and incremental tax avoidance. *The Accounting Review, 94*(2), 229–247.

Huisman, W., & Erp, J. (2013). Opportunities for environmental crime. *British Journal of Criminology, 53*, 1178–1200.

Iannacci, F., Seepma, A. P., Blok, C., & Resca, A. (2019). Reappraising maturity models in e-government research: The trajectory-turning point theory. *Journal of Strategic Information Systems, 28*, 310–329.

Kempa, M. (2010). Combating white-collar crime in Canada: Serving victim needs and market integrity. *Journal of Financial Crime, 17*(2), 251–264.

King, M. (2020). Out of obscurity: The contemporary private investigator in Australia. *International Journal of Police Science and Management.* Published online https://doi.org/10.1177/1461355720931887.

Lange, D. (2008). A multidimensional conceptualization of organizational corruption control. *Academy of Management Journal, 33*(3), 710–729.

Mannucci, P. V., Orazi, D. C., & Valck, K. (2021). Developing improvisation skills: The influence of individual orientations. *Administrative Science Quarterly, 66*(3), 612–658.

Masood, T. (2020). A machine learning approach for performance-oriented decision support in service-oriented architecture. *Journal of Intelligent Information Systems.* Published online https://doi.org/10.1007/s10844-020-00617-6.

McElwee, G., & Smith, R. (2015). Towards a nuanced typology of illegal entrepreneurship: A theoretical and conceptual overview. In G. McElwee & R. Smith (Eds.), *Exploring criminal and illegal enterprise: New perspectives on research, policy & practice* (Contemporary issues in entrepreneurship research) (Vol. 5). Bingley.

Michel, C. (2016). Violent street crime versus harmful white-collar crime: A comparison of perceived seriousness and punitiveness. *Critical Criminology, 24*, 127–143.

Olav, H. E. (2014). *Det store selvbedraget: Hvordan statsmakt ødelegger menneskeverd og velferd* [The grand self-deception: How state power harms human dignity and welfare]. Kolofon Publishing.

Olav, H. E. (2015). *The grand self-deception: A libertarian manifesto against the deep state – The failed welfare-taxation model of Norway.* Kindle Edition, printed in Great Britain by Amazon.

Oslo tingrett. (2015, January 12). Case number 14-067448MED-OTIR/06, *Oslo tingrett* (Oslo District Court).

Petrocelli, M., Piquero, A. R., & Smith, M. R. (2003). Conflict theory and racial profiling: An empirical analysis of police traffic stop data. *Journal of Criminal Justice, 31*(1), 1–11.

Pinto, J., Leana, C. R., & Pil, F. K. (2008). Corrupt organizations or organizations of corrupt individuals? Two types of organization-level corruption. *Academy of Management Review, 33*(3), 685–709.

Pratt, T. C., & Cullen, F. T. (2005). Assessing macro-level predictors and theories of crime: A meta-analysis. *Crime and Justice, 32*, 373–450.

Ramoglou, S., & Tsang, E. W. K. (2016). A realist perspective of entrepreneurship: Opportunities as propensities. *Academy of Management Review, 41*, 410–434.

Rashid, A., Al-Mamun, A., Roudaki, H., & Yasser, Q. R. (2022). An overview of corporate fraud and its prevention approach. *Australasian Accounting, Business and Finance Journal, 16*((1), Article 6), 101–118.

Reyns, B. W. (2013). Online routines and identity theft victimization: Further expanding routine activity theory beyond direct-contact offenses. *Journal of Research in Crime and Delinquency, 50*, 216–238.

Röglinger, M., Pöppelbuss, J., & Becker, J. (2012). Maturity model in business process management. *Business Process Management Journal, 18*(2), 328–346.

Scheaf, D. J., & Wood, M. S. (2021). Entrepreneurial fraud: A multidisciplinary review and synthesized framework. *Entrepreneurship: Theory and Practice*, pp. 1–36. Published online https://doi.org/10.1177/0422587211001818.

Smets, M., Morris, T., & Greenwood, R. (2012). From practice to field: A multilevel model of practice-driven institutional change. *Academy of Management Journal, 55*(4), 877–904.

Smith, R. (2009). Understanding entrepreneurial behavior in organized criminals. *Journal of Enterprising Communities: People and Places in the Global Economy, 3*(3), 256–268.

Solli-Sæther, H., & Gottschalk, P. (2015). Stages-of-growth in outsourcing, offshoring and back-sourcing: Back to the future? *Journal of Computer Information Systems, 55*(2), 88–94.

Tonoyan, V., Strohmeyer, R., Habib, M., & Perlitz, M. (2010). Corruption and entrepreneurship: How formal and informal institutions shape small firm behavior in transition and mature market economies. *Entrepreneurship: Theory & Practice, 34*(5), 803–831.

Transparency. (2018). Corruption perceptions index 2018. *Transparency International.* www.transparency.org/cpi2018

Welter, F., Baker, T., Audretsch, D. B., & Gartner, W. B. (2017). Everyday entrepreneurship: A call for entrepreneurship research to embrace entrepreneurial diversity. *Entrepreneurship: Theory and Practice, 41*(3), 323–347.

Wheelock, D., Semukhina, O., & Demidov, N. N. (2011). Perceived group threat and punitive attitudes in Russia and the United States. *British Journal of Criminology, 51*, 937–959.

Williams, M. L., Levi, M., Burnap, P. & Gundur, R. V. (2019). Under the corporate radar: Examining insider business cybercrime victimization through an application of routine activities theory. *Deviant Behavior, 40*(9), 1119–1131.

Chapter 13
Conclusion

All case studies in this book help illustrate the shortcomings of only legal perspectives in the work of fraud examiners when conducting internal investigations for client organizations. Bestseller headquartered in Denmark was dependent on the social license to operate and therefore terminated its business in Myanmar. Obos in Norway was dependent on member acceptance and will therefore avoid deviance from their basic idea of social housing. Samherji in Iceland was dependent on local acceptance by the government as well as citizens in the country and therefore made an apology for corruption, although without accepting the blame. Wirecard in Germany helplessly requested fraud examiners to provide a clean bill of health to continue their accounting manipulation.

Anecdotal evidence from these investigation reports illustrates the emerging perspective of the social license to operate becoming important. It seems not sufficient anymore for acceptance of business practice simply based on legal perspectives. In knowledge societies such as Denmark, Norway, Iceland, and Germany, citizens do not trust the criminal justice system to the extent that all forms of wrongdoing are covered in statutes and that all incidents of wrongdoing are prosecuted. In a criminological perspective, crime is defined by two characteristics. The first is that an incident is wrong. The second is that an incident should be punished. Crime is then wrongdoing that requires punishment, while law is statutory principles, which may or may not cover the specific wrongdoing. In this line of reasoning, Friedrichs (2020: 19) mentioned humanistic definition of crime:

> A humanistic definition of crime focuses on demonstrable harm, more often than not coming from powerful elements of society, rather than legal status as the basis for something being designated a crime.

Perceived seriousness has been studied as a factor that can influence the involvement or lack of involvement of the criminal justice system in cases of white-collar and corporate crime. For example, Cullen et al. (2020) studied public opinion about white-collar crime, and they found public willingness to punish white-collar

P. Gottschalk, *Financial Crime Issues*,
https://doi.org/10.1007/978-3-031-11213-3_13

offenders. However, they found that public opinion about inflicting punishment on white-collar criminals varies depending on clarity of culpability, typical harm, violation of trust, and need to show equity. Sources of authority for assessing violations of the social license to operate can, however, apply different criteria when determining the seriousness of wrongdoing.

There are important implications of perspectives presented in this book for future fraud examinations as well as corporate crime research. Fraud examiners might look beyond legal issues when conducting internal investigations in client organizations, as the reasons for harm and punishment might be found in social issues. Similarly, corporate crime research might consider punishment beyond the criminal justice system of prison and fine by looking at executive terminations and changes in business practices.

Studies as well as examinations of white-collar and corporate crime tend to apply the legal definition of crime where corporate escape from allegations and accusations is assumed if there is no involvement of the criminal justice system. The emerging perspective of a social license to operate tells a different story. As illustrated by case studies in this book, violations of the social license do have consequences. There is an interesting avenue here for future white-collar and corporate crime research in distinguishing between punishment from violations of the legal license and punishment from violations of the social license to operate where perceived seriousness can be introduced as an important factor.

References

Cullen, F. T., Chouhy, C., & Jonson, C. L. (2020). Chapter 14: Public opinion about white-collar crime. In M. L. Rorie (Ed.), *The handbook of white-collar crime* (pp. 211–228). Wiley.
Friedrichs, D. O. (2020). Chapter 2: White collar crime: Definitional debates and the case for a typological approach. In M. Rorie (Ed.), *The handbook of white-collar crime* (pp. 16–31). Wiley.

Bibliography

Agnew, R. (2014). Social concern and crime: Moving beyond the assumption of simple self-interest. *Criminology, 52*(1), 1–32.

Ashforth, B. E., Gioia, D. A., Robinson, S. L., & Trevino, L. K. (2008). Re-reviewing organizational corruption. *Academy of Management Review, 33*(3), 670–684.

Baba, S., Hemissi, O., Berrahou, Z., & Traiki, C. (2021). The spatiotemporal dimension of the social license to operate: The case of a landfill facility in Algeria. *Management Internationl – MI, 25*(4), 247–266.

Baer, M. D., Frank, E. L., Matta, F. K., Luciano, M. M., & Wellman, N. (2021). Untrusted, over-trusted, or just right? The fairness of (in)congruence between trust wanted and trust received. *Academy of Management Journal, 64*(1), 180–206.

Beare, M. E., & Martens, F. T. (1998). Policing organized crime. *Journal of Contemporary Criminal Justice, 14*(4), 398–427.

Benson, M. L. (1985). Denying the guilty mind: Accounting for involvement in a white-collar crime. *Criminology, 23*(4), 583–607.

Benson, M. L., & Simpson, S. S. (2018). *White-collar crime: An opportunity perspective* (3rd ed.). Routledge.

Bentzrød, S. B. (2022a). Jernbanen i Moss står bom fast i kvikkleire – For ett år siden fant Bane Nor mer kvikkleire i Moss sentrum enn de visste om (The railway in Moss is stuck in quick clay – A year ago, Bane Nor found more quick clay in the center of Moss than they knew about), daily Norwegian newspaper *Aftenposten*, Sunday, February 20, p. 1.

Bentzrød, S. B. (2022b). Aksjonsgruppe i Moss tapte ny rettssak – Lagmannsretten konkluderer med at vedtak som ble gjort om jernbaneutbygging i Moss var lovlig (Action group in Moss lost a new lawsuit – The court of appeal concludes that decisions made on railroad development in Moss were legal), daily Norwegian newspaper *Aftenposten*, Wednesday, February 23, p. 21.

Berghoff, H., & Spiekermann, U. (2018). Shady business: On the history of white-collar crime. *Business History, 60*(3), 289–304.

Bestseller. (2021). *Not placing new orders in Myanmar*, Bestseller, www.bestseller.com, published August 27.

Beukel, J., & Geuns, L. (2019). *Groningen gas: The loss of a social license to operate*. Hague Centre for Strategic Studies.

Bittle, S., & Hébert, J. (2020). Controlling corporate crimes in times of de-regulation and re-regulation, chapter 30. In M. L. Rorie (Ed.), *The handbook of white-collar crime* (pp. 484–501). Wiley & Sons.

P. Gottschalk, *Financial Crime Issues*,
https://doi.org/10.1007/978-3-031-11213-3

Bjarnadóttir, S. M. (2020). *Iceland's Involvement in Bribes and Corruption in Namibia's Fishing Industry – Discourse Analysis of the Media* (Master thesis in culture communication and globalization, September 15). Aalborg University.

Bloomberg. (2021). Jailed ex-Wirecard CEO sues chubb to pick up his legal bills, *Bloomberg*, www.bloomberg.com, published May 10.

Borgerud, I. M., Christensen, E., Finstad, L., Kassman, A., & Nylund, M. H. (2021, May 26). *Politikorrupsjon – Lederskap, risikoerkjennelse og læring (Police Corruption – Leadership, Risk Assessment and Learning)*. Report by the evaluation committee, Oslo, Norway.

Bosse, D. A., & Phillips, R. A. (2016). Agency theory and bounded self-interest. *Academy of Management Review, 41*(2), 276–297.

Bråthen, T., Fjørtoft, T., Refsholt, H., Minde, S. W., Kronborg, A. K., Allgot, B., & Boye, E. (2022, February 15). *Demokratiutvalgets innstilling (The democracy committee's recommendations)*, Obos, www.obos.no, Oslo.

Brooks, G., & Button, M. (2011). The police and fraud investigation and the case for a nationalized solution in the United Kingdom. *The Police Journal, 84*, 305–319.

Brustad, L., & Hustadnes, H. (2016). -Bjerke har forsømt lederansvaret uansett (-Bjerke has neglected the management responsibility regardless), daily Norwegian newspaper *Dagbladet*, www.dagbladet.no, published April 11.

Bruun Hjejle. (2018). *Report on the non-resident portfolio at Danske Bank's Estonian branch* (p. 87). Law Firm Bruun Hjejle.

Bugge, W. (2020). Wirecard-revisor i trøbbel for å ikke ha avdekket milliardsvindelen (Wirecard auditor in trouble for failing to uncover billionaire fraud), daily Norwegian business newspaper *Dagens Næringsliv*, www.dn.no, published June 26.

Buhmann, K. (2016). Public regulators and CSR: The 'social license to operate' in recent United Nations instruments on business and human rights and the juridification of CSR. *Journal of Business Ethics, 136*, 699–714.

Bundy, J., & Pfarrer, M. D. (2015). A burden of responsibility: The role of social approval at the onset of a crisis. *Academy of Management Review, 40*(3), 345–369.

Bunt, H. G., & Schoot, C. R. A. (2003). *Prevention of organised crime – A situational approach*. Willan Publishing.

Campbell, J. L., & Göritz, A. S. (2014). Culture corrupts! A qualitative study of organizational culture in corrupt organizations. *Journal of Business Ethics, 120*(3), 291–311.

Chan, J., Logan, S., & Moses, L. B. (2020). Rules in information sharing for security. *Criminology & Criminal Justice*. Published online pages 1–19. https://doi.org/10.1177/1748895820960199

Chazan, G. (2021). Wirecard given no 'privileged treatment' says German finance deputy, *Financial Times*, www.ft.com, published April 21.

Chazan, G., & Storbeck, O. (2020a). Wirecard: The scandal spreads to German politics, *Financial Times*, www.ft.com, published September 29.

Chazan, G., & Storbeck, O. (2020b). Wirecard's Markus Brown says regulators not to blame in scandal, *Financial Times*, www.ft.com, published November 20.

Chen, Y., & Moosmayer, D. C. (2020). When guilt is not enough: Interdependent self-construal as moderator of the relationship between guilt and ethical consumption in a Confucian context. *Journal of Business Ethics, 161*, 551–572.

Chown, J. (2021). The unfolding of control mechanisms inside organizations: Pathways of customization and transmutation. *Administrative Science Quarterly, 66*(3), 711–752.

Chrisman, J. J., Chua, J. H., Kellermanns, F. W., & Chang, E. P. C. (2007). Are family managers agents or stewards? An exploratory study in privately held family firms. *Journal of Business Research, 60*(10), 1030–1038.

Christoffersen, J., & Mikkelsen, M. S. (2021, May 10). *Redegjørelse: Bestseller A/S' samfundsansvar i Myanmar (Statement: Bestseller Ltd.'s social responsibility in Myanmar)* (p. 122). Law Firm Offersen Christoffersen.

Ciric, J. (2022). Namibia requests Interpol's aid in extraditing former Samherji executives, *Iceland Review*, www.icelandreview.com, published February 21.

Clifford Chance. (2020). *Report of investigation on Swedbank* (p. 218). Law Firm Clifford Chance.

Cotterill, J. (2019). Two Namibian ministers resign in Icelandic fishing scandal, *Financial Times*, www.ft.com, published November 14.

Cui, J., Jo, H., & Velasquez, M. G. (2016). Community religion, employees, and the social license to operate. *Journal of Business Ethics, 136*, 775–807.

Cullen, F. T., Chouhy, C., & Jonson, C. L. (2020). Public opinion about white-collar crime, chapter 14. In M. L. Rorie (Ed.), *The handbook of white-collar crime* (pp. 211–228). Wiley & Sons.

Davidson, J., & Gottschalk, P. (2012). *Police deviance and criminality – Managing integrity and accountability*. Nova Science Publishers.

Demuijnck, G., & Fasterling, B. (2016). The social license to operate. *Journal of Business Ethics, 136*, 675–685.

Desai, V. M. (2016). Under the radar: Regulatory collaborations and their selective use to facilitate organizational compliance. *Academy of Management Journal, 59*(2), 636–657.

Desmond, S. A., Rorie, M., & Sohoni, T. (2022). Working for God: Religion and occupational crime and deviance. *Deviant Behavior*, published online https://doi.org/10.1080/01639625.2021.2022968.

Direnzo, M. S., & Greenhaus, J. H. (2011). Job search and voluntary turnover in a boundaryless world: A control theory perspective. *Academy of Management Review, 36*(3), 567–589.

Dodge, M. (2009). *Women and white-collar crime*. Prentice Hall.

Durand, R., Hawn, O., & Ioannou, I. (2019). Willing and able: A general model of organizational responses to normative pressures. *Academy of Management Review, 44*(2), 299–320.

Eberl, P., Geiger, D., & Assländer, M. S. (2015). Repairing trust in an organization after integrity violations. The ambivalence of organizational rule adjustments. *Organization Studies, 36*(9), 1205–1235.

Eggen, S., Andersen, G., Tommelstad, B., Widerøe, R. J., Hengingeng, T., & Hopperstad, M. S. (2016). Han var politiets 'wonderboy' – Nå er Eirik Jensen korrupsjonssiktet (He was the police 'wonderboy' – Now Eirik Jensen is charged with corruption). Daily Norwegian newspaper *VG*, www.vg.no, published February 12.

Einarsdottir, I. E. (2021). Bestseller får kritikk for påståtte militærforbindelser i kriserammede Myanmar (Bestseller receives criticism for alleged military connections in crisis-stricken Myanmar), fashion industry magazine *Melk & Honning*, www.melkoghonning.no, published April 20.

Eisenhardt, K. M. (1989). Agency theory: An assessment and review. *Academy of Management Review, 14*(1), 57–74.

Ekroll, H. C., Breian, Å., & NTB (2019). Økokrim starter etterforskning av DNB i forbindelse med islandsk fiskerisak (Økokrim is launching an investigation into DNB related to the Icelandic fisheries case), daily Norwegian newspaper *Aftenposten*, www.aftenposten.no, published November 29.

Eren, C. P. (2020). Cops, firefighters, and scapegoats: Anti-money laundering (AML) professionals in an era of regulatory bulimia. *Journal of White Collar and Corporate Crime*, 1–12. Published online https://doi.org/10.1177/2631309X20922153

Erikstad, T. (2020). Wirecard kan ha blitt tappet for midler før konkurs (Wirecard may have been drained of funds before bankruptcy), daily Norwegian business newspaper *Dagens Næringsliv*, www.dn.no, published August 11.

Ernst & Young. (2022, February 14). *Rapport Vestre Toten kommune til Kontrollutvalget (Report Vestre Toten Municipality to the Control Committee)*. Audit Firm Ernst & Young.

Finanstilsynet. (2020, December 4). Tilsynsrapport fra undersøkelser av DNBs etterlevelse av hvitvaskingsloven (Review report from investigation of DNB's compliance with the Money Laundering Act), The Financial Supervisory Authority of Norway, www.finanstilsynet.no

Fitzgibbon, W., & Lea, J. (2018). Privatization and coercion: The question of legitimacy. *Theoretical Criminology, 22*(4), 545–562.

Fjeld, J. T. (2020). BI-professor: -Justismord (BI professor: -miscarriage of justice), daily Norwegian newspaper *Dagbladet*, www.dagbladet.no, published June 19.

Friedrichs, D. O. (2020). White collar crime: Definitional debates and the case for a typological approach, chapter 2. In M. Rorie (Ed.), *The handbook of white-collar crime* (pp. 16–31). Wiley.

Galvin, B. M., Lange, D., & Ashforth, B. E. (2015). Narcissistic organizational identification: Seeing oneself as central to the organization's identity. *Academy of Management Review, 40*(2), 163–181.

Gangloff, K. A., Connelly, B. L., & Shook, C. L. (2016). Of scapegoats and signals: Investor reactions to CEO succession in the aftermath of wrongdoing. *Journal of Management, 42*, 1614–1634.

Garoupa, N. (2007). Optimal law enforcement and criminal organization. *Journal of Economic Behaviour & Organization, 63*, 461–474.

Gill, M. J. (2019). The significance of suffering in organizations: Understanding variation in workers' responses to multiple modes of control. *Academy of Management Review, 44*(2), 377–404.

Goldstraw-White, J. (2012). *White-collar crime: Accounts of offending behavior*. Palgrave Macmillan.

Gomulya, D., & Mishina, Y. (2017). Signaler credibility, signal susceptibility, and relative reliance on signals: How stakeholders change their evaluative processes after violation of expectations and rehabilitative efforts. *Academy of Management Journal, 60*(2), 554–583.

Gottschalk, P. (2012). White-collar crime and police crime: Rotten apples or rotten barrels? *Critical Criminology, 20*(2), 169–182.

Gottschalk, P. (2016). Private policing of financial crime: Key issues in the investigation business in Norway. *European Journal of Policing Studies, 3*(3), 292–314.

Gottschalk, P. (2018). Opportunistic behavior in the principal-agent model of policing: The case of a convicted field officer in Norway. *International Journal of Police Science & Management, 20*(2), 109–115.

Gottschalk, P. (2020). Private policing of white-collar crime: Case studies of internal investigations by fraud examiners. *Police Practice and Research, 21*(6), 717–738.

Gottschalk, P. (2021). *Private policing of economic crime – Case studies of internal investigations by fraud examiners*. Routledge.

Gottschalk, P., & Benson, M. L. (2020). The evolution of corporate accounts of scandals from exposure to investigation. *British Journal of Criminology, 60*, 949–969.

Gottschalk, P., & Gunnesdal, L. (2018). *White-collar crime in the shadow economy: Lack of detection, investigation, and conviction compared to social security fraud*. Palgrave Pivot, Palgrave Macmillan, Springer Publishing, UK.

Gottschalk, P., & Markovic, V. (2016). Transnational criminal organizations (TCOs). The case of combating criminal biker gangs. *International Journal of Criminal Justice Sciences, 11*(1), 30–44.

Gottschalk, P., & Tcherni-Buzzeo, M. (2017). Reasons for gaps in crime reporting: The case of white-collar criminals investigated by private fraud examiners in Norway. *Deviant Behavior, 38*(3), 267–281.

Grimstad, E. (2021). *Rapport etter saksbehandling av varslingssak i Nittedal kommune (Report after case processing of notification case in Nittedal municipality)* (p. 29). Law Firm Grimstad.

Grønningsæter, F. (2022). Russlands svarte økonomi (Russia's black economy), Norwegian business magazine. *Kapital, 5*, 16–23.

Haines, F., Bice, S., Einfeld, C., & Sullivan, H. (2022). Countering corporate power through social control: What does a social licence offer? *The British Journal of Criminology, 62*, 184–199.

Håkensbakken, S. (2022). Vestre Toten må forstå hvorfor det har blitt som det har blitt (Vestre Toten must understand why it has become as it has become), daily local newspaper *Oppland Arbeiderblad*, www.oa.no, published February 15.

Håland, S. (2020). De elendige: Hva feiler det tyske banker? (The miserable: What is wrong with German banks?), daily Norwegian business newspaper *Dagens Næringsliv*, www.dn.no, published July 27.

Harenbrock, K., & Mergenthaler, T. (2021). Wirecard shareholders pay the price for fraud scandal, Deutsche Welle, www.dw.com, published March 19.

Harfield, C. (2008). Paradigms, pathologies, and practicalities – Policing organized crime in England and Wales. *Policing, 2*(1), 63–73.

Hegtun, H. (2021). Granskere har gått inn i PC-en og telefonen hans. «Helt greit», sier presset Obos-sjef (Investigators have entered the PC and his phone. "Quit all right", says the Obos boss, weekly magazine *A-magasinet*, www.aftenposten.no, published June 12.

Hjort. (2016). *Rapport til styret i DNB (report to the board at DNB), bank mentioned in the Panama Papers, report of investigation* (p. 18). Law Firm Hjort.

Holm, E. D. (2021). Er Obos løsningen eller problemet? (Is Obos the solution or the problem?), daily Norwegian newspaper *Aftenposten*, www.aftenposten.no, published June 21.

Huang, L., & Knight, A. P. (2017). Resources and relationships in entrepreneurship: An exchange theory of the development and effects of the entrepreneur-investor relationship. *Academy of Management Review, 42*(1), 80–102.

Hurst, B., Johnston, K. A., & Lane, A. B. (2020). Engaging for a social license to operate. *Public Relations Review, 40*. Published online https://doi.org/10.1016/j.pubrev.2020.101931

Ismail, K. (2022). Swedbanks tidligere ledelse i Estland mistenkt for hvitvasking (Swedbank's former management in Estland suspected of money laundering), daily Norwegian business newspaper *Dagens Næringsliv*, Monday, March 28, p. 7.

Ivkovic, S. K. (2009). The Croatian police, police integrity, and transition toward democratic policing. *Policing: An International Journal of Police Strategies and Management, 32*(3), 459–488.

Jacobsen, S. (2020). Har solgt 182 leiligheter for 936 millioner (Have sold 182 apartments for 936 million), daily Norwegian business newspaper *Finansavisen*, www.finansavisen.no, published December 3.

Johannessen, S. Ø., & Christensen, J. (2020). Swedbank vil ikke betale sluttpakke til toppsjef som matte gå av etter hvitvaskingsskandale (Swedbank will not pay final package to top executive who had to leave after money laundering scandal), daily Norwegian business newspaper *Dagens Næringsliv*, www.dn.no, published March 23.

Johnsen, N. (2014). Frank Aarebrot om first house: -vi vet ikke hvem de representerer (Frank Aarebrot about first house: -we do not know who they represent), daily Norwegian newspaper *VG*, www.vg.no, published May 21.

Jonnergård, K., Stafsudd, A., & Elg, U. (2010). Performance evaluations as gender barriers in professional organizations: A study of auditing firms. *Gender, Work and Organization, 17*(6), 721–747.

Jordanoska, A. (2018). The social ecology of white-collar crime: Applying situational action theory to white-collar offending. *Deviant Behavior, 39*(11), 1427–1449.

Jørgensen, G., & Mannsåker, H. (2022). Blir sjuk av støyen fra vindturbinene (Get sick from the noise from the wind turbines), Norwegian Public Broadcasting *NRK*, www.nrk.no, published February 21.

Jung, J. C., & Sharon, E. (2019). The Volkswagen emissions scandal and its aftermath. *Global Business & Organizational Excellence, 38*(4), 6–15.

Kagge, G. (2021). Merkel må forklare seg om hjelp til selskap anklaget for milliardsvindel (Merkel must explain herself about help to companies accused of billion fraud), daily Norwegian newspaper *Aftenposten*, Thursday, April 22, p. 24.

Kakkar, H., Sivanathan, N., & Globel, M. S. (2020). Fall from grace: The role of dominance and prestige in punishment of high-status actors. *Academy of Management Journal, 63*(2), 530–553.

Kamerdze, S., Loughran, T., Paternoster, R., & Sohoni, T. (2014). The role of affect in intended rule breaking: Extending the rational choice perspective. *Journal of Research in Crime and Delinquency, 51*(5), 620–654.

Kibar, O. (2020a). Varsleren (the whistleblower), daily Norwegian business newspaper *Dagens Næringsliv*, Saturday, August 8, pp. 32–37.

Kibar, O. (2020b). Både ryddet opp for og gransket fiskerikjempe (Both cleaned up and investigated fishing giant), daily Norwegian business newspaper *Dagens Næringsliv*, Tuesday, September 1, pp. 18–19.

Kim, P. H., Dirks, K. T., & Cooper, C. D. (2009). The repair of trust: A dynamic bilateral perspective and multilevel conceptualization. *Academy of Management Review, 34*(3), 401–422.

King, M. (2012). The contemporary role of private investigators in Australia. *Criminal Justice Matters, 89*(1), 12–14.

King, M. (2020). Financial fraud investigative interviewing – Corporate investigators' beliefs and practices: A qualitative inquiry. *Journal of Financial Crime.* Published online https://doi.org/10.1108/JFC-08-2020-0158

King, M. (2021). Profiting from a tainted trade: Private investigators' views on the popular culture glamorization of their trade. *Journal of Criminological Research Policy and Practice.* Published online https://doi.org/10.1108/JCRPP-07-2020-0050

Kleinfeld, J. (2019). Anatomy of a Bribe: A deep dive into an underworld of corruption, news organization *Al Jazeera*, www.aljazeera.com, published December 1.

Kleinfeld, J. (2020). Corruption allegations in Namibian 5G deal with Huawei, news organization *Al Jazeera*, www.aljazeera.com, published July 15.

Kleinfeld, J. (2021). Namibian president caught in new fishing corruption allegations, news organization *Al Jazeera*, www.aljazeera.com, published April 2.

König, A., Graf-Vlachy, L., Bundy, J., & Little, L. M. (2020). A blessing and a curse: How CEOs' trait empathy affects their management of organizational crisis. *Academy of Management Review, 45*(1), 130–153.

Kostova, T., Roth, K., & Dacin, M. T. (2008). Institutional theory in the study of multinational corporations: A critique and new directions. *Academy of Management Review, 33*(4), 994–1006.

Kownatzki, M., Walter, J., Floyd, S. W., & Lechner, C. (2013). Corporate control and the speed of strategic business unit decision making. *Academy of Management Journal, 56*(5), 1295–1324.

KPMG. (2020, April 27). *Report concerning the independent special investigation at Wirecard AG* (p. 74). Audit Firm KPMG.

KPMG. (2021). *Ulven-transaksjonen – Granskingsrapport til styret i Obos (The Ulven transaction – Investigation report to the board at Obos)* (p. 34). Law Firm KPMG.

Lange, D., Bundy, J., & Park, E. (2022). The social nature of stakeholder utility. *Academy of Management Review, 47*(19), 9–30.

Langset, M., Ertesvåg, F., & Ensrud, S. (2016). BI-professor: -Det vil bli rettssaker (BI professor: -there will be court cases), daily Norwegian newspaper *VG*, Wednesday, April 6, p. 7.

Langton, L., & Piquero, N. L. (2007). Can general strain theory explain white-collar crime? A preliminary investigation of the relationship between strain and select white-collar offenses. *Journal of Criminal Justice, 35*, 1–15.

Larsen, B. E. (2021a). Noen betraktninger før Obos' generalforsamling 2021 (Some considerations before Obos' general assembly 2021), *Benjamin E. Larsen's blog*, www.benjaminlarsen.net, posted June 19.

Larsen, M. (2021b). Danish company Bestseller urges EU to take action on Myanmar, *ScandAsia*, Nordic News and Business Promotion in Asia, www.scandasia.com, published April 21.

Leigh, A. C., Foote, D. A., Clark, W. R., & Lewis, J. L. (2010). Equity sensitivity: A triadic measure and outcome/input perspectives. *Journal of Managerial Issues, 22*(3), 286–305.

Leinfelt, F., & Rostami, A. (2012). *The Stockholm gang model – Panther – Stockholm gang intervention and prevention project.* Stockholm County Police.

Li, S., & og Ouyang, M. (2007). A dynamic model to explain the bribery behavior of firms. *International Journal of Management, 24*(3), 605–618.

Lorch-Falch, S., & Tomter, L. (2021). Slaget om Obos (The battle of Obos), public Norwegian broadcasting corporation *NRK*, www.nrk.no, published June 22.

Lorch-Falch, S., Tomter, L., & Lydersen, T. (2020). Nekter å vise frem regnestykkene som feilet (Refuses to show the calculations that failed), Norwegian Public Broadcasting *NRK*, www.nrk.no, published October 9.

Lorch-Falch, S., Tomter, L., & Engebretsen, D.K. (2021). Obos-opprøret tapte kamp om maktseter (The Obos uprising lost the battle for seats), Norwegian Public Broadcasting *NRK*, www.nrk.no, published June 22.

Loyens, K., Claringbould, I., Heres-van Rossem, L., & van Eekeren, F. (2021). The social construction of integrity: A qualitative case study in Dutch football. *Sports in Society*. Published online https://doi.org/10.1080/17430437.2021.1877661

Lundgaard, H. (2022). Hun hadde ikke sjanse til å kjøpe leilighet. Nå skal flere tusen få samme muligheten (She had no chance of buying an apartment. Now several thousand will have the same opportunity), daily Norwegian newspaper *Aftenposten*, Thursday, February 24, p. 6.

Lundgaard, H., & Sørgjeld, C. (2021). Milliardene renner inn i Obos-kassen. Men mer enn 80 prosent kommer ikke fra boligbygging (The billions are floating into the Obos cash register. But more than 80 percent do not come from housing construction), daily Norwegian newspaper *Aftenposten*, www.aftenposten.no, published June 21.

Madshus, K., & Hageskal, A. (2019). Langer ut mot politiet etter Jensen-saken, daily Norwegian newspaper *Dagbladet*, www.dagbladet.no, published January 30.

Mannucci, P. V., Orazi, D. C., & Valck, K. (2021). Developing improvisation skills: The influence of individual orientations. *Administrative Science Quarterly, 66*(3), 612–658.

Maslow, A. H. (1943). A theory of human motivation. *Psychological Review, 50*(4), 370–396.

Mauno, H. (2017). Han er pinsevenn og BMW-eier. Men ikke si at han er fra Flekkefjord (He is a Pentecostal friend and BMW owner. But do not say that he is from Flekkefjord), daily Norwegian newspaper *Dagsavisen*, www.dagsavisen.no, published June 25.

McClean, E. J., Martin, S. R., Emich, K. J., & Woodruff, T. (2018). The social consequences of voice: An examination of voice type and gender on status and subsequent leader emergence. *Academy of Management Journal, 61*(5), 1869–1891.

McCrum, D. (2015). The house of Wirecard, *Financial Times*, www.ft.com, published April 27.

McCrum, D. (2019). Wirecard's suspect accounting practices revealed, *Financial Times*, www.ft.com, published October 15.

McCrum, D. (2020). Wirecard: The timeline, *Financial Times*, www.ft.com, published June 25.

Meerts, C. (2020). Corporate investigations: Beyond notions of public-private relations. *Journal of Contemporary Criminal Justice, 36*(1), 86–100.

Meerts, C. (2021). Struggles in cooperation: Public-private relations in the investigation of internal financial crime in the Netherlands. In N. Lord, E. Inzelt, W. Huisman, & R. Faria (Eds.), *European white-collar crime: Exploring the nature of European realities*. Bristol University Press.

Meixler, E., & Creery, J. (2022). EU targets Myanmar's lucrative energy sector in latest sanctions. *Financial Times*, www.ft.com, published February 22.

Melé, D., & Armengou, J. (2016). Moral legitimacy in controversial projects and its relationships with social license to operate: A case study. *Journal of Business Ethics, 136*, 729–742.

Menges, W. (2020). Fishrot lawyer fights to stay on as executor, *The Namibian*, www.namibian.com, published August 6.

Mesmer-Magnus, J. R., & Viswesvaran, C. (2005). Whistleblowing in an organization: An examination of correlates of whistleblowing intentions, actions, and retaliation. *Journal of Business Ethics, 62*(3), 266–297.

Mikalsen, K. S., Gustavsen, Ø., Acharki, F., & Vissgren, J. (2020). Ordføreren i Nittedal er tiltalt for grov korrupsjon (The mayor of Nittedal is accused of gross corruption), Norwegian Public Broadcasting Corporation *NRK*, www.nrk.no, published December 16.

Mitnick, B. M. (1975). The theory of agency: The policing 'paradox' and regulatory behavior. *Public Choice, 24*(1), 27–42.

Mjelde, K. N. (2022). Obos-selskap får krass kritikk og bot (Obos company receives harsh criticism and fine), daily Norwegian business newspaper *Dagens Næringsliv*, Friday, February 25, p. 31.

Mpho, B. (2017). Whistleblowing: What do contemporary ethical theories say? *Studies in Business and Economics, 12*(1), 19–28.

Mulinari, S., Davis, C., & Ozieranski, P. (2021). Failure of responsive regulation? Pharmaceutical marketing, corporate impression management and off-label promotion of enzalutamide in Europe. *Journal of White Collar and Corporate Crime, 2*(2), 69–80.

Müller, S. M. (2018). Corporate behavior and ecological disaster: Dow chemical and the Great Lakes mercury crisis, 1970–1972. *Business History, 60*(3), 399–422.

Nason, R. S., Bacq, S., & Gras, D. (2018). A behavioral theory of social performance: Social identity and stakeholder expectations. *Academy of Management Review, 43*(2), 259–283.

Oesterud, T. I. (2016). The prices for OBOS housing in Oslo increased by 11.5 percent, *Norway Today*, www.norwaytoday.info, published April 1.

Panda, S. S., & Sangle, S. (2019). An exploratory study to investigate the relationship between social license to operate and sustainable development strategies. *Sustainable Development, 27*, 1085–1095.

Park, H., Bjørkelo, B., & Blenkinsopp, J. (2020). External whistleblowers' experiences of workplace bullying by superiors and colleagues. *Journal of Business Ethics, 161*, 591–601.

Paruchuri, S., Han, J. H., & Prakash, P. (2021). Salient expectations? Incongruence across capability and integrity signals and investor reactions to organizational misconduct. *Academy of Management Journal, 64*(2), 562–586.

Paternoster, R., Jaynes, C. M., & Wilson, T. (2018). Rational choice theory and interest in the "fortune of others". *Journal of Research in Crime and Delinquency, 54*(6), 847–868.

Paybarah, A. (2021). Burning of police station after George Floyd's death draws 4-year sentence, *The New York Times*, www.nytimes.com, published April 28.

Petrocelli, M., Piquero, A. R., & Smith, M. R. (2003). Conflict theory and racial profiling: An empirical analysis of police traffic stop data. *Journal of Criminal Justice, 31*(1), 1–11.

Piening, E. P., Salge, T. O., Antons, D., & Kreiner, G. E. (2020). Standing together or falling apart? Understanding employees' responses to organizational identity threats. *Academy of Management Review, 45*(2), 325–351.

Pillay, S., & Kluvers, R. (2014). An institutional theory perspective on corruption: The case of a developing democracy. *Financial Accountability & Management, 30*(1), 95–119.

Poensgen, K., Mikalsen, K. S., & Tolfsen, C. (2020). Ordføreren i Nittedal er siktet for grov korrupsjon (The mayor of Nittedal is charged with gross corruption), Norwegian Public Broadcasting Corporation *NRK*, www.nrk.no, published June 23.

Prenzler, T., & Lewis, C. (2005). Performance indicators for police oversight. *Australian Journal of Public Administration, 64*(2), 77–83.

Punch, M. (2003). Rotten orchards. «Pestilence», police misconduct and system failure. *Policing and Society, 13*(2), 171–196.

PwC. (2022). *Nittedal kommune: Håndtering av varsel mot ordfører (Nittedal municipality: Handling of notification against mayor), fraud investigation report*. PricewaterhouseCoopers.

Reed, J. (2022). Stay or go: The dilemma for multinationals in Myanmar, *Financial Times*, www.ft.com, published January 25.

Reed, J., & Nilsson, P. (2021). H&M and Primark resume Myanmar orders for first time since coup, *Financial Times*, www.ft.com, published May 21.

Rehg, M. T., Miceli, M. P., Near, J. P., & Scotter, J. R. V. (2009). Antecedents and outcomes of retaliation against whistleblowers: Gender differences and power relationships. *Organization Science, 19*(2), 221–240.

Reuters. (2019). Norway's DNB investigates allegedly improper Samherji payments to Namibia, *Under Current News*, www.undercurrentnews.com, published November 15.

Reuters. (2020). Germany's DAX index gets shake-up in wake of Wirecard scandal, *Reuters*, www.reuters.com, published November 24.

Ritzau. (2021). Kofod fortørnet over Bestsellers brug af fabrikker i Myanmar (Kofod upset over Bestseller's use of factories in Myanmar), Danish broadcasting *TV2*, www.nyheder.tv2.dk, published April 18.

Rooney, D., Leach, J., & Ashworth, P. (2014). Doing the social in social license. *Social Epistemology, 28*(3–4), 209–218.

Routh, R. (2022). Kanyangela accused of 'holding back', *New Era*, www.neweralive.na, published February 22.

Saenz, C. (2019). Building legitimacy and trust between a mining company and a community to earn social license to operate: A Peruvian case study. *Corporate Social Responsibility and Environmental Management, 26*(2), 296–306.

Sale, H. A. (2021). The corporate purpose of social license. *Sothern California Law Review, 94*(4), 785–842.

Samherji. (2019a). *Statement from Samherji: Press release*, www.samherji.is, published November 11 by margret@samherji.is.

Samherji. (2019b). *Samherji CEO steps aside while investigations are ongoing*, www.samherji.is, published November 14 by margret@samherji.is.

Samherji. (2020a). *Samherji's Namibia investigation finalized*, Samherji ice fresh seafood, website https://www.samherji.is/en/moya/news/samherjis-namibia-investigation-finalized, Akureyri, Iceland, published by margret@samherji.is.

Samherji (2020b). *Fees for quotas were in line with market prices in Namibia*, Samherji seafood, www.samherji.is, published September 25 by Margrét Ólafsdóttir, margret@samherji.is.

Samherji. (2021). *Statement and apology from Samherji*, Samherji seafood, www.samherji.is, published June 22.

Sanger, S. W., Duke, E. A., James, D. M., & Hernandez, E. (2017, April 10). *Independent directors of the Board of Wells Fargo & Company: Sales practices investigation report* (pp. 113). https://www08.wellsfargomedia.com/assets/pdf/about/investor-relations/presentations/2017/board-report.pdf. Downloaded 2018, September 7.

Schoen, J. L., DeSimone, J. A., Meyer, R. D., Schnure, K. A., & LeBreton, J. M. (2021). Identifying, defining, and measuring justification mechanisms: The implicit biases underlying individual differences. *Journal of Management, 47*(3), 716–744.

Schoultz, I., & Flyghed, J. (2021). Performing unbelonging in court – Observations from a transnational corporate bribery trial – A dramaturgical approach. *Crime, Law and Social Change*. Published online https://doi.org/10.1007/s10611-021-09990-x

Schultz, J. (2019). Wikborg Rein-gransker om Samherji: -Planen er å være ute av Namibia innen få måneder (Wikborg Rein investigator about Samherji: -The plan is to be out of Namibia within a few months, daily Norwegian business newspaper *Dagens Næringsliv*, www.dn.no, published December 1.

Schultz, J., & Trumpy, J. (2019a). NRK: DNB brukte mer enn et år på å stenge Samherji-kontoer (NRK: DNB spent more than a year to close Samherji accounts), Norwegian daily business newspaper *Dagens Næringsliv*, www.dn.no, published August 26.

Schultz, J., & Trumpy, J. (2019b). Björgolfur Johannsson ble Samherji-sjef etter hvitvaskingsavsløring: -Jeg tror ikke det har vært noen bestikkelser, Norwegian daily business newspaper *Dagens Næringsliv*, www.dn.no, published December 13.

Seljan, H., Kjartansson, A., & Drengsson, S. A. (2019). What Samherji wanted hidden, Kveikur at *RUV*, public broadcasting on Iceland, www.ruv.is/kveikur/fishrot/fishrot

Shadnam, M., & Lawrence, T. B. (2011). Understanding widespread misconduct in organizations: An institutional theory of moral collapse. *Business Ethics Quarterly, 21*(3), 379–407.

Shawver, T., & Clements, L. H. (2019). The impact of value preferences on whistleblowing intentions of accounting professionals. *Journal of Forensic and Investigative Accounting, 11*(2), 232–247.

Shepardson, D., & Burden, M. (2014). GM recalls 778K cars to replace ignition switches after fatal crashes, *Detroit News*, February 13, https://infoweb.newsbank.com/apps/news/document-view?p=AWNB&t=&sort=YMD_date%3AA&maxresults=20&f=advanced&val-base-0=ignition%20switch%20failure&fld-base-0=alltext&bln-base-1=and&val-base-1=GM&fld-base-1=alltext&bln-base-2=and&val-base-2=cobalt&fld-base-2=alltext&bln-base-3=and&val-base-3=2014&fld-base-3=YMD_date&bln-base-4=and&val-base-4=learned&fld-base-4=alltext&docref=news/14BF79CC1A B3B180

Shepherd, D., & Button, M. (2019). Organizational inhibitions to addressing occupational fraud: A theory of differential rationalization. *Deviant Behavior, 40*(8), 971–991.

Sheptycki, J. (2007). Police ethnography in the house of serious and organized crime. In A. Henry & D. J. Smith (Eds.), *Transformations of policing* (pp. 51–77). Ashgate.

Skolnick, J. H. (2002). Corruption and the blue code of silence. *Police Practice & Research, 3*(1), 7–19.

Solberg, F. (2022). Rydd opp i våre medlemseide organisasjoner som eksempelvis Coop og Tobb (Clean up our member-owned organizations such as Coop and Tobb), web-based discussion forum *Trønderdebatt*, www.tronderdebatt.no, published March 29.

Solgård, J. (2020). «Bestemors favorittbank» ga milliardlån til tidligere Wirecard-sjef («Grandma's favorite bank» gave billions in loans to former Wirecard boss), daily Norwegian business newspaper *Dagens Næringsliv*, www.dn.no, published July 9.

Solgård, J., & Trumpy, J. (2019). Økokrim har startet etterforsking av DNB (Økokrim has started investiging DNB), Norwegian daily business newspaper *Dagens Næringsliv*, www.dn.no, published November 28.

Solhaug, E. A., Sønstelie, E., & Fosslien, H. R. (2022). Stor støtte til hjemmetjenestens tidligere leder: "Jobbet døgnet rundt" (Great support to the home sevice's former leader: "Worked around the clock"), daily local newspaper *Oppland Arbeiderblad*, www.oa.no, published February 15.

Solsvik, T. (2017). Norwegian policeman jailed for 21 years in drugs case, www.reuters.com, *Reuters*, September 18.

Sonnenfeld, J. (2022a). The great business retreat matters in Russia today – Just as it mattered in 1986 South Africa, *Fortune*, www.fortune.com, published March 7.

Sonnenfeld, J. (2022b). Over 300 companies have withdrawn from Russia – But some remain, Yale School of Management, www.som.yale.edu, published March 10.

Sønstelie, E., Solhaug, E. A., & Fosslien, H. R. (2022). Hjemmetjeneste-sjefen mener topplederne sviktet henne: -De har gjort meg urettmessig til syndebukk, local daily newspaper *Oppland Arbeiderblad*, www.oa.no, published February 15.

Sørgjeld, C. (2021). På utsiden demonstrerte Obos-opprøret. På innsiden ble de nedstemt (On the outside, the Obos demonstration revolted. On the inside, they were voted down), daily Norwegian newspaper *Aftenposten*, www.aftenposten.no, published June 22.

Spaberg, C., Zachariassen, S., & Gunnarshaug, S. (2021). Økokrim anker frifinnelsen av ordfører: -Jeg er sønderknust (Økokrim appeals the acquittal of the mayor: -I am totally broken), local Norwegian daily newspaper *Romerikes Blad*, www.rb.no, published November 1.

Stang, F. (2021). Obos saboterer sitt eget samfunnsoppdrag (Obos sabotages its own social mission), daily Norwegian newspaper *Aftenposten*, www.aftenposten.no, published June 21.

Storbeck, O. (2020a). Wirecard: The frantic final months of a fraudulent operation, *Financial Times*, www.ft.com, published August 25.

Storbeck, O. (2020b). Whistleblower warned EY of Wirecard fraud four years before collapse, *Financial Times*, www.ft.com, published September 30.

Storbeck, O. (2021a). Prosecutors delayed arrest warrant for Wirecard's Jan Marsalek, *Financial Times*, www.ft.com, published January 29.

Storbeck, O. (2021b). German parliament expands probe into EY's audits of Wirecard, *Financial Times*, www.ft.com, published April 22.

Storbeck, O., & Morris, S. (2021). BaFin files insider trading complaint against Deutsche Bank board member, *Financial Times*, www.ft.com, published April 19.

Sutherland, E. H. (1939). White-collar criminality. *American Sociological Review, 5*(1), 1–12.

Sutherland, E. H. (1983). *White collar crime – The uncut version*. Yale University Press.

Svendsen, E. (2021). Advokatfirma skal evaluere varslingsrutinene i Nittedal (Law firm to evaluate the whistleblowing routines in Nittedal), Norwegian municipal journal *Kommunal Rapport*, www.kommunal-rapport.no, published November 5.

Tanum, A. C. (2016). DNB *Luxembourg – Redegjørelse fra styret (DNB Luxembourg – Statement from the board)*, brev til Nærings- og fiskeridepartementet ved statsråd Monica Mæland (letter to the department of industry and fishery attention minister Monica Mæland), April 11, Oslo, Norway.

Thaxton, S., & Agnew, R. (2018). When criminal coping is likely: An examination of conditioning effects in general strain theory. *Journal of Quantitative Criminology, 34*, 887–920.

Tomter, L. (2021). Varsleren på Island: -DNB burde vært stilt til ansvar for hvitvasking (The whistleblower in Iceland: -DNB should have been held responsible for money laundering), Norwegian broadcasting corporation *NRK*, www.nrk.no, published February 12.

Turner, J. (2021). Johannes Stefansson, *Whistleblower Network News*, www.whistleblowersblog. org, published March 1.

Waheed, A., & Zhang, Q. (2022). Effect of CSR and ethical practices on sustainable competitive performance: A case of emerging markets from stakeholder theory perspective. *Journal of Business Ethics, 175*, 837–855.

Welsh, D. T., & Ordonez, L. D. (2014). The dark side of consecutive high performance goals: Linking goal setting, depletion, and unethical behavior. *Organizational Behavior and Human Decision Processes, 123*, 79–89.

Williams, J. W. (2008). The lessons of 'Enron' – Media accounts, corporate crimes, and financial markets. *Theoretical Criminology, 12*(4), 471–499.

Williams, M. L., Levi, M., Burnap, P. & Gundur, R. V. (2019). Under the corporate radar: Examining insider business cybercrime victimization through an application of routine activities theory. *Deviant Behavior, 40*(9), 1119–1131.

Witbooi, E., Ali, K. D., Santosa, M. A., Hurley, G., Husein, Y., Maharaj, S., Okafor-Yarwood, I., Quiroz, I. A., & Salas, O. (2020). Organized crime in the fisheries sector threatens a sustainable ocean economy. *Nature*. Published online https://doi.org/10.1038/s41586-020-2913-5

Zhong, R., & Robinson, S. L. (2021). What happens to bad actors in organizations? A review of actor-centric outcomes of negative behavior. *Journal of Management, 47*(6), 1430–1467.

Zondag, M. H. W., Brekke, A., Aasen, K. R., & Holm-Nilsen, S. (2021). Knallhard kritikk av Oslo-politiet etter Jensen-saken: -Grunnleggende svikt i ledelsen (Strong criticism of the Oslo police after the Jensen case: -Basic failure in management), Norwegian Public Broadcasting *NRK*, www.nrk.no, published May 26.

Zvi, L., & Elaad, E. (2018). Correlates of narcissism, self-reported lies, and self-assessed abilities to tell and detect lies, tell truths, and believe others. *Journal of Investigative Psychology and Offender Profiling, 15*, 271–286.

Index

Milton Keynes UK
Ingram Content Group UK Ltd.
UKHW010705040923
428018UK00006B/587

9 783031 112157